AF729699

PRAISE FOR *MONEY TALKS*

"Diana Isern is one of the sharpest minds out there teaching kids financial literacy—from budgeting to blockchain. Practical, inclusive, and research-backed, *Money Talks* offers teachers a fun-to-read road map that will transform students' lives—and their own."

—BETH KOBLINER, *New York Times* best-selling author of *Get a Financial Life: Personal Finance in Your Twenties and Thirties*

"Teaching money is deeply personal, and Isern handles it with the warmth and wisdom of a true veteran. By prioritizing vulnerability over perfection, she shows us how to foster a 'you belong here' vibe that sticks with students long after graduation. Isern treats financial education as a mission, not just a math problem."

—ALEX LAMON, award-winning high school business teacher and executive director of New Jersey Council for Economic Education

"In *Money Talks*, Diana Isern shares her experience and passion for financial literacy, inspiring educators and providing practical ideas to make personal finance meaningful for every student."

—COURTNEY POQUETTE, personal finance educator at Winooski High School (Vermont)

"*Money Talks* helps you examine your own relationship with money so you can show up authentically for your students. Diana treats financial education as personal, inclusive, and joyful. I wish every educator in the financial literacy movement had this book in their hands right now!"

—YANELY ESPINAL, author of *Mind Your Money* and director of Educational Outreach at Next Gen Personal Finance

"*Money Talks* is a must-read for all financial educators! The book empowers you to uncover your own unique teaching style and shows you how to create a financial literacy curriculum that leaves your students feeling seen, confident, and ready to master their finances."

—GIOVANNA GONZALÉZ, award-winning author of *Cultura & Cash: Lessons from the First Gen Mentor for Managing Finances & Cultural Expectations*

"Diana Isern makes the subject of financial literacy relatable and empowering for students from all economic backgrounds. Her focus on abundance, rather than scarcity—both in financial literacy and in the classroom—offers a welcome way to reframe economics and reach more students."

—HALLE AMORE BAUER, award-winning high school economics and world history teacher at Ethical Culture Fieldston School (Bronx, NY)

MONEY
TALKS

MONEY TALKS

AN EDUCATOR'S GUIDE TO TEACHING FINANCIAL EMPOWERMENT

DIANA ISERN

BEACON PRESS, BOSTON

BEACON PRESS
24 Farnsworth Street
Boston, Massachusetts
www.beacon.org

Beacon Press books
are published under the auspices of
the Unitarian Universalist Association of Congregations.

© 2026 by Diana Isern

All rights reserved
Printed in the United States of America

29 28 27 26 8 7 6 5 4 3 2 1

This book is printed on acid-free paper that meets the uncoated paper ANSI/NISO specifications for permanence as revised in 1992.

Text design and composition by Kim Arney

Library of Congress Cataloguing-in-Publication Data is available for this title.
Paperback ISBN: 978-0-8070-2262-7
E-book ISBN: 978-0-8070-2263-4
Audiobook: 978-0-8070-2625-0

The authorized representative in the EU for product safety and compliance is Easy Access System Europe 16879218, Mustamäe tee 50, 10621 Tallinn, Estonia: https://beacon.org/eu-contact.

To KJ and Zoe,
my favorite humans on Earth.

Work hard, have fun,
get your wealth on, lift others. Pa'lante.

CONTENTS

MONEY TALKS

INTRODUCTION

WHY TEACHING MONEY BECAME MY MISSION

Educators don't often have the time to focus on the larger whirlwind forces that shape our work, including ever-changing educational policies, relentless administrative paperwork, and high-stakes testing demands. As an educator with twenty years of experience in New York City Public Schools, I know firsthand that we focus on what we can control. We load up on vitamin C, bust out the disinfecting wipes, and make learning happen. Educators harness passion and creativity to drive change, working within constraints of curriculum, time, budget, and space. In this spirit, I center my financial literacy work on what I can directly influence, determined to create hopeful opportunities within and beyond systemic confines.

Without fail, every time I say I teach and advocate for financial education, I get the same exact response: "I wish I learned that when I was in high school."

So do I.

And that's why I titled this book *Money Talks*—because money is loud. It tells stories about our values, choices, and opportunities. It has a megaphone in our lives, announcing the urgent needs we have right now, and the long-term dreams. Yet for all the noise money makes, our society has been strikingly hush-hush about it. It's taboo. But surprise: It doesn't have to be. My goal is to make sure money conversations aren't silent anymore, especially for the next generation. Educators are already creating spaces where our finances can be discussed openly and authentically, in ways that empower. This book, this guide, is written for those "money talks."

My personal finance journey, like that of many others, started with a few rude awakenings that exposed major gaps in my knowledge. Growing up, we didn't have financial wealth, but I watched my hardworking, self-educated parents model resilience and determination. My father, who started as a building caretaker, became an administrator in the New York City Housing Authority. He came from Puerto Rico and taught himself English using flash cards scattered throughout our home. My mother pursued her higher education in her forties, all the while juggling the invisible labor that so many women do. On top of that, as building supers, they kept up an apartment complex with us kids lending our labor—shoveling snow, washing windows, and taking out *mucha basura* (lots of trash).

Inspired by their example, I dove headfirst into my own financial education in my late twenties, consuming every book, podcast, and video I could find about personal finance. This self-education transformed my life, but as any true educator knows, knowledge isn't meant to be hoarded, it's meant to be shared.

It was time to spread the wealth.

BRIDGING THE FINANCIAL EDUCATION GAP

As an assistant principal, I had finance books stacked around my office, and soon enough, students started stopping by to ask about savings, budgeting, and taxes. Teachers and family members reached out too, looking for guidance on retirement planning and investing. My nerdy secret was out.

For years, I welcomed students and teachers during lunch and after school as we bonded over a shared curiosity about money. Eventually, combining their eagerness with my passion, I advocated for a stand-alone finance course for all eleventh graders. Even though finance courses are still not required in New York State, as an administrator, I was uncomfortable with kids graduating from my school—located in the financial capital of New York City—without a formal foundation in the wealth around them. They could walk past the New York Stock Exchange and pet the bull on Wall Street but not learn the skills to build wealth.

And that excitement for financial education was continuous. After launching the finance course, students kept asking deeper questions—about real estate, stocks, and cryptocurrencies—so I created a second course, Making Money Move$, to explore investments in greater depth. Every semester, the demand is huge. Almost half the school tries to enroll, including students who want to take the class again.

Plus, the impact doesn't stop in the classroom. Students take these ideas home. I hear stories like: "Miss, I showed my mom how to check her credit report!" Or "I explained to my uncle how to analyze a rental property—I never knew he used to own one!" I live for a sharing-the-wealth moment.

WHY YOUR WORK MATTERS

Right now, we're at a pivotal moment where students, parents, teachers, and communities are hungry for financial knowledge. While information is everywhere, it is often overwhelming, confusing, or untrustworthy. That's where educators step in.

Educators can be the bridge between curiosity and credible financial information. You hold a unique power to teach financial concepts *and* help students understand their own agency in financial spaces. I teach students wealth-building skills despite educational and societal constraints. This is my small, determined contribution toward a more equitable future. And in doing so, I continue the self-education legacy my parents instilled in me.

A VISION FOR FINANCIAL EMPOWERMENT

My goal in writing this book is to make teaching financial education feel accessible, mission-driven—and fun! I have read *a lot* of educational books. Many are inspiring and helpful; others are loaded with jargon that doesn't help put educational theory into practice for thirty students five times a day for 180 days. This book addresses a gap in financial education. Written by an educator for educators across the country, it breaks down concepts like investing and credit and translates them into lessons that are tangible and relevant to the diverse experiences of their students. This book supports people working to bring financial education to their communities. Teaching is deeply personal. Money is deeply personal. So it makes sense that teaching about money is twice as personal. When approached with reflection, financial education becomes deeply empowering and can create opportunities for both students and teachers to enact real change in their lives.

Throughout this book, students, educators, and other changemakers share authentic anecdotes about their financial journeys. Their stories illustrate the profound impact financial education has on real lives. After all, the best learning happens when we share our experiences and realize we're not alone. Some stories may inspire us, others may challenge us, but all serve as powerful reminders that financial learning is a collective process, and we are all learning about money together.

To bring this transformation into classrooms, educators must personally connect with financial concepts. I envision financial knowledge moving throughout our entire community like a 4 x 100 relay. In the first leg, I'm deepening my own financial literacy, consuming one gazillion books, podcasts, and videos. In the second leg, I share what I'm learning with colleagues, strengthening our collective financial confidence. In the third leg, educators engage students with inclusive resources, turning financial discussions into practical, empowering learning experiences. And in the final leg, students take the baton, applying financial knowledge to align their lives with their values and uplift their communities. In this relay, we all win—not just with financial competence but with the abundance that comes from collective knowledge and empowerment.

But for many educators, it's hard to grab the baton when they are feeling uncertainty or discomfort around financial topics. As financial expert Paco de Leon states in *Finance for the People*, "The recipe is perfect: negative emotions + gaps in information about the world of money and our own minds x inequality = weirdness and problems."[1] My hope is to help educators confront those insecurities without judgment, through reflection and action. This book offers both personal and professional insights, guiding educators to explore:

- their own beliefs and emotional relationship with money
- financial goals that align with their values
- practical tools to navigate financial systems with clarity

When educators are honest, reflective, and empowered in their financial literacy, they create learning environments where students feel capable, confident, and included.

There are systemic barriers that many face in accessing financial stability, which I discuss further in chapter 2. And there are also actionable steps we can take amidst these systemic challenges. Educators stand at the forefront of a financial empowerment movement, shaping the future through every conversation and every lesson they bring to their students. By combining societal awareness with practical tools, we can help students not just navigate the financial world as it exists but actively shape the financial world as it could be.

THE LANGUAGE OF FINANCIAL EDUCATION

Being intentional with our words is important: Language shapes how we make meaning of the world and how we understand our place in it. Language also shapes how we understand financial systems and how we engage with money. In financial literacy discussions, you will hear different terms and understanding the intention behind them is key. People use different terms to highlight goals like fostering agency, expanding access, or ensuring inclusion. These terms include:

financial knowledge = having financial information

financial literacy = understanding and applying financial concepts

financial capability = literacy and access to resources

financial education = structured learning to build knowledge, literacy, and capability

financial well-being = having financial security, financial control, and freedom of choice

financial empowerment = confidence and agency in financial decision-making

financial activism = using financial knowledge to advocate for systemic change

I prefer the term *financial education*—an ongoing process of understanding how money moves throughout our lives. That is the term I use primarily throughout this book. Depending on the context, I may also use *financial literacy*, since it's commonly referenced in media and legislation. At times, I use *financial empowerment* or *financial activism* to highlight how financial education goes beyond the classroom and into community action.

WHO THIS GUIDE IS FOR

Do you want to learn about money and help others do the same? Then this book is for you. While grounded in classroom practice, it's designed for anyone providing financial education—from classroom teachers and school leaders to financial coaches, community educators, and parents—no matter the setting or format. Whether you're teaching in a K–12 classroom, leading after-school workshops, or having money conversations at home, this book offers reflective approaches and practical tools to make financial education more inclusive and effective. It's also for anyone who loves learning and wants to educate themselves.

Before we dive deeper, I want to clarify that when I say "parents" throughout this book, I'm including caregivers, guardians, mentors, and other supportive figures who shape a young person's financial understanding. Similarly, "home" isn't a physical residence but any environment where financial values, habits, and knowledge are shared.

Inclusive Educators

Have you ever felt like you didn't belong in money conversations? Same here. Financial spaces should be open to everyone, not just for access but for empowerment. Belonging means engaging, questioning, and shaping the financial systems that impact our lives. *You* belong here because you understand that financial knowledge is deeply personal and transformative.

This guide is for educators who believe every person has a place in financial learning spaces. It's for those who know that all students deserve to see themselves represented as financial decision-makers and wealth builders. It's for those who foster genuine inquiry, encouraging students to ask, "Why does money work this way?" instead of just accepting "That's how it is."

Financial educators know content is most powerful when it connects abstract concepts to real life. A lesson on compound interest hits differently when it's tied to a student's dream of buying their grandmother a house. This guide is for those who believe financial education should be accessible to everyone. It's for those who embrace holistic thinking, recognizing that students arrive with forms of wealth and knowledge that are valuable in building financial futures. This book is for educators committed to recognizing abundance in themselves and their students. If you're ready to shift toward asset-based thinking, this book is for you.

These principles—Representation, Inquiry, Connection, and Holistic thinking—form the RICH framework, a model I developed to create financial learning spaces where all students feel they belong. (I just couldn't resist the acronym.) Chapter 3 dives into the framework in depth, but throughout the book, we put the pillars into practice. Together, we'll explore how these four elements can reshape classrooms and make financial education more inclusive, less intimidating, and truly empowering. My goal is to offer both the philosophy and practical tools to help you create that "you belong here" vibe in your own classroom.

Reflective Educators

Good news: You don't have to be a financial expert to teach financial education. You just have to be curious and willing to reflect on your own money stories and how they shape your relationship with money and teaching practices. To truly connect with students, we will ask ourselves questions like:

- Why am I teaching this financial concept?
- How does my own financial background influence my approach?
- Is my money story helping—or unintentionally reinforcing barriers?
- How might different learners experience this lesson based on their own financial realities?
- What do I want my students to remember forever about this topic?

Financial education requires us to adapt our teaching methods, just as we do in math, history, or science, but teaching financial knowledge deserves even more reflection, as it can be deeply personal. The self-reflection sections in this guide invite educators to explore their own relationship with money, building deeper connections to financial topics.

This guide is for educators willing to learn alongside their students. There's no need to have all the answers. I know I don't. Magic happens in classrooms where teachers are open to learning together. Throughout these pages, I share real experiences and strategies for creating environments where authentic learning happens through shared discovery, honest conversations about money, and collective problem-solving.

Authentic Educators

Students value authenticity. When we show up as our true selves in the classroom, they engage more deeply. Plus, let's be honest: They can spot inauthenticity a mile away, so we might as well be ourselves before they find us out.

The amazing part is that there's no "right" teaching style. I've seen analytical, by-the-book educators, energetic performers, and Zen-like teachers all connect with their students. In these reflection activities, you'll discover your own authentic approach. All you need is curiosity about money topics, intentionality in your lessons, and a willingness to keep growing.

MY APPROACH TO FINANCIAL EDUCATION

Through both my leadership and this book, I want to share an approach to learning that is deep, meaningful, and infused with humor and fun. After nearly two decades in the educational system, I've learned that sustaining this work requires uplifting one another and holding onto joy.

Interacting with hundreds of personalities every day is emotionally demanding. Anyone who says otherwise has likely never taught a full week of classes, maybe not even a full day. Of course, teaching is deeply rewarding, but we also need to take care of ourselves. The key? Focusing on the big ideas, the learning moments, and the meaningful connections that replenish our energy and fill our buckets. Teaching, reflecting, and thinking systemically about financial topics can be intense, yet we can still approach them in ways that feel hopeful for both our students and ourselves.

Teaching Teens: Playing the Long Game

Let's talk about teenagers for a moment. They can be prickly bundles of contradictions, but they're also hysterical. I find this age extremely amusing, and I think they keep me youthful. But I know that teaching them means riding the emotional roller-coaster they bring to class each day. I've learned to embrace a "short memory" approach, where every day is a fresh start. We reset, reconnect, and jump back into learning about money together.

Teaching financial literacy—teaching in general—is about playing the long game. When students clam up during a discussion or seem overwhelmed by financial calculations, I remind myself that transformation rarely happens in one class period. Sometimes, the impact comes in real time, like when students teach their families what they've learned that day. Other times, it appears years later, when returning alumni tell you about the financial decisions they made because of a lesson, a discussion, or even a single moment in your classroom. Financial education, like all meaningful teaching, is an investment in a future we don't always get to see—but one we know changes lives.

Finding the Joy

I firmly believe that part of our charm as educators is our ability to teach enthusiastically with zero regard for our social status. My passionate rants "Pay yourself first!" or "Take the company match!" make me look completely unhinged. And I'm good with that.

Finding the fun in learning is why I named my course Making Money Move$. It's why I wear finance-themed clothing, even though it's a tough crowd. On February 14, I wore a T-shirt that said "VTSAX Is My Valentine," which is clearly funny and clever. When I asked if they liked my shirt, I was met with blank stares and some nods. No problem, they didn't get it because we hadn't done the stock unit yet. "My Keeping It Real." Estate T-shirt was another objectively funny clothing choice. I got some slow claps for that one.

Teens. They laugh on the inside.

These moments of lightheartedness show students that important financial topics can be approached with passion and joy. When educators bring genuine excitement to the classroom, students pick up on that energy and appreciate it—even if they pretend not to.

HOW THIS GUIDE IS ORGANIZED

This guide is designed by an educator in the field, which means practical application is always at the forefront. It's organized into two sections. Each chapter ends with reflections and resources to support educators in their teaching journey.

Foundations of Financial Education (Chapters 1–5)

Chapters 1–5 lay the groundwork for understanding financial education through the lens of personal impact, systemic context, inclusive teaching practices, and youth development. These chapters explore why financial literacy matters, why your work matters, and what it means to create belonging in financial learning spaces. They also invite educators to reflect on their own money stories and consider how those experiences shape their teaching.

Teaching Financial Literacies (Chapters 6–11)

Chapters 6–11 focus on practical strategies for teaching key financial topics, including money mindset, savings, credit, the stock market, real estate, and Web3. These topics were chosen for their impact on students' financial futures. They are also my favorite to teach, and educators ducators have expressed the greatest need for resources in these areas. While topics like earning, taxes, and risk management aren't covered, this guide is designed to build your confidence so you can integrate additional financial topics based on your students' needs.

Each application chapter begins with an overview of the topic and its purpose—to clarify why the topic matters, how it shows up in students' lives, and why it holds power in shaping their financial futures. From there, we explore the academic and pedagogical foundation of each topic, grounding lessons in research and practice. (In a fun way, I promise.) Midway through each chapter, you'll find a pause for educator self-reflection before transitioning into tangible classroom strategies.

These chapters also include:

- learning objectives and inquiry questions to frame the topic
- suggested content and student discussion prompts to deepen engagement
- sample lesson plans and activities designed for turnkey use
- Your Financial Learning Tool Kit (the appendix and online), with additional resources to support implementation and ongoing learning

These resources have been used in my classroom and school community. They will continue to be updated to reflect evolving needs and best practices.

MAKING THE MOST OF THIS GUIDE

While we all love a good turnkey resource to photocopy and use ASAP, I strongly recommend starting with the first five foundational chapters. These chapters lay the groundwork for why financial education matters and will get you fired up to teach wealth building in ways that stick. And when that mid-semester adrenaline crash hits? Having a strong foundation in how you're changing the world can give you the motivation to keep on keeping on.

After reading these foundational chapters, feel free to explore the rest of the guide based on the topics you're teaching. You can also read it start to finish for a big-picture approach to structuring an inclusive and empowering financial education course.

Thank you for picking up this book. Thank you for being an educator, a learner, a changemaker. We might not all have grown up with access to financial wealth, but together, we can change that story for the next generation.

Your work matters more than you know. Now let's teach this money.

EDUCATOR REFLECTION

- What experiences motivated you to become an educator?
- How do you hope to feel more confident with money, in your life and in your teaching?
- Which financial literacy term resonates with your teaching approach?
- How do you bring joy into your teaching?
- Which topics in this guide do you feel most confident teaching? Which do you want to explore further?
- Is reflection something you regularly do, or is it new for you?
- How do you hope to use this guide in your teaching practice?

SECTION I

FOUNDATIONS OF FINANCIAL EDUCATION

CHAPTER 1

THE IMPACT

How Financial Education Changes Lives

Money touches everything—where we live, what jobs we have, what food we eat, and who we want to become in the future. Yet even though money is fundamental to our lives, few of us learned financial literacy foundations growing up. Our schools, and many of our homes, were devoid of financial guidance.

This chapter explores how our early money messages, financial reality checks, and adversities influence our relationship with money. I share my own journey—along with those of students, families, and community leaders—to showcase the power and potential of financial education to break cycles of scarcity and create generational change.

Your own financial journey was shaped by early influences too. This is your moment to pause, reflect, and choose which teachings to carry forward—and which to leave behind.

We begin with the money messages I received early in life and their impact, and then examine how financial knowledge creates ripple effects across families and communities.

EARLY MONEY MESSAGES

I never realized it growing up, but my parents could not have been more different when it came to money. Their contrasting financial philosophies shaped my relationship with money for decades. My mother emphasized frugality and independence while my father was big on generosity and living in the moment. Both taught me powerful lessons about money, lessons I still carry today and am now passing on to my own children.

Let me share a few snapshots from my parents, Margaret and Juan, that illustrate these formative money messages:

"Keep the carcass; we can use it for soup."
—MARGARET

My mother is an expert at frugality: There was never food wasted—she didn't mess around with that—and she'd use every part of the animal for someone's soup. She knew how to stretch a pound of ground beef into what felt like fifty meals for our relatives. Our humble dollars stretched, too, because she had a distaste for debt and refused to live above her means. She never wanted to owe anyone and still avoids carrying balances on credit cards.

The idea that money was scarce was passed down for generations in her family, all the way back to the Great Depression. Her mother used the same tea bag for days during hard times. That sense of scarcity lingered. To protect us from similar uncertainties, she spent very little and saved whenever she could. Even now, we talk through her lingering fear that there still isn't enough. But her deep commitment to financial security taught me the value of saving, the power of living within your means, and the importance of being genuinely appreciative of what we have.

"We work hard, and enjoy that Meximelt."
—JUAN

In contrast, my father emphasized working hard and spending freely. He grew up in a small home in beautiful Vega Alta, Puerto Rico, and experienced financial poverty as a child, growing up with four sisters in a household where food and even clean water wasn't always guaranteed. He often said they had one outfit and, most times, no shoes on their feet. Perhaps because of that early uncertainty, he took pride in being a dependable provider for our extended family. He worked multiple jobs to ensure everyone was taken care of. It gave him joy to make sure everyone always had food on the table, plus our favorite . . . Taco Bell every other month.

However, his generosity often had no limits, and he often struggled to set financial boundaries, giving his last dollar to family members in need even when it meant sacrificing his own financial stability. This pattern of overextending himself to care for others became a recurring dynamic in our family. Yet seeing how fulfilled he felt when helping others taught me that money can connect us and make us more human.

"Always have your own money, no matter what."

—MARGARET

Throughout my life, my mother always reinforced the importance of my having my own career and not being financially dependent on anyone else. When I was sixteen, she took me to get an old-school bankbook because she insisted that I start saving in my own account. Her insistence on saving makes sense given her experiences. She saw the one-sided power dynamic of her mother depending on her father financially. Like many female baby boomers, she depended on her husband, my father, as the financial breadwinner and decision-maker. Laws preventing women from opening bank accounts without a husband's permission ended only in the 1960s.

Another wish my mother held was to own a home. She often talks about wishing they could have purchased one to pass down to her children. Yet it wasn't until 1974, when the Equal Credit Opportunity Act passed, that women were finally guaranteed the right to get a mortgage in their own name without needing a man to cosign. Even after the laws changed, society lagged behind, and the belief that men were the primary financial decision-makers persisted for decades. As much as Mom tried, my father was not interested on planning ahead, investing, or owning a home, so it never happened. With that history, it makes perfect sense that my mother was so insistent that I establish financial independence. And thanks to her, I did.

"No te preocupes por el dinero, la vida es una."

—JUAN

After he was drafted and served in Germany during the Vietnam War, my father (Papi) moved to New York City with my *tía* and lived very humbly. To be content, he needed little more than a chair and a TV to watch *béisbol*. Maybe because he didn't need much, he had a "don't worry about money" philosophy. I knew we didn't have a lot, so whenever I asked if the coconut FrozFruit cost too much, Papi would say, "*Nena, no te preocupes por el dinero, la vida es una*," a Puerto Rican version of "YOLO!"

Perhaps because my father was raised with so little, he became an incredibly generous adult. To this day, I consider him to be the most worry-free and unselfish person I have ever known. While he was more focused on living in the present and often uncomfortable talking about finances or planning for the future, he taught me something equally important: Sometimes the best financial decision is to invest in experiences and relationships that make life worth living.

Their extreme and opposing financial behaviors—my mother's frugality and my father's YOLO spending—were survival strategies born of scarcity. For many, poverty can be traumatic. If you have ever gone without food or stable housing, you understand the instinct to guard every penny, often going to extreme lengths to hold on to cash just in case you need it later. Past hardships train you to expect the worst whenever setbacks occur. When parents have lived through financial trauma, they may overstress the importance of earning and saving money as a survival tactic.[1] This is an impulse I find myself fighting against.

Therapists use the term *intergenerational financial trauma* to describe the ways our family's financial struggles shape how we relate to money, often without realizing it. As mental health author Nicole Russell-Wharton explains in *Breaking Generational Silence*, these problems often come from families staying silent about their struggles, allowing hidden pain to pass from one generation to the next.[2]

Financial stress can be so intense that it manifests in physical symptoms like headaches and stomachaches, as well as in behaviors like avoiding bills and fixating on worst-case outcomes.[3] My mother still experiences many of these reactions to her finances. Her physical tension and sleepless nights have been shaped not only by her experiences but also by the financial stress endured by our ancestors decades—even centuries—before.

As you can imagine, these financial behaviors also created tensions in their relationship. My mother wanted structure and control, which clashed with my father's go-with-the-flow approach to life. Research on financial conflict in relationships shows that disagreements over spending, wages, salary, and bills are more stressful and threatening for couples than conflicts about other topics. These disputes lasted longer, recurred more often, and held higher current and long-term importance for relationships. Couples also displayed more depressive behavior, including physical distress, withdrawal, sadness, and fear, during conflicts about money than disagreements about other topics.[4] Scarcity reared its head in every one of my parents' money conversations and resulted in these types of reactions in both of them. Financial decisions were tense whether they involved something minor, like paying the phone bill, or something major and impulsive, like buying a used car for six hundred dollars. (RIP to our janky red Pinto!) Their arguments weren't really about the dollars themselves, but about the deep-seated money beliefs that shaped how each of them saw the world.

Ultimately, I feel deep gratitude and empathy for my parents. I often reflect on their choices through the quote, "All behavior makes sense with enough information."[5] Juan and Margaret were humans doing their best to navigate the challenges they faced with the resources available to them. From their contrasting approaches, I learned invaluable lessons that continue to shape my financial journey. My mother taught me that preparation and stability create lasting security, not just for ourselves but for our children. She showed me the importance of thinking about the future and being intentional with my money. My father, through his joy, taught me that wealth isn't just about accumulation, but about using money to live a full life. Money, he showed me, is meant to create experiences, support others, and bring joy to our fleeting time on earth. Their wisdom is woven into my own money story, and for that, I am endlessly grateful.

Who knew that these childhood lessons would one day ignite a joyful passion for financial education, a passion that would ripple outward to touch the lives of students, families, and communities throughout my career? My financial journey continues to be about valuing their wisdom while finding my own way forward.

FINANCIAL REALITY CHECKS

It took me years to truly understand how these early money messages had shaped me. Like many of us, I needed my own financial wake-up calls to recognize the narratives I had inherited.

The first wake-up call came in 2010, when a co-teacher casually asked how much I was saving from each paycheck. At the time, I was making $40K a year, living in New York City, paying off student loans, and partying every weekend. These circumstances were not ideal for financial empowerment. My colleague's simple question felt like a spotlight on my financial reality. I mumbled something about contributing to my retirement account, but the truth was embarrassing: I wasn't saving anything meaningful, and something had to change.

Until then, I had accepted the narrative that educators were meant to live paycheck to paycheck. Weren't we public servants? My family was deeply involved in our church and genuinely believed in serving others and practicing selflessness. Somewhere along the way, I interpreted that as meaning financial struggle was normal, maybe even virtuous. Inheriting those beliefs, along with my own lack of financial knowledge, reinforced a mentality of scarcity. It felt uncomfortable—but also familiar—to barely have enough to make ends meet.

By the time I reached adulthood, I assumed saving was something I'd do "someday," after my student loans were paid off. Like many first-generation college graduates, I prioritized attending a prestigious university without comprehending the financial implications. Despite generous financial aid, graduating a year early, and my family helping where they could, I still graduated with about fifty thousand dollars in student loans.

Like many millennials, I started my adult life best friends with Sallie Mae, paying her five hundred dollars a month.

In quiet moments, the burden of debt weighed on me: sitting on the bus tallying the seemingly endless years of payments ahead, growing angry with myself for accepting so many loans without appealing or exploring other options, even feeling guilty for ordering Domino's cheesy bread during my deferment. I felt trapped by my debt, and my dreams of traveling now seemed completely out of reach. Financial anxiety became a constant hum in the background, not loud enough to force immediate change, but persistent enough to dull my sense of possibility.

My student loan experience is typical for my generation. According to research from the Global Financial Literacy Excellence Center, 55 percent of college-educated millennials have an outstanding student loan, and 47 percent of those borrowers worry about their ability to fully repay them.[6] Despite being the most educated generation in American history, we entered adulthood burdened with significant financial baggage. I wanted more financially, but without clear direction or mentors I connected with, achieving "more" felt abstract. How could I plan for the future when my current life seemed to require every dollar I earned?

Then came the second reality check: homeownership in New York City. Remembering conversations with my mother about her lifelong desire to own a home inspired me. At this point, my financial mindset shifted from survival mode to thinking about generational goals. Pulling my credit report for the first time and spotting negative marks sent my stomach into knots. I learned to dispute errors quickly, but the bigger shock came when I calculated a 20 percent down payment on a Queens apartment. New York City home prices still send a chill down my spine. The gap between my reality and my dreams was undeniable, but for the second time, I felt motivated to change my financial habits. The fire to be the first in my family to own a home became impossible to ignore and would fuel my learning journey for years to come. Also impossible to ignore: I would be renting for a while.

LOSS AND LEGACY

My third financial reality check came crashing into my life when Papi suddenly passed away. When he died, everything shifted. We were incredibly close, spending time together at the gym, dancing salsa, making green juices, and getting every answer wrong on *Cash Cab*. His absence changed my view of money forever and in multiple ways.

First, having to manage finances after my dad's death was completely overwhelming. Untangling accounts, sorting through family requests, locating documents, and making financial decisions while mourning enveloped me in darkness. For years, the stress made my loss even harder to bear. Through my father's passing, I saw firsthand how being financially unprepared can make the experience of death far more painful.

His death was sudden, and I wish we had talked more openly about money and planning while he was still with us. Trust me, the last people you want to be dealing with are lawyers and accountants while wading through your tears and trying to choose a prayer card quote. Planning ahead doesn't erase the heartbreak of losing your person, but it can ease some of the burden when you're already navigating deep grief.

Second, Papi was the financial cornerstone of our family. He was a generous soul, often to a fault, whom everyone called when they needed help. He was extremely proud of my college education. Whenever we went anywhere, and I mean *anywhere*—the beach, the pharmacy, the bodega, Shea Stadium—he would tell every unfortunate person near us about how I was a teacher: *la profe*. Back then, I'd cringe. Now, I carry that pride with me.

But he also made it clear that my education and career placed me in a position of privilege in our community, and he urged me never to forget the importance of giving back. My father entrusted me with the responsibility of financially supporting my family, a responsibility I felt deeply then and continue to feel fifteen years later. From that moment, I vowed to excel and become highly financially literate in his honor. His hard work and generous spirit are the legacies that inspire me to pursue financial stability and to help as many people as I can.

I recognize now that caring for those we love includes giving to others. The aftermath of Papi's passing taught me that financial literacy is not just about individual accumulation of money. It is about creating security for those who depend on us and keeping alive the values of those we've lost.

KNOWLEDGE IMPACT: MY SELF-EDUCATION JOURNEY

My financial reality checks lit a fire inside of me. I wanted to do more than just survive; I wanted to build a legacy. But first, I needed to get a handle on my money. I needed knowledge. That motivation led me to my first deliberate step: downloading a free e-book called *The No-Spend Challenge Guide*. It had a bright pink cover with dollar signs, which obviously seemed like a good place to start.

That little book did something profound: It made me *reflective*. I began to question my spending habits and financial choices. I asked myself questions like, "Self, do you really need party clothes from Express every weekend?" For the first time, I realized my spending was within my control, and being broke was actually avoidable. At that moment, learning how to spend less was the accessible starting point I needed. I quickly realized, though, spending less was only the beginning of understanding money.

As I began to learn the financial education lingo, I kept hearing about emergency funds, also known as contingency or rainy-day funds. Up to that point, imagining having three zeroes (after a number) in my bank account was unfathomable. I wasn't alone; building emergency savings is challenging for many Americans. The FINRA Foundation National Financial Capability Study shows that half of Americans report they would struggle to cover an unexpected two thousand dollar expense.[7] Little by little, I started building my own emergency savings, setting a goal of one thousand dollars. My newfound financial knowledge gave me the tools to achieve that goal, which I did later that year.

The power of financial education extends far beyond individual experiences. Recent research from the National Endowment for Financial Education analyzed seventy-six financial education experiments across thirty-three countries and consistently found positive results. This research concluded that "financial education improves financial knowledge and financial behaviors" and that these interventions were "three to five times as effective in improving financial knowledge and behaviors" than previously thought.[8]

The research aligns with my personal experience: Financial knowledge translates directly to dollars and cents. A study by Harvard and MIT researchers found that even modest improvements in financial literacy can significantly impact wealth accumulation. The study focused on Chilean households, but the researchers accounted for structural differences between Chile's financial system and that of the US. They found that relatively small increases in financial literacy scores led to an average $13,800 boost in net wealth across retirement accounts, housing equity, and other assets.[9]

Increasing my savings fueled a hunger to learn everything I could about finances. Over the next several years, my education came from countless books, podcasts, articles, and videos. My knowledge progressed through what I consider the natural stages of financial education: first spending less, then saving more, addressing credit and debt issues, learning to invest, and continually aligning my finances with my values. There was, and continues to be, so much amazing content created by diverse voices, which I share in the appendices. Through these resources, I became fascinated by the power of money to build wealth, impact lives, and do good in the world. My journey of financial learning never ends. To deepen my knowledge and help more people understand how money can improve their lives, I decided to become an Accredited Financial Counselor.

Financial knowledge transformed my wallet and my mindset too, replacing (half of my) scarcity with a sense of empowerment. Research supports this powerful connection between financial literacy and overall well-being. A report titled *Health Is Wealth* examining the connections between financial, mental, and physical well-being found that 75 percent of US adults believe improving financial literacy would enhance their health.[10]

Similarly, the Federal Reserve System's *Economic Well-Being of US Households* documents how financial literacy impacts wellness. According to this report, financially knowledgeable individuals:

- are three times more likely to have emergency savings
- report 27 percent higher financial well-being scores
- experience significantly lower stress levels—and 62 percent fewer sleepless nights about money!
- demonstrate greater confidence in long-term planning[11]

Feeling financially empowered has improved my well-being in ways I never imagined as a kid. Gaining knowledge allowed me to define wealth on my own terms and align my spending with my values instead of society's expectations. Financial choices are personal and should reflect what you most care about. Research from the Consumer Financial Protection Bureau (CFPB) shows that financial well-being isn't measured by your bank balance alone, but by having "security and freedom of choice, in the present and in the future," no matter your income. The study emphasizes that financial well-being is highly personal and cannot be fully captured by objective financial measures.[12]

For me, freedom means choosing to purchase a modest apartment, not owning a car, and prioritizing spending on meaningful experiences. I have been able to take my mother abroad for the first time, to Scotland; travel with my kids; attend the Paris Olympics with my crew; and surprise my partner with tickets to see Jey Uso win the WWE Royal Rumble—epic moments I'll never forget. I can also donate to causes that my parents cared about, like St. Jude and Samaritan's Purse, and continue their legacy of giving back. Though I still catch myself falling into scarcity habits, like only buying toothpaste with coupons at CVS or checking my banking app daily, I've developed a healthier relationship with money. My holistic financial journey shows how financial literacy creates both security today and freedom tomorrow. Financial empowerment isn't just a lofty theory but the difference between constant money anxiety and freedom to focus on what truly matters, like ordering that feta and spinach cheesy bread whenever the craving hits.

As my money confidence grew, so did my professional capabilities. Surprisingly, I felt more prepared for leadership roles, like becoming an assistant principal. The CFPB research explains that financial well-being creates "control over day-to-day finances" and "freedom to make choices that allow you to enjoy life."[13] This foundation carried over to my work, helping me approach school leadership with the same clarity I was developing in my personal finances. The CFPB studies confirm that financial capability boosts decision-making confidence, reduces stress at work, and improves overall life satisfaction.

TRANSFORMATIVE IMPACT: SHARING THE WEALTH

Since becoming an assistant principal, I've maintained an open-door policy. People consistently came to talk about financial wellness, and they still do. These conversations made me realize that most of my students and colleagues were navigating the same knowledge gaps I had. This realization transformed my calling as a teacher. My financial education came a little later in life, and I am thankful for it, but I know many others still struggle to access trustworthy resources.

Inspired by each conversation and question, I set out on a mission to help educators, students, and honestly, anyone else with a pulse, to gain the financial knowledge they need to live comfortably and true to their values. I began holding informal financial counseling sessions with teachers during lunch, prep periods, after school, and even happy hours. There's nothing quite like walking into a bar after a long week and having a coworker call out, "Hey, Isern, I need help with this debt." But I'd pull up a stool next to them, and we'd talk. We had thoughtful, nuanced conversations about what was important to them and how their money could support the type of life they wanted to live, both now and in the future.

What excited me was how often these conversations about money revealed deeper values. There was the teacher who dreamed of traveling during school breaks but was overwhelmed by student loan repayment. The teacher who couldn't figure out where the money from his raises was going. The first-year teacher torn between paying down credit card debt and building an emergency fund. The teacher worried they hadn't contributed enough to their 403(b) for retirement. Over time, hallway conversations turned into weekly meetups where we discussed financial topics together.

The conversations with students covered different topics, but the underlying concerns were the same. I remember Luis coming to my office to ask whether he should get a credit card when he turned eighteen the following month. Lucia needed a Parent PLUS loan, but didn't have a cosigner with good credit. Ray wondered if his dream of owning a business someday meant he shouldn't pursue a traditional college degree. These questions weren't just about dollars, they were really about values, family dynamics, hopes, and fears. And they lit a fire in me to go beyond one-on-one conversations.

Beyond school educators, there are many faces in the financial empowerment movement. Whether you're teaching high schoolers like me, coaching adults through their own money stories, leading community workshops in an after-school program, hosting a money podcast, or talking about spending with your kids at Five Below, you are carrying the work forward. I've watched district leaders transform entire school systems with thoughtful financial education policies and volunteer mentors change lives in a one-hour session. I've seen staff at nonprofits inspire kids with SMART goals. I've spoken to college professors who describe students' eyes lighting up when they see the connection between mental well-being and financial well-being. I've heard podcast hosts who empathetically break down the emotional barriers that prevent others from reaching financial goals. I know people who run financial workshops that guide parents toward more mindful spending for themselves and their families.

We might have different job titles, but we share the same mission: to ignite financial confidence in others. The stories from my classroom are also happening in your living room, community centers, and podcast studios everywhere. Whatever your role, you are helping people take control of their finances—and planting seeds with an unimaginable impact.

STUDENT IMPACT: SPARKING THE FINANCIAL LITERACY FIRE

My conversations with young people and adults reinforced my belief in the power of financial literacy. I could see the potential to reach far more students. When we feel confident in our own finances, we inevitably pass these lessons to the next generation and the impact continues to shape their future lives. A Moneyzine study found that 80 percent of Americans wished they had learned more about personal finance in high school, and 76 percent believed it would have reduced their stress.[14] Recognizing this need, I advocated for a standalone financial literacy course and later introduced a second class, which I taught myself, focused on investments. Sharing information isn't just our job; the best educators I know have an intrinsic drive to empower others.

The research confirms the life-changing impact of financial knowledge. In states that require financial education, students develop smarter financial habits, increase their credit scores, avoid payday loans, and make better decisions about college funding.[15] A study in *Economics of Education Review* examined the credit reports of young adults who had completed financial education and found they had fewer defaults and higher credit scores than peers without it.[16] If we know financial mistakes are preventable, how can we not ensure students are prepared?

One of my financial education alums, Naiymah, describes its impact: "Before, I didn't fully understand credit or how important it was to use it in a responsible way. Now, I see credit as a tool that can help or hurt me depending on my decisions."[17] Research shows that young adults like Naiymah who participate in rigorous financial education programs see improvements in credit outcomes, including fewer late payments and higher credit scores, translating to thousands of dollars saved over a lifetime through better interest rates and fewer fees.[18]

Beyond credit, financial literacy helps students avoid costly mistakes that drain wealth. Overdraft fees, credit card costs, and identity theft add up to a lot. Americans now pay roughly $160 billion per year in credit card interest and fees—about $1,300 per household.[19] On top of that, overdraft and non-sufficient funds (NSF) fees totaled over $12.1 billion in 2024 alone.[20] It is encouraging that the Consumer Financial Protection Bureau has pushed for major banking reforms, including a rule to cap many of these overdraft fees at five dollars.[21] Still, while the system is improving, individuals have to stay informed to navigate these pitfalls. When students understand how credit, banking, and fees actually work, they make smarter decisions that ripple outward, benefiting families, communities, and the broader economy. Knowledge directly impacts financial outcomes.

Financial education also transforms mindsets. "After taking your class, my thinking completely shifted," Ryan, an alum who I taught in eleventh grade, shared. "I used to just focus on my next purchase. Now I focus on my next investment. I had planned on taking out major student loans for an expensive college, but after learning how debt works, I changed my decision."[22] States with rigorous financial education mandates see improved debt management and smarter financial decisions among young adults.[23] Ryan's understanding of debt and investing empowered him to make informed money management decisions.

Amazing transformations can happen when young people apply financial literacy to their everyday lives. Naiymah is a great example. She told me, "Financial literacy classes empowered me to take control of my money. It taught me how important it is to think before I make a financial decision, not just to spend without thinking."

All my ranting about automating savings actually worked! Naiymah adds, "I remember what you said, and I started setting up automatic transfers to my savings account so that some of my income goes right into savings each time I get paid. This way, I'm building my savings without even thinking about it, and it's helped me develop better discipline." I've seen that same shift in so many young people, as they move from impulse spending to thoughtful planning. Learning to separate true needs from momentary wants and creating spending habits that support our goals is a powerful outcome of financial education.

You know that teaching moment when you pause, survey the room, and wonder, "Are they hearing me right now, or am I just talking to myself?" Have no fear, those financial concepts are taking root in ways we can't immediately see. Anais, now studying business in college, recalls, "Ever since I took my first financial course in Brooklyn Prep, it truly opened my eyes to realize how important money is. When I learned about credit cards and how to have a good credit score, I had no idea this new thing I was learning in class was something so important. Now as a nineteen-year-old, I think back heavily about it because I see how much it will affect my life in the future!"[24]

Beyond practical skills, financial literacy courses ignite students' passions. Anais shares: "This class opened my eyes to how important money is. It also allowed me to find something I was passionate about. I love business, and I now want to learn all about income statements and balance sheets and even cash flow and how all these things are extremely important . . . I want to have my own business one day. Just because of that class I started to have that drive in me to learn what we can really do with money."

What I love most about financial education is seeing students bring their aha moments home. Naiymah tells me, "I've shared several budgeting tips from class with my family, helping track income and expenses and create a plan that works for our needs." Another former student, Lexi, became her family's "money coach," discussing credit cards and scores with her parents, and even Roth IRAs. She later returned to ask me about my thoughts on Roth

IRAs. If that's not a feel-good, full-circle moment of financial education, I don't know what is. Newfound knowledge can spark family conversations about money that improve financial behaviors across generations.

FAMILY IMPACT: RIPPLE EFFECTS ON THE HOME

Financial education creates an organic bridge between the classroom and home. I have found that when students feel confident about a money topic, they often share it immediately with family. Countless students return the next day or even months later and say, "Miss, I talked to my mother about her credit score," or "I spoke with my uncle about his rental property." They essentially become financial ambassadors, and their enthusiasm creates ripples of change beyond their individual benefit. Students sharing knowledge with their families is called reverse mentoring; it transforms how financial knowledge spreads across generations.

Your students might share similar anecdotes with you, and this ripple effect is backed by research. School-based financial education programs lead to measurable spillover effects on parents, improving financial behaviors within families. In particular, parents in disadvantaged households showed notable improvements in credit scores and reduced default rates after their children learned financial literacy in school.[25] The impact of financial education is expansive: It not only prepares students for their own financial futures but also strengthens financial knowledge within entire households.

Even if we didn't receive financial education ourselves, parents and caregivers overwhelmingly recognize its importance. An article analyzing a Chase study of two thousand American parents found that 83 percent wish they had learned more about money growing up.[26] My mother is one of them, which is why she wholeheartedly supports my advocacy for financial education.

It is encouraging to see families today breaking taboos and becoming more financially educated. Seventy percent of parents are actively teaching their children fundamental concepts like saving, investing, and using banking services. I am excited that families are becoming more transparent about money, with 62 percent of parents discussing their own family's financial situation, including purchasing decisions and budgets for activities. Many parents (66 percent) take practical steps to prepare their children's financial future, helping them open bank accounts and save for major purchases. These home discussions revolve around key financial principles, with teaching children about saving (32 percent) and increasing general financial conversations (26 percent) ranking as top financial goals for families.[27]

Likewise, in my own journey as a parent, I've started conversations about money and values with my thirteen- and ten-year-old children. They know how much our mortgage costs, how buying in bulk cuts food costs, and what the price of our monthly electricity is, hence the reminders: "Turn off the lights when you're not in the room!" and "Why is the TV watching itself?" They can't believe what we spend on the magical Wi-Fi that keeps us all digital zombies. I explain that our air fryer gets daily use because we prioritize eating at home instead of ordering in—and those consistent savings help fund experiences like our family trip to Iceland. We talk about how these intentional choices reflect what we collectively value: adventure and memories. I even share with them how I pay myself first through savings, even if it's just one cent as we build the habit.

I also make sure they know that our decisions don't have to be their future decisions. If they want a car, a house with a lawn, a yurt, an RV, or whatever other lifestyle choices feel right to them, they can choose that when it makes sense financially and personally. These are simply the choices we're making for our values. When they're grown, they can go wild and live in that RV—as long as they save me a seat.

I won't pretend these conversations are always smooth. My kids, like so many others, are constantly comparing their lives to what they see on YouTube—the endless unboxings, the influencers with perfect rooms, the giveaways that make $100K look like a drop in the bucket, plus the everyday spending temptations that show up in real life. The magnetic pull of fast food and Pokémon cards are a constant force in our budgeting lessons. Just last month, my son spent his entire two-week allowance in a single morning buying protein bars and electrolyte drinks to share with friends. Yet, real-world financial situations create powerful teachable moments. His 7-Eleven haul led to a nuanced conversation where I reinforced that spending all your money immediately meant he'd have $0 until his next allowance. But I also shared my pride in his generosity to others. We talked about how financial responsibility doesn't mean losing the spirit of giving but learning to balance it with our own needs. There's no perfect script. What matters is our willingness to be transparent about how money works in our household and how our spending reflects what we truly value. When my ten-year-old stood in Five Below, weighing the cost of two Squishmallows against her budget, I knew the lessons were starting to sink in, at least for that moment.

In addition to teaching about expenses, these intergenerational conversations have long-term impact on financial behaviors. High schoolers who regularly talk about money with their parents develop healthier financial habits than their peers who do not. These home discussions lay the groundwork for financial confidence that carries into adulthood, helping students break cycles of financial insecurity that often persist across generations.[28]

When students share what they've learned at home, they are creating lasting change through family financial socialization. According to an article in the *Journal of Family Psychology*, families shape financial behavior in three primary ways:

1. Parent financial modeling: Kids observe how their parents manage money.
2. Parent-child financial discussions: Having open conversations builds financial confidence for both parties involved.
3. Experiential learning: Hands-on financial decision-making strengthens their understanding about money.[29]

Financial education is far more impactful when it connects to personal values and comes from someone close and trusted. Children learn more about money—intentionally or not—from their parents than from school, work, media, or peers, making parents the primary source of financial socialization.[30] Families influence not just knowledge of concepts like budgeting but also behaviors like saving and deeper attitudes toward money and value.

I love seeing how financial education creates a beautiful interchange between the classroom and home. Financial educators at all levels play a critical role in encouraging students to engage in discussions at home. *The Journal of Financial Counseling and Planning* emphasizes that financial education in the home is essential. Financial educators should encourage students to discuss personal finance with their families and provide activities designed to spark these money talks.[31] In chapter 3, we explore ways to intentionally incorporate family wealth and wisdom into financial education, and in the later application chapters, I provide specific strategies for integrating families into lessons. By doing so, we can make financial literacy a shared experience rather than an isolated academic subject.

For many families in this country, their relationship with money is deeply emotional and layered. Reflecting on my own journey with both financial scarcity and unchecked spending, I know how complex these dynamics can be. The good news? Financial education equips students with the tools to appreciate, question, and even reshape these inherited financial patterns.

COMMUNITY IMPACT: RIPPLE EFFECTS FOR SOCIETY

Educators know that meaningful learning doesn't stop at the classroom door. As we have seen with our students, it can transform dinner table conversations, spark neighborhood workshops, and even inspire local business growth. Financial knowledge can empower entire communities.

When I spoke with renowned financial educator and author Tiffany Aliche, aka the Budgetnista, she explained that real magic unfolds when everyday financial lessons are shared among family members, friends, and neighbors. When someone learns how to budget or understand credit, that knowledge naturally spreads, empowering others to challenge old habits and embrace new ways of thinking about money. She explained, "You don't have to be a financial expert to start making better money choices."[32]

Aliche illustrates this ripple effect beautifully through her classroom and community experiences. In her workshops, she encourages learners to analyze businesses in their communities by calculating potential revenue: "Next time you go to a restaurant, see how much you and your family spent. Then multiply. How many people are inside that restaurant? How much is that restaurant making at that moment? Fifty times . . . there's four other families. That's two hundred." This simple exercise expands into multiplying by days, weeks, and years, creating powerful aha moments of financial awareness.

Financial education has the power to spark natural conversations that extend beyond school walls, explains Aliche. "If you do a really good job of introducing financial education in a way that's meaningful, it ripples because it makes them say, 'But Mom . . . about the pizza place around the corner. How much do you think they're making?'" This real-world approach pulls back the curtain on economic systems, helping students see possibilities both for financial awareness ("How is my mom affording this?") and entrepreneurial thinking ("How is this business making money?"). As she puts it, "Not every student is going to be an entrepreneur, but it allows them to realize that there's a wider world happening around them."

Aliche takes it even further by designing projects that move learning from theory to practice. "What if we did a class project where, let's just say, in the next six months, can we collectively make six thousand dollars?" she suggests. "Week one, let's do some ideas and put them on a board. Week two, maybe we have entrepreneurs from the community come in to talk to us about ways they made money when they were younger. Week three, let's map out the plan."

This creates a powerful progression: Students first learn concepts, then meet people who've applied them successfully, and finally work together to achieve shared financial goals. It's a perfect example of Aliche's three components for transformation: "knowledge, access, and community." I've implemented similar approaches in my classroom. When teaching about real estate, I begin by having students analyze properties and run the numbers. Then, I invite real estate agents and investors to share their experiences—successes and failures. Students are encouraged to take these conversations home, asking parents about property values in their neighborhoods or discussing family members' experiences with investing.

I love seeing conversations travel from classroom to living rooms and community centers. John Hope Bryant notes in *Time* magazine that teaching smart financial choices can create pathways to economic stability that can lift entire neighborhoods. I've witnessed firsthand that when people understand how to budget, save, invest, and manage debt, they gain the confidence to change their lives. This combination of knowledge and agency can break generational cycles of poverty. Empowerment comes when individuals develop a healthy relationship with money and convert that understanding into tangible assets, businesses, and community development.[33] Financial education ripples out from the personal, functioning as a public good that strengthens entire communities.

Meaningful financial education creates what they call in business "positive network effects." When one person in a community becomes financially literate, they don't keep it to themselves. They share what they've learned with others, make different choices, and inspire change. As more people build stronger financial knowledge, the benefits multiply across the community.[34]

I've seen this happen time and again. One family learns about credit repair and shares tips with neighbors. A community budgeting workshop leads to a neighborhood savings challenge. As financial knowledge spreads, communities grow stronger together, showing more economic resilience during tough times, launching more small businesses, and building wealth that passes between generations. This impact spreads because financial education isn't just about adding money to someone's bank account. It's about enriching lives. I've watched students figure out compound interest for the first time, then head home eager to explain it to their parents that night. The excitement of financial knowledge flows naturally through families and neighborhoods.

When we teach financial concepts—in classrooms, communities, and even casual conversations—something magical happens. A student who calculates restaurant revenue might help their family price items for their food truck. Another may explain APR (annual percentage rate) to an older sibling applying for their first credit card. In these moments, financial success becomes a shared goal. This is why I believe financial education is not just another subject. It's a movement that strengthens our entire society, one informed decision at a time.

What's inspiring is how financial education thrives in so many different settings: community organizations that run financial workshops for small business owners, universities where college professors teach economics, podcast studios where hosts share money tips, and nonprofit after-school programs where kids play money management games. When financial educators at any level share knowledge in accessible, relevant ways, they're planting seeds that grow far beyond their immediate audience.

PATHWAYS TO PRO$PERITY: THE TRANSFORMATIVE IMPACT OF FINANCIAL KNOWLEDGE

Here's the mind-blowing part: our individual money choices can influence people's lives fifty or one hundred years from now. When we become good with money, we share that financial knowledge with students, who then bring it home. Family members pass it along to their communities, and the learning goes on forever. Financial knowledge has the power to transform individuals, families, neighborhoods, and entire communities.

The question is no longer whether financial literacy matters, but how we can bring it to every corner of society. Despite persistent gaps in access, there is also unprecedented momentum for change. In the next chapter, we explore innovations, policies, and mandates that are helping to spread financial education to the masses.

SELF-REFLECTION

We've explored how simple classroom lessons unfold into life-changing knowledge that students carry far beyond our school walls. Take a moment to reflect on these questions as you shape your teaching approach.

Personal Reflection

- $ What financial lessons did you learn from your own parents or caregivers? How do these still influence your relationship with money today?
- $ What was your first significant financial reality check, and how did it change your approach to money?

- $ What financial books, podcasts, courses, or people changed your perspective on money?
- $ Who have you shared your financial knowledge with? Family members, friends, students, parents, community organizations, or followers on social media?
- $ What is something you have done financially that you are really proud of?
- $ What financial concept do you wish you had learned earlier in life?

Educator Reflection

- $ How do your personal financial experiences influence your approach to teaching money concepts?
- $ Which financial education concepts do you find students connect with most deeply, and why?
- $ Have you noticed your students sharing financial concepts with their families? What stories have they brought back to the classroom?
- $ How might you intentionally design lessons that encourage students to bring financial conversations home?
- $ In what ways could you involve parents in your financial education program?
- $ How do you navigate cultural differences in financial values when teaching students from diverse backgrounds?

EDUCATOR RESOURCES

Student Discussion Questions

Quick prompts designed to ignite student conversation

- Are you too young to learn about finances? If not, why not? Or if so, when is an ideal age?
- What's something about money that confuses you or makes you curious?
- What money goal would make the biggest difference in your life right now?
- Which ideas about money do you agree with? What do you argue with?
- Who do you know who seems to handle money well? What do you notice about them?
- How do you and your family talk about money? Is it a comfortable topic or something rarely discussed?
- What is something you will share with someone when you get home?
- What financial goals do you have for your future? How did you decide on these goals?

- What have you observed about how different people in your community handle money?
- What's one thing you wish adults in your life would understand about money from your perspective?

Standalone Activities (20–50 minutes)

Exercises that can fit into any lesson, with added discussion to extend learning

- **MONEY STORY EXCHANGE**
  - **Purpose:** Help students recognize diverse financial experiences and histories while honoring the wisdom that exists within families and communities.
  - **Process:** Students conduct interviews with family members to uncover financial stories, then share these narratives to build understanding across different backgrounds.

    1. Provide students with thoughtful questions that go beyond surface-level financial facts: What was your first job and what did it teach you about money? What's your earliest money memory, and how did it shape you? What financial advice would you give your younger self?
    2. Students conduct interviews at home, creating space for intergenerational dialogue. They then create brief narratives highlighting the most meaningful insights from their interviews, focusing on wisdom gained rather than specific financial details.
    3. Display stories in the classroom, creating a rich tapestry of diverse financial experiences. Facilitate discussion identifying common themes across different backgrounds—resilience, sacrifice, hope—while celebrating the unique perspectives each family brings.

- **FAMILY VISION BOARD**
  - **Purpose:** Encourage families to envision their financial future and articulate their values through creative expression.
  - **Process:** Students and their families collaborate to create a visual board representing their financial goals, values, and aspirations.

    1. Provide guidelines and examples showing how vision boards can incorporate images, quotes, and symbols that represent both practical goals and deeper values. Students ask family members questions about hopes, dreams, and values: What does security mean to our family? How do we want to impact our community?

2. Families collect images, words, and symbols from magazines, digital resources, or their own artwork that resonate with their shared financial vision. They work together to arrange elements on a physical board or digital collage, ensuring every family member's voice is represented.
3. Host a gallery walk where students explain the significance of their family's vision, celebrating the diverse ways families define financial success and well-being.

CHAPTER 2

THE MOMENTUM

Policies and Practices in Financial Education

Financial literacy is finally having its red-carpet-at-the-Met-Gala moment. On the legislative stage, states are racing to mandate personal finance courses for high school graduation. Currently, thirty states—up from just five in 2020—require them. Major media outlets like CNBC, the *New York Times*, and *Forbes* regularly feature financial literacy stories like "Why Financial Literacy Is the Civil Rights Issue of This Generation" and "The New Financial Literacy Gen Z Needs." Budgeting trends like "loud budgeting" and "soft saving" are going viral on social media. This subject has grown increasingly popular for its powerful impact on individuals, families, and communities.

Financial education can't exist in isolation. As with any national movement, many stakeholders are working together to drive change. To visualize how people and organizations are collaborating for communal financial well-being, the National Endowment for Financial Education developed an insightful framework called the Personal Finance Ecosystem. According to the framework, teaching students about budgeting or investing makes us knowledge influencers—a major force in shaping the financial future of the next generation. The framework also shows that our financial education work is most effective when supported by structural policies, behavioral interventions, and strong social support systems.[1]

In this chapter, we explore how this ecosystem is coming to life through two key dimensions. First, we highlight innovative programs led by pioneering organizations, companies, governments, and financial institutions working to narrow long-standing wealth gaps and empower communities. With our population clamoring for trustworthy financial information, creative thinkers are stepping forward with fresh, impactful solutions.

Second, we dive into school-based practices that embed financial literacy into classrooms. States are rapidly expanding mandates requiring graduates to complete personal finance courses, prompting educators and school districts to rethink how we teach and learn about money.

Throughout this chapter, you'll see how the programs and policies I highlight represent different forces of the financial literacy movement—from building knowledge and expanding access to creating supportive structures and fostering positive behaviors. These approaches are most effective when they work together. That's how real change happens: not from one lesson or one law but from many people and ideas aligning to build financial well-being for our young people.

FOCUSING ON PROGRESS OVER PERFECTION

This work isn't easy, and there are real challenges. But educators are not in it alone. Here, I highlight people who are making financial education more inclusive, relevant, and accessible for the next generation. It's encouraging to see this work becoming a shared priority.

Is it perfect? Nope. But that's not the point. It's about progress. And there is clear progress being made to bring financial information into classrooms and beyond. Like physician and statistician Hans Rosling writes in his fantastic book *Factfulness*, "Does saying 'things are improving' imply that everything is fine, and we should all relax and not worry? No, not at all. Is it helpful to have to choose between bad and improving? Definitely not. It's both. It's both bad and better. Better, and bad, at the same time. That is how we must think about the current state of the world."[2] There are systemic barriers and structural challenges in implementing nationwide financial education. Materials still need to reflect diverse experiences, and we must recognize that not every student has the same financial starting point.

But the momentum toward inclusive access to financial education is undeniable. Let's take a closer look at current financial realities and how we got here, so we can move forward with care, inclusion, and purpose.

FACING WEALTH GAPS IN OUR CLASSROOMS

Let me share a truth that we might not often say out loud: Wealth gaps in our world silently impact students every day. Some hesitate to go out with friends to expensive Brooklyn lunch spots because their family is on a tight budget. Some work twenty-plus hours a week to help cover family expenses while also keeping up with high school classes. Some students come from cash-only households hesitant to open bank accounts, often due to negative experiences with banking services, here or abroad. Different financial realities walk into our classrooms every single day. For centuries, opportunities to build wealth have not been distributed fairly. These issues persist today and shape our students' financial realities. That's why we need to be aware of what is happening with wealth and economic opportunity right now.

Socioeconomic Gaps

The beauty of compounding is that assets grow exponentially, but the painful truth is that many were never able to board the train to benefit. Since 1989, the richest 10 percent of US households have continued to increase their share of total wealth exponentially while the bottom half's share has declined.[3] Families with lower incomes are far less likely to invest in the stock market, while wealthy families are pretty much all in. Those who need chances to grow their wealth often have the least access.[4] When I read those numbers, I think of how I felt as a teen—and of the students who come into class believing financial success is for other people, not for them. The system has stacked wealth toward the top. That's why I'm on a mission to help young people get on the wealth-building train.

Income levels deepen these disparities. Homeownership, which is usually how people build wealth, remains far more accessible to higher-income families. In 2023, only 47 percent of households in the lowest income group owned homes, while 81 percent of those in the top owned theirs.[5] Owning property has helped people build wealth for generations, so this big gap continues to impact wealth building. In 2022, the wealth gap between homeowners and renters was nearly $390,000.[6] This kind of inequality shapes peoples' lives for years to come. These statistics can feel overwhelming, but they're important for our work together.

Racial Gaps

Racial gaps in wealth are even more striking and persistent. According to the Federal Reserve, in 2022, the typical white person held about $285,000 in median wealth. Black and Hispanic families had far lower medians, with about $44,900 and $61,600, respectively. These disparities are the result of decades of housing discrimination, unequal education, and lending practices that excluded entire communities. It's encouraging to see wealth ratios narrowing somewhat, as non-white families have seen faster growth in home, stock, and business ownership. Still, there's much work to do, as the absolute differences in wealth remain huge.[7]

Another interesting nuance of the racial wealth gap is that not all assets build wealth at the same rate. Historically, stocks have outperformed housing by nearly five times. While white households hold a larger share of wealth in financial assets like stocks, Black households hold much more of their net worth in housing and physical assets.[8] Hispanic families show a similar pattern, with lower rates of stock ownership widening wealth gaps.[9] These differences are a reminder that families don't all have the same access to growing wealth. However, this doesn't mean dismissing the wealth our students' families have built through homeownership and physical assets. That's real wealth, quite literally earned through blood, sweat, and tears. Our job is to honor that foundation while opening doors to additional wealth-building opportunities—and to teach them that homes and stocks aren't rivals, but besties in the wealth journey.

Gender Gaps

The gender wealth gap—complete with its pink tax—adds another challenging layer. In 2019, the median wealth of families headed by women was about half that of families headed by men. This gap stems from interrelated factors including the pay gap, uneven caregiving responsibilities, and limited access to tax breaks and employment-related benefits that support wealth building.[10] On top of that, women often pay more for everyday items like razors, shampoo, and hygiene products simply because they are marketed to them.[11]

Gender plus race makes the disparities even more striking. Families headed by Black and Hispanic women had just five and ten cents, respectively, for every dollar of median wealth held by families headed by white men. White women had fifty-six cents in median wealth for every dollar held by white men.[12] These statistics affect the young women sitting in our classroom. They deserve to know what the reality is so we can set them up to change it.

Leading a female-focused investing group is one way I push back and reimagine a different future. We bring thirty teens together during lunch to build confidence, teach practical wealth-building strategies, and create a supportive community. (Shout-out to the Council for Economic Education's awesome—and free—Invest in Girls partnership!) Our squad talks honestly about how money shapes spending, goals, relationships, and careers. It's my small but mighty way of helping the next generation rewrite the wealth rules in a way that truly serves them.

WHEN EQUITY GROWS, WE ALL GROW

Even more powerful news: Closing racial and gender wealth gaps is a national game changer. Bridging these divides could potentially add $1 trillion to $1.5 trillion to the US economy over the next ten years, driven by increased consumption, tax revenue, and productivity.[13] The Kellogg Foundation also found that reducing these gaps could boost gross domestic product (GDP) by up to 12 percent by 2050. This economic growth would benefit communities who need it most, as well as businesses, local areas, and our nation overall.[14] It's a win-win-win situation.

The larger impact reframes financial education from a "nice to have" into an economic necessity. The economic benefits of financial capability extend far beyond the individual. When more people are empowered with resources to build wealth, they invest in homes that strengthen community tax bases, launch small businesses that create local jobs, and contribute to retirement accounts that fuel broader market growth. And most importantly, they model financial wellness for the next generation, creating a momentum of financial well-being.

Providing accessible financial education isn't only about lifting individuals; it's a social and economic movement. Education alone won't narrow wealth gaps, but it is an impactful system within our control, so let's lock in and power through to meaningful change.

BREAKING THE MYTH OF BEING "BAD WITH MONEY"

Understanding wealth gaps is essential to our teaching because financial education doesn't happen in a vacuum. Students enter our classrooms carrying their own financial experiences, along with their families' financial histories, cultural attitudes toward money, and varying levels of trust (or distrust) in financial institutions. Some students are interested in long-term wealth building. Others are drawn to the riskier assets after years of exclusion and a desire to "catch up." Some don't trust the stock market and prefer investing in a physical asset like a home, something they can see and hold. Others, like my own family growing up, had little exposure to wealth-building tools at all. These differences shape children's expectations, their sense of what's possible, and their access to intergenerational wealth. As educators, we need this context to meet students where they are, explain these gaps, and show practical ways to build their financial futures.

Likewise, financial choices are not made in isolation. It's important for students to understand that wealth gaps are rooted in systemic forces, not personal failures. When people ask me for help, they often say things like, "I'm just not good at saving," or "I'm bad with money." That fixed mindset is unfortunate, but is totally understandable given the systems at play. We don't want our students to internalize the idea that they are not "good" with money, a misconception that can leave students feeling discouraged instead of empowered.

Every year, at least one of my students inevitably tells me they are taking this course because they are "bad with money." That usually inspires one of my signature motivational monologues: "Let me stop you there. Don't let me hear you saying you are 'bad' with money again. You are learning. You are growing. You are going to make a lot of decisions. There are systems at play impacting every money move we make from birth. Our goal is to equip you with information to make the best decisions you can at each moment in your life, then make adjustments along the way. Stop saying you are 'bad' at things. We are growing here, people! Got it?" After the unexpected rant, they might be more likely see me as someone who cares about them—and as a total lunatic. My sweet spot.

TEACHING FINANCIAL EMPOWERMENT

The goal is to replace shame with empowerment and action.

When it comes to teaching about wealth gaps, I use a framework called the Cortés triad, developed by Carlos E. Cortés of the University of California, Riverside.[15] It's perfectly simple—just fourteen words—and it helps me acknowledge the weight of history without getting stuck in anger or despair:

Look unflinchingly at the past.
Apply it to the present.
Pivot to the future.

In my financial classroom, we look at how systems like discriminatory lending and unequal access to employment have excluded communities from wealth building. Then we apply that history to today, to see why wealth gaps persist for women, people of color, and low-income families. The past gives us the context to understand the present and imagine new ways forward.

Then comes my favorite part. We pivot to the future, where hope sashays into the ballroom. As Doc Brown reminds us in *Back to the Future III*: "Your future is whatever you make it. So make it a good one." Here we ask: Now that we understand how we got here, what tools and strategies can create different outcomes? What policies must change? What financial knowledge can we share? What wealth-building opportunities exist today that didn't before?

By teaching students wealth-building "secrets" like taking the company match, harnessing the power of compound interest, and spotting predatory lending, we give them knowledge that can change their lives. Education may not erase decades of inequity, but it equips students to navigate current systems and push for a more inclusive financial future.

Our learning spaces offer tremendous reasons for optimism. Research shows that younger generations are eager to learn, with 73 percent of teens expressing a desire for more financial knowledge.[16] This enthusiasm provides an exciting foundation, one that allows us to teach financial concepts that instill confidence and agency in every student.

OPENING DOORS TO FINANCIAL ACCESS

Education is a powerful tool for change, and innovative individuals and organizations are making finance more accessible than ever. Entrepreneurs share financial content across the world, policymakers add coaching to public services, educators connect lessons to real life, community leaders run neighborhood workshops, and podcast hosts break down money topics for millions. Even established institutions are rethinking how people access their financial information.

Closing wealth gaps isn't a one-person job. It requires educators offering passion and pedagogy, tech designing for accessibility, government officials pushing policy change, community organizers building grassroots support, and financial institutions offering long-term expertise. This multi-sector approach is how we make real, lasting progress.

Transforming Money Lessons with Digital Learning

Knowledge changes everything.

—ELLY VALDEZ, senior content creator
for financial literacy, Khan Academy

As content creator for Khan Academy's personal finance curriculum, Elly Valdez is redefining how financial education is delivered. Her personal journey from a cash-only belief to financial expertise illustrates the transformative power of financial education. Elly, a financial advisor and former math educator, shared, "I had to learn financial literacy to teach it. Now I own my home, manage credit cards strategically, and invest. Knowledge changes everything."

Khan Academy's approach has already reached 1.6 million users organically by focusing on relatable content. "We don't discuss lavish vacations," Elly notes. Instead, they emphasize making financial concepts applicable to everyday life. "We're really trying to be like, 'Okay, your car breaks down. How much is a set of used tires?'"[17] I use several of their resources, particularly their financial goals unit and postsecondary planning videos like "Real World: The Menu of Opportunities."

Another way they make it relatable is by speaking directly to the learner. "We wrote in second person—you need tires, you are buying life insurance," Elly explains. "It's not abstract. It's personal." This seemingly small tweak created a major difference in engagement, making financial topics personal to the learner.

Elly Valdez knows what captivates learners. "When I taught math, students groaned," she recalls. "Now, strangers ask me to teach their kids about money. Financial literacy has become the class everyone wants." She emphasizes that even a little knowledge can be transformative. "Financial literacy creates money. The knowledge alone—understanding topics like retirement and savings—empowers people to build wealth."

Platforms like Khan Academy show how free, high-quality digital resources can make financial education more accessible. People like Elly Valdez make a difference by breaking down complex financial ideas. Connecting abstract concepts to everyday experiences makes learning about money more relatable and engaging.

Government Policies for Financial Empowerment

I'm going to give you the information that empowers you to make an informed decision.

—VILDA VERA MAYUGA, commissioner, New York City Department of Consumer and Worker Protection

Financial empowerment is about equipping people with the skills and confidence to manage their money and support their communities. In New York City, Vilda Vera Mayuga, commissioner of the Department of Consumer and Worker Protection, brings genuine passion and energy to tackling obstacles that keep people from accessing financial education.

In 2025, approximately 238,900 households in New York City didn't have bank accounts. Encouragingly, over 66,000 households have gained bank access since 2021.[18] To continue expanding access, Commissioner Mayuga told me about her work championing Financial Empowerment Centers across school districts, supporting both students and parents. People I know who've used these centers rave about their nonjudgmental approach and helpful support. The commissioner's long-term goal is to place an educator in every public school district by 2030: "Financial educators are the glue that's going to keep the whole initiative together." These centers offer free counseling and education and have already served over 73,000 clients to reduce debt by over $127 million and increase savings by more than $14 million.[19] For Mayuga, financial literacy is a win for all of us: "It's feel-good work . . . who doesn't want to help people pay off their debt, increase savings, and have the tools to succeed? It helps the economy."[20]

Mayuga's commitment to this work is deeply personal. She knows firsthand how difficult it is to navigate financial systems without the right knowledge. Reflecting on her childhood in Puerto Rico, she remembers, "Happiness and simplicity were the wealth of my youth." Her awareness of financial literacy began with the challenges of student loans and credit card offers in college, and becoming a mother solidified her drive: "I don't think I started to be so conscious about it until I had kids and had to make sure we could give them the opportunities we wanted."

Her core beliefs center on learning as empowerment: "I'm going to give you the information that empowers you to make an informed decision. Maybe it's not the 'right' decision by some standards, but it's your decision, made with all the information you need." Local government leaders like Commissioner Mayuga are a major driver of financial empowerment.

Building Confidence Through Industry Innovation

We're not just building financial knowledge.
We're building confidence that lasts a lifetime.

—ANDREW KADJESKI, head of brokerage and investments, Vanguard

Banks, investment firms, and financial services can feel out of reach for those who were not raised with the vocabulary, skills, or confidence to participate. That narrative is starting to change. Industry leaders like Andrew Kadjeski, head of brokerage and investments at Vanguard, are shining a light on how money works, especially for young people.

Andrew shares with me that the biggest barrier to investing isn't just money, it's confidence. "What holds many young people back from investing isn't just a lack of funds—it's a lack of confidence. Without foundational financial education, they often don't feel equipped to ask questions, explore options, or take that first step," he explains.[21]

That's why Vanguard created free programs like My Classroom Economy, which bring real-world money lessons directly into K–12 classrooms. I've seen this program in action with elementary students, and it's fascinating how it shapes their thinking about money. Teachers create a classroom economy where students earn income for things like completing outside reading assignments and face expenses if they miss work or are late. Andrew emphasizes creating safe spaces for learning: "A huge part of any type of curriculum, whether it's financial literacy or otherwise, is creating an environment where it is safe to ask questions and try new things and fail. Programs like My Classroom Economy lay the groundwork. They introduce foundational concepts that spark curiosity, build confidence, and encourage students to keep learning."

This work is about lasting generational change. When I asked Andrew what could the world look like in twenty years if every kid graduated with a solid financial background, he said, "For me, it's about seeing a generation grow up with the confidence to make smart financial decisions, take control of their future, and break free from the limitations of their environment. When students graduate with a strong foundation of financial knowledge, they're equipped to do things differently—and that's how lasting change begins."

Whether through digital platforms like Khan Academy, government initiatives like Commissioner Mayuga's Financial Empowerment Centers, or established institutions like Vanguard supporting young people, increasing access to wealth requires a multi-sector approach. This Captain Planet–style "let our powers combine" approach has the potential to transform how an entire generation understands and interacts with money.

THE STATE OF FINANCIAL LITERACY TODAY

With all these innovative efforts, you might wonder: Where do we stand with financial literacy education in America today? Understanding some history might help explain the current momentum for change.

Financial literacy education isn't new. We just put it on the back burner for a while. Remember how we used to learn cooking and sewing in home economics class? In seventh grade, I sewed a basketball hoop pillow. My mother was very proud. Well, those classes also used to teach us about managing money. But something interesting happened in 1957 that changed everything.

Trivia question: What does Sputnik have to do with financial literacy?

According to research by Dan Otter, a former teacher and longtime advocate for financial literacy in schools, when the Soviet Union launched the

Sputnik satellite into space in 1957, America got worried about falling behind. Schools quickly shifted focus to math and science, pushing aside practical life skills classes where we learned about money.[22] For decades, money education took a back seat.

But in the 1990s, things changed. Many people were struggling with credit card debt, paying their mortgages, and saving for retirement, especially as pension plans became less common. So, in 1995, a group called Jump$tart Coalition formed to bring financial education back to schools. Their goal was simple but important: Every kid in America should learn how to manage money. The government followed suit, creating the Financial Literacy and Education Commission in 2003.

We have made progress, but there is still a long way to go. Many Americans struggle with basic personal finance concepts. They get only about half of the basic questions right on the Financial Industry Regulatory Authority (FINRA) financial literacy quiz.[23] Younger people, especially Gen Z and millennials, fare worse, answering just 38 percent and 45 percent correctly, respectively.[24] While financial education is more accessible, there is still work to be done to make sure everyone gains the money skills they need.

Financial Knowledge Quiz: Pulling Back the Curtain

So how do we determine if someone is financially literate? What's the measuring stick experts use? And if we're going to teach financial literacy, what knowledge are we aiming for?

One of the standard measuring tools for financial literacy is surprisingly simple. It's just seven questions from FINRA that cover basic money concepts.[25] As educators, we should be aware of these tools, so we can support students and address gaps in our own understanding.

Here are the seven FINRA financial knowledge questions. (Cover the answers with a piece of paper in case you are a nerd like me and want to test yourself.)

1. **Compound Interest:** Suppose you have $100 in a savings account earning 2 percent interest per year. After five years, how much would you have?

   a) More than $102
   b) Exactly $102
   c) Less than $102

   Answer: a) More than $102 (The balance would grow to about $110.40 due to compound interest.)

2. **Inflation:** Imagine the interest rate on your savings account is 1 percent per year and inflation is 2 percent per year. After one year, would the money in the account buy more, the same, or less than today?

   a) More than today
   b) Exactly the same
   c) Less than today

   Answer: c) Less than today (The inflation rate is higher than the interest rate.)

3. **Bond Pricing:** If interest rates rise, do bond prices typically rise, fall, stay the same, or is there no relationship?

   a) They will rise
   b) They will fall
   c) They will stay the same
   d) There is no relationship between bond prices and the interest rate

   Answer: b) They will fall (Bond prices move in the opposite direction of interest rates.)

4. **Mortgage Terms:** A fifteen-year mortgage typically requires higher monthly payments than a thirty-year mortgage, but the total interest paid over the life of the loan will be less.

   a) True
   b) False

   Answer: a) True (A fifteen-year loan costs less in interest than a thirty-year loan because the principal is paid off faster.)

5. **Risk Diversification:** Buying a single company's stock usually provides a safer return than a stock mutual fund.

   a) True
   b) False

   Answer: b) False (Diversification through a mutual fund reduces risk.)

6. **Compound Interest Calculation:** Suppose you owe $1,000 on a loan and the interest rate you are charged is 20 percent per year compounded annually. If you didn't pay anything off, at this interest rate, how many years would it take for the amount you owe to double?

   a) Less than two years
   b) Two to four years
   c) Five to nine years
   d) Ten or more years

Answer: b) Two to four years (That's about 3.6 years, using the Rule of 72, a shortcut where 72 ÷ interest rate = years to double money.)

7. **Probability and Risk Understanding:** Which of the following indicates the highest probability of getting a particular disease?
   a) One-in-twenty chance of getting the disease
   b) 2 percent of the population will get the disease
   c) Twenty-five out of every one thousand people will get the disease

   Answer: a) One-in-twenty chance (That means a 5 percent chance, while b is 2 percent, and c is 2.5 percent.)

How did you do? I have a confession: The bond question always makes my brain hurt. According to FINRA's latest findings, as a nation, we are still struggling with basic concepts of money. Overall, only 27 percent of respondents answered at least five out of seven questions correctly, a figure that hasn't changed much over the years. There's some good news, though: More people understand how inflation affects their savings compared to a few years ago.[26]

The urgency is real when we look at young adults specifically. More research based on the Personal Finance Index found that 30 percent of young adults (ages eighteen to forty-four) have a relatively low level of financial literacy across key areas like earning, saving, investing, and debt.[27]

The reason why this data matters is the same reason you are here: "Basic personal finance behavior and habits often become established early in adulthood. Young adults also confront a range of financial decisions with ramifications for their financial well-being decades into the future, as well as the present. Yet they are working from a limited base of personal finance knowledge."[28] So, at eighteen, when young people think they are adults all of a sudden, we're asking them to make life-altering financial decisions—student loans, credit cards, apartment leases, first jobs—without the foundational knowledge to guide them.

Financial knowledge gaps are not just an individual problem. They highlight systemic issues in education and economic opportunity across the country. Expecting people to figure it out on their own clearly isn't working. In order to close those gaps, we need thoughtful policy decisions and collective action.

Fortunately, Americans are overwhelmingly in favor of changing this situation. Public support for financial education is strong. A National Endowment for Financial Education nationwide poll found that 88 percent of Americans believe their state should require a semester or yearlong personal finance course for high school graduation, with 80 percent wishing they had taken such a course themselves.[29] Widespread support for teaching financial skills creates a strong foundation for advocacy and policy change. Like John Cena sings, "The time is now." Let's look at how financial education is evolving in our classrooms, where we stand today, and the incredibly promising paths ahead.

THE METEORIC RISE OF FINANCIAL LITERACY MANDATES

By 2030, we project that the number of students required to take standalone personal finance courses will triple.

—CHRISTIAN SHERRILL, director of Teacher Success, Next Gen Personal Finance

As a country, we are done being clueless about money. A staggering 90 percent of Americans agree that financial literacy should be a required subject in schools, and more than half (57 percent) strongly agree.[30] When was the last time 90 percent of Americans agreed on anything? Ultimately, we understand, as a nation, teaching financial skills helps everyone and hurts no one.

That's why financial education is making a grand comeback in schools across America. The mandate movement requiring high school students to graduate with one semester of standalone personal finance is riding a huge wave of support. Of the thirty states currently requiring such a course, Utah led the way—so early to the party, it ended up helping set up the chairs. More recently, Delaware, Kentucky, Colorado, and Texas have joined the financial-literacy fiesta.[31] This isn't a small educational trend; it's a passionate movement that is changing how an entire generation will understand money. "By 2030, we project that the number of students required to take standalone personal finance courses will triple," says Christian Sherrill, director of advocacy at Next Gen Personal Finance (NGPF). NGPF's mission is to ensure that all students graduate high school with the financial skills needed to thrive in adulthood that year.

Christian brings both classroom and policy experience to his advocacy work. When I spoke with him, he emphasized that this movement isn't driven by politicians but by families. "In all these states, we almost never frame it as a mandate," he explains, "because ultimately this is like an 85 to 90 percent issue, meaning people are clamoring to be required to take a personal finance class or for their children to be required to take a personal finance class." Christian stresses that the momentum comes from the community level. "It's not the state level or federal level prescribing this because it's 'good for us,'" he tells me. "No, this is something that people are asking for. They're not asking for a couple of workshops at the end of another class. They're asking for the whole enchilada—a full course required for graduation."[32]

The best part is that this change is fueled by grassroots energy—caregivers emailing school boards, kids advocating in student government, and educators like us pushing for financial literacy in schools. There's a reason why people always say they wish they learned this in school. It's because talking about money often brings us back to our own past struggles with things like credit card debt, student loans, or budget stress. It makes us realize how powerful it would have been to learn these skills sooner. That belief in financial literacy spreads, reaching parents, school boards, and legislators, driving real change. Thanks to these efforts, soon two-thirds of high school graduates will step into adulthood with real money skills.

Grassroots change happens alongside larger organizations like the Council for Economic Education (CEE), which is making a significant impact on the mandate movement. Its FinEd50 initiative in partnership with Visa is about bringing financial empowerment to all fifty states. They provide professional development for teachers, curriculum resources, and advocacy efforts, to ensure every student, regardless of zip code, has access to high-quality financial education.[33]

The Council for Economic Education holds a special place in my heart. First, because the organization co-wrote the National Financial Literacy Standards that guide so much of our teaching. Second, for CEE, it's all about human impact. I had the honor of presenting at their Women's History Month workshops, where I met caring people across fields who genuinely want our youth to feel financially confident and capable. CEE's leadership recognizes that financial education is both an academic subject and a pathway to economic mobility. At their national conferences, I met dedicated teachers from rural, suburban, and urban areas helping students navigate complex financial realities. CEE's resources speak to all these experiences, recognizing that financial empowerment looks different for every student—but is essential for all.

Their 2026 *Survey of the States* shows the remarkable progress we're making nationwide. Each state that adopts financial education requirements is doing so on behalf of thousands of young people, students who will enter adulthood better equipped to build wealth, avoid predatory lending, and make financial choices aligned with their values.[34]

I see the profound impact of this work in my own journey to break financial scarcity, and in my students' journeys too. Big opportunities to reshape patterns of financial inclusion for generations don't come often. Educators around the country have known this for years, and it's important to recognize the grassroots work happening in classrooms alongside policy from the start.

Authentic Teaching That Sparked a Movement

She told me, "Thank you. You have changed my family tree."

—JOEL CHRISLER, director of teacher engagement and support, Jump$tart Coalition

Joel Chrisler returned to his high school in Wisconsin as a teacher and found himself assigned to consumer economics—a class he once took and remembered for only one lesson: how to write a check. Looking back, he told me: "What a waste! This subject has the potential to be truly impactful, and I need to do everything I can to make that happen."[35]

Joel's personal connection to financial struggle—watching his family farm go through bankruptcy—fueled his determination. "I saw firsthand what economics can do to a family-run business," Joel said. "It was horrible." That experience motivated him to teach a course that would be not only useful, but memorable.

Joel discovered something powerful about authenticity: "A willingness to share bad stuff as well as the good stuff made all the impact in the world." Students connected with his honest approach. That authenticity led to breakthrough moments, like when a student told him, "I've lived my whole life watching my parents struggle paycheck to paycheck, argue about money, fighting about money. I'm never going to have to live that way. Thank you. You have changed my family tree."

Building Movements from the Ground Up

Moments like these helped Joel see the broader potential of his work, and he embraced advocacy. "This has to be bigger," he stated, as the momentum shifted from the classroom to the wider community. Collaborating closely with his now superintendent, he channeled enthusiastic parent feedback into collective action. "I asked parents to direct their support to the school board," he recalls. Their voices were heard, and by 2017, his consumer economics course became a graduation requirement.

His approach created a powerful ripple effect by:

- establishing meaningful classroom curriculum
- driving student engagement that led to parent advocacy

- amplifying parent voices at the school board
- turning one district's requirement into a model for others
- attracting statewide attention through district success

It all started in Joel's classroom with his authenticity, meaningful lessons, and strong student connection. This genuine approach is what fuels the financial education movement across the nation. Today, Joel serves as the director of teacher engagement and support at the Jump$tart Coalition, where he's still advocating for financial education at a national level. His journey shows how passionate educators can influence their local communities and even help shape national educational policy. Passionate individuals are bringing personal finance to college campuses too. Drew Barksdale, dean of Undergraduate Student Success at Boston College, noticed that students were mastering *corporate* finance but no one was teaching them to manage their *own* money. So he built a personal finance seminar called Gen-Z Money. (I wish this course existed when I was on campus eating ramen.) Three cohorts and 300+ students later, Drew says of the impact: "One small decision has been compounding ever since."

LEARNING FROM STATE IMPLEMENTATION EXPERIENCES

There's no one-size-fits-all for financial education.

—CARLY URBAN, professor of economics,
Montana State University

Okay, I'm sold. So how do we get financial education going for the rest of us across the country? And what can we learn from the trailblazing states that already pioneered personal finance courses and navigated implementation challenges?

For over a decade, Carly Urban, professor of economics at Montana State University, has studied financial education's impact. A research legend in financial education, she is also an expert at translating complex policy insights into practical tools for educators and policymakers. When I reached out to understand what truly works in financial education policy, she shared her wealth of knowledge.

Urban's report, *Best Practices Implementing Financial Education in High Schools*, examines eight states and identifies key patterns behind successful mandates.[36] Her report outlines key characteristics of effective financial education programs, whether implemented by state legislation or local initiatives. If you're ready to advocate for implementation at your school, district, or state level, à la Joel Chrisler in Wisconsin, I highly recommend reading the full report. It's accessible and full of actionable steps.

Let's explore Urban's core findings about how they can help us create more effective financial literacy programs.

The People Matter

In our conversation, Carly Urban emphasized that successful implementations begin with committed people. Every successful state started by building what she calls "a coalition of stakeholders." These coalitions often included local nonprofits, Federal Reserve branches, credit union leagues, and teachers already passionate about financial literacy, and perhaps most importantly, students themselves.[37]

Passionate people matter even more than the size of the coalition. As one leader put it, "If you have a continuous appetite for the conceptual idea, you are way ahead of the game, and the rest is in the details." I have seen this in my own advocacy work. The passion and commitment must be genuine and sustained as the implementation challenges are real.

Implementation, just like personal finance, is personal. Transforming financial education is driven by relationships. The states that succeeded were those that fostered strong human connections: between state officials and local educators, between veteran teachers and newcomers to financial education, and between schools and their communities.

Professional Development as the Key

Every state leader Urban interviewed emphasized the same point: Teacher professional development was "the most important component of successful implementation." States that succeeded didn't just throw curriculum links at teachers in a long email and hope for the best. They created systematic training programs that spanned multiple years.

The approaches varied, with some states offering intensive summer institutes with stipends, others providing flexible online modules, and some doing both. But they all recognized a fundamental truth: You can't teach what you don't understand. Most teachers weren't formally trained in financial concepts during their own education, so we need to support them first. High-five to you reading this right now.

The Funding

State mandates often require funding in two key areas: teacher professional development and dedicated staff to oversee implementation. Successful states found creative ways to support teacher training, often partnering with local foundations and other organizations to provide stipends for educators completing professional development hours.

Even more encouraging was what Urban heard from one state representative: "Personal finance is the most resource-rich environment in public education." Unlike other subjects, where teachers may struggle to find quality materials, financial education offers a wealth of vetted, no-cost resources and professional development opportunities.

This abundance can create its own challenge. How do you choose from so many good options? The most successful states solved this by creating curated lists of recommended resources, often in partnership with organizations like the Federal Reserve System, to vet materials and ensure quality.

Allowing for Flexibility

The most effective mandates provided clear standards while allowing local flexibility. States that were too rigid in their requirements faced resistance. States that were too loose saw inconsistent implementation. The sweet spot seemed to be what is called *principled flexibility*: being clear about what students need—comprehensive financial education—while remaining open about how and when schools achieve it, choosing vetted approaches that fit their contexts.

Let's start with when we teach it. Many educators and policymakers I've spoken with believe eleventh grade is the ideal time for a standalone personal finance course. An NGPF survey found that eight out of ten personal finance teachers recommend teaching it in eleventh or twelfth grade.[38] Students of this age have started working, received paychecks (with deductions), and begun thinking seriously about their next steps in adulting, which makes the content immediately relevant. Still, what's possible varies by district, with some schools offering the course earlier and others reserving it for twelfth grade to meet scheduling or graduation requirements.

Teacher requirements are a clear example of this balance. Some states took a broad approach, allowing any certified teacher to instruct financial literacy, while others imposed strict criteria, requiring specific endorsements or training. Both approaches have challenges. If you are too broad, teachers are unprepared and struggle with the content. If you are too specific, schools with fewer teachers like rural schools can't find qualified teachers, limiting students' access to the course. Successful states balanced establishing clear standards and offering multiple pathways for teachers to acquire credentials.

Flexibility is also important in selecting a curriculum. Some states that mandated a specific textbook or program faced pushback from districts with a mix of student needs and resources. The more successful approaches were in states that laid out clear standards but also provided a range of vetted options. This structured flexibility empowered schools to choose what worked best for their communities.

This structured flexibility is key because every school district has unique student populations, resources, and community needs. The most effective mandates honored those differences while maintaining commitment to the goal: ensuring every student graduates with meaningful financial knowledge and skills.

A Mindset of Continuous Improvement

Successful states built feedback loops from the very beginning. They didn't treat implementation as a one-time event to check off—"Yay, we did it!"—but as an ongoing process requiring continuous attention and adaptation.

Utah set a strong example for continuous improvement with its comprehensive state auditor's report, which assesses not only whether schools are providing financial education but also the real impact on students. Other states gather feedback through teacher surveys, student transcript reviews, and regular school visits to ensure policy translates into meaningful learning.

IMPLEMENTING FINANCIAL EDUCATION IN MY SCHOOL COMMUNITY

Today, New York State lacks a standalone personal finance requirement, but our students still need essential money skills. So we need to figure out ways to make it happen. The scheduling puzzle is real. In my own school, we wrestled with the same questions you're probably asking: Where does this fit? What gets displaced? Will this overload students who are already juggling core classes and testing requirements?

Constraints

These aren't just theoretical concerns. In my school, we had heated debates about these same questions. The truth of leadership is that when we commit time, energy, and resources to one initiative, something else inevitably slides down the priority list. That's just the real deal of working within finite hours and limited resources. In places like New York City, where union contracts and graduation requirements create additional constraints, the puzzle becomes even more complex.

Creativity

But we got creative. We started by initially adding a financial literacy component to our existing economics class. It was one unit in the spring semester where students would complete tasks around taxes, create budgets, and learn about opening bank accounts. As student interest grew, we developed a standalone elective that all eleventh graders now take. It became a math class where students run the numbers for budgets around realistic situations like housing and vacations, analyze rental leases, and dive deep into savings and interest calculations.

What I discovered through this process is that I couldn't allow scheduling challenges to become excuses for inaction. Yes, academic policy and schedules are complicated. Yes, it requires creative solutions. Yes, scheduling conversations are mind-numbing. But we must stay the course, because we are changing lives here, people!

Expansion

The student demand didn't stop there. We expanded further, creating an additional standalone elective I decided to teach that focused more deeply on topics like money mindset and investing. Now students in my school can graduate with both a financial literacy and an investment elective course, creating multiple entry points and pathways for students to explore money topics that matter to them. Having the vision and flexibility to implement financial education allowed us to respond to what our students truly wanted and needed.

Circumstances are always changing; our students need schools that can respond to new realities. For us, that meant recognizing that while core classes remain essential, financial literacy was not optional anymore. We couldn't wait for a mandate; we had to build it into our graduation requirements ourselves. The boldest change is to question what we've always done.

Innovation means admitting that our current structure, while well intentioned, may not serve students as well as it once did.

EDUCATORS AT THE HEART OF IMPLEMENTATION

Teaching financial literacy feels different from algebra, history, or even physical education. While these subjects have established curricula and teaching methods honed over decades, financial education is still the new kid on the block in many ways. Teachers also lack a frame of reference from their own education. Financial education became a formal requirement in schools only recently, with Utah breaking ground with the first state mandate in 2008 following the global financial crisis. Most of us never took financial courses during our own schooling, and we certainly weren't trained in the pedagogy for teaching these concepts during teacher preparation programs.

As states across the country increasingly mandate financial literacy education, teachers need meaningful professional development to teach these skills with confidence. That's the primary reason I wrote this book. "The teachers who are already teaching personal finance don't have it yanked away from them," notes Christian Sherrill. "This is something they raised their hand to do." This book grew out of classroom experiences and conversations with hundreds of educators nationwide who face the same challenge: They want to equip students with financial knowledge but often lack the training and confidence to do so effectively.

The newness of financial education as a subject in schools, combined with no personal frame of reference, makes many educators feel unprepared. I felt that same flutter of nervousness when I first started teaching financial concepts. The thought of standing in front of a class of thirty teenagers feeling unprepared is the stuff nightmares are made of. But then I discovered an incredible ecosystem of free resources built specifically for educators like us.

Finding Your Financial Education Community

What helped me feel prepared was finding organizations that understand our challenges and provide ready-to-use materials that don't require a finance degree to teach effectively. I started with NGPF's professional development courses on career planning and cryptocurrency, which were incredibly helpful. The teaching credits and professional development swag were nice bonuses, but more important, their materials strengthened my content knowledge and showed me how to present complex topics in engaging ways for students.

Through CEE's master teacher program, I met educators whose energy and creativity in making financial education relevant fundamentally changed my approach. Their webinars guided me through topics like taxes and insurance, where my own knowledge was weakest. At the CEE national conference in Cleveland, I presented workshops and found like-minded passionate educators from across the country. Conversations about topics like the business of youth sports in the elevator made me realize, "These are my people." Eventually, I found myself leading CEE sessions, sharing strategies that worked in my classroom with others just beginning their financial education journey.

The momentum continued when I joined the Intuit Educator Community. Suddenly, I wasn't alone in this work. Our monthly virtual meetings became a highlight, with educators from across the country sharing creative ways to make tools like TurboTax and Credit Karma relevant to teenagers. Those virtual connections blossomed into in-person professional development and student events in cities like New Orleans, Washington, DC, and Los Angeles.

Your Professional Development Road Map

If you're feeling that familiar teacher anxiety about diving into financial concepts, know that there's a community of practice waiting to welcome you. Here are some standout organizations offering free professional development.

- **Banzai** offers free webinars and on-demand courses with professional development credit for teachers. *banzai.org/professional-development*
- **Council for Economic Education** provides webinars, conferences, and resources. *econedlink.org/webinar-catalogue/*
- **Intuit for Education** offers professional development events, certifications, and curricular resources. *intuit.com/solutions/education/*
- **Jump$tart Coalition** offers professional development events and online distance learning and resources. *jumpstart.org/education/jsffe/*
- **Next Gen Personal Finance (NGPF)** offers webinars, courses, certifications, and curricular resources. *ngpf.org/ondemand*

As Marsha Iverson, a financial literacy consultant for New York City Public Schools, tells me, "Effective financial education needs to help teachers in both content and confidence." That dual focus makes all the difference.

REMEMBER: YOUR STUDENTS NEED YOU

Here's the beautiful truth about teaching financial literacy: Your students need you exactly as you are. Your confidence and capability come from your curiosity, your willingness to learn with them, and your ability to make complex concepts accessible. They don't need you to be a certified financial planner or investment advisor. Unless you are, in which case, that's also awesome!

When a student asks about calls and puts and you're still learning about investing yourself, you can say, "I'm learning about this too. Let's research it together and figure out what reputable sources tell us about the risks and benefits." (This is me every time.) This intellectual honesty strengthens your credibility and models lifelong learning for students.

You don't need to know everything about money. You just need to create spaces where your students can explore, question, and grow. Your willingness, combined with the incredible resources available, is more than enough to transform young lives.

PATHWAYS TO PRO$PERITY: SUSTAINING THE MOMENTUM

The momentum is undeniable. We have public support, legislative backing, proven implementation models, and passionate educators ready to transform financial education. The challenges of crowded schedules, teacher preparation, and diverse student needs aren't roadblocks. They're the very problems we're uniquely positioned to solve.

What gives me hope is that this movement isn't a top-down policy forcing change on reluctant schools. It's grassroots energy bubbling up from classrooms, dinner tables, and community conversations. A teacher discovers the power of authentic money discussions and becomes an advocate. Parents watch their children ask thoughtful financial questions and approach school leaders. Students graduate with confidence to navigate their financial futures and spread that knowledge to their families. Everyday people figure out their finances and start podcasts to help others avoid their mistakes.

Whether you're a classroom teacher guiding students through credit scores, a caregiver navigating your first budgeting conversations, a community workshop leader addressing local economic challenges, or a financial coach helping clients untangle debt, you're an educator who is part of this collective effort. Through financial education, we're unlocking possibilities for our youth that our ancestors could only dream of.

In my experience, I've learned that even the snazziest mandate loses impact if students don't see themselves reflected in it. The question isn't just about getting students to calculate financial formulas, it's about whether they believe those concepts apply to their lives and futures. When financial education is built on a foundation of belonging, it can transform generations. In the next chapter, we explore how to create inclusive spaces where every student has value and a voice in money conversations.

SELF-REFLECTION

Throughout this chapter, we've explored the incredible work happening across public and private sectors to promote financial literacy education. Take a moment to think about these questions as you shape your teaching approach.

Personal Reflection

- $ How has your understanding of wealth gaps and systemic barriers evolved throughout your career? Were there moments that shifted your perspective?
- $ What financial programs, tools, or resources have you personally found most helpful in your own financial journey? What made them effective for you?
- $ When you think about innovation in financial services or education, what excites you most? What concerns you most?
- $ How comfortable do you feel discussing policy changes or systemic issues related to finance? What helps you navigate these complex conversations?
- $ What's one financial topic where you've experienced significant personal growth in understanding, and how did that growth happen?
- $ If you could change one aspect of how financial education is structured nationally, what would it be and why?

Educator Reflection

- $ How do you make abstract financial policies or systems tangible and relevant for your specific students?
- $ How do you balance teaching immediate money skills with encouraging students to question and improve financial systems?
- $ How do you currently navigate financial education within your school's scheduling constraints? What creative approaches have you tried?
- $ What professional development experiences have been most valuable in building your confidence to teach financial concepts? What made them effective?
- $ What partnerships—with businesses, nonprofits, or community organizations—have enhanced your financial education efforts, or which would you like to develop?

EDUCATOR RESOURCES

Student Discussion Questions

Quick prompts designed to ignite student conversation

- Given that financial literacy hasn't always been required in school, why are you excited to take this course?
- What financial topics feel most immediately relevant to your life right now?
- How does your personal background affect how you experience financial systems? What perspectives might you bring that others don't have?

- What local, state, or national changes do you think could narrow wealth gaps?
- When a teacher shares their own financial experiences—both successes and mistakes—how does that affect how you connect with the topic?

Standalone Activities (20–50 minutes)

Reflective activities for educators to assess their teaching context, resources, and approach

- **FINANCIAL PROGRAM MAPPING ACTIVITY**
  - **Purpose:** Evaluate your organization's current financial education practices to find strengths and areas of growth.
  - **Process:** Form a cross-stakeholder team of teachers, administrators, students, parents, community members, and create a structured chart covering current offerings, teacher confidence, student engagement, parent involvement, community connections, resources, and challenges. Collaboratively identify current strengths for each category before noting gaps. Gather perspectives of multiple stakeholders through surveys, focus groups, or individual interviews. Identify two to three "quick wins" and one to two longer-term goals based on capacity and community needs. Create an action plan with responsible parties and timelines.

- **LOCAL RESOURCE MAPPING**
  - **Purpose:** Find resources to build financial education in your community.
  - **Process:** Create a visual mind map of your school community identifying both formal institutions (banks, credit unions, nonprofits, government offices, tax assistance centers, local businesses) and informal networks (parents with financial expertise, alumni in finance, cultural organizations). For each resource, note potential contributions, contact information, and cultural relevance. Develop an outreach plan for three to four promising connections, honoring authentic relationship-building approaches. (Shout-out: This embodies *ujamaa*, or cooperative economics, the fourth principle of Kwanzaa, emphasizing community-based resources for shared prosperity!)

- **FINANCIAL EDUCATION IMPLEMENTATION TIMELINE**
  - **Purpose:** Create a realistic road map for intentional, sustainable implementation.
  - **Process:** Map out one to two school years, marking key decision points, including curriculum planning periods, budget cycles, professional

development days, and parent-teacher conferences. Schedule touchpoints for teacher training, curriculum development, resource acquisition, parent engagement, and community partnerships. Build in regular assessment points, celebrations, and course corrections to maintain momentum. Identify potential obstacles (funding, resistance, competing priorities) and develop strategies to deal with those anticipated issues.

CHAPTER 3

THE BELONGING

Creating Inclusive Financial Spaces

When I think about the powerful moments in my classroom—the ones that make spiraling down a planning wormhole feel worth it—I think about Sherry lighting up during our unit on credit. We were watching a video of credit expert Shonda Martin discussing how she learned to build credit from scratch and then shared those resources with her community.

Sherry turned to me and said, "Ooh, Miss, I didn't know people like us did this stuff." I smiled at her comment and my little educator heart did the Tootsie Roll.

It wasn't just the thrill of a student understanding the lesson. It was because Sherry saw someone who she connected to speaking confidently in a financial space. Financial spaces often feel exclusionary, especially for students from communities historically left out of wealth conversations. Because it's not just about learning the jargon of money. It's about facing a deeper question that plagues many people: *Do I belong in these financial conversations? Is this world for me?*

For much of my life, I asked myself the same questions. *Does someone from my background belong in conversations about money, wealth, and power?* The answer I've discovered—and the one I'm passionate about helping my students discover—is a resounding YES.

SEEING YOURSELF IN THE FINANCIAL WORLD

When I ask students to define wealth at the beginning of our course, their answers are predictable: money, mansions, luxury cars, private jets. Who can blame them? Our culture and social media reinforce this narrow vision daily. I admit, my own wealth dreams might include an overwater bungalow in Bora Bora.

Yet true financial belonging begins when we expand that definition. Wealth isn't only what we own; it's also the skills, resilience, and community we offer to the world. By widening that lens, we create classrooms where student strengths are valued.

As Aisha Nyandoro explains in her inspiring TED Talk, "We have a poverty of imagination about what makes you wealthy." She defines wealth as a sense of agency, a sense of freedom, the collective well-being of the whole, not an individual pathological pursuit.[1] We need to expand our understanding of wealth to honor the diverse strengths people bring to their financial lives.

This view of wealth is what is referred to as an asset-based approach or a lens of abundance. This perspective shift is transformational because instead of just looking at what students don't have when it comes to money, we see the strengths and resources they already have. Students aren't empty vessels waiting to be filled with financial knowledge, but individuals who already possess valuable forms of wealth that we can leverage.

When creating inclusive financial education spaces, I'm reminded of renowned scholar Rudine Sims Bishop's powerful "windows, mirrors, and sliding glass doors" framework. Bishop is known for her work in children's literature and multicultural education, and she created this concept to show how diverse stories help children see into other lives, reflect on their own, and step into new experiences.[2]

According to Bishop's framework, financial education serves three essential functions:

- **As windows:** Materials offer views into experiences that may be unfamiliar, allowing students to glimpse financial realities and approaches different from their own.
- **As mirrors:** Content reflects students' own identities and experiences, validating that their financial lives and cultural approaches to money are legitimate and valuable.
- **As sliding glass doors:** Experiences invite students to actively participate in conversations, empowering them to see themselves as capable financial actors rather than passive observers.

Bishop's framework serves as a blueprint for designing curricula that reflect students' identities in financial contexts so that they feel they belong. When a student like Sherry sees herself reflected in a credit expert, she's experiencing a mirror moment where financial success feels accessible and relevant to her own life. This plants a seed for Sherry to participate in the financial world in ways she might never have considered before.

This chapter promotes that vision of inclusivity for everyone who enters our learning spaces, educators and students alike.

The Many Forms of Wealth We Carry

Finances are just one form of wealth; we each bring far more to the classroom than our bank accounts. Our wealth is also found in cultural capital, community resources, linguistic abilities, and generational knowledge. These forms of capital are lived, tangible strengths we carry every day. Growing up, I viewed my humble beginnings through a deficit mindset, equating a lack of financial wealth with being "poor." As I've done a lot of self-growth work, and connected with people across backgrounds, I now recognize the many forms of wealth that exist beyond money. Let me share some I've discovered in my own life:

- **Knowledge wealth:** My mother is one of the most well-read, educated people I know. She wasn't able to finish her formal schooling, so she got her GED and went back to college and earned credits in her forties. She's bilingual, loves learning languages, and sends me *mamá chancleta* memes of mothers everywhere wielding the disciplinary slipper. We went to the library every day and read the *World Book* encyclopedia. To this day, she constantly sends me articles, books, and videos from all different perspectives. Her commitment to learning is an invaluable asset that shapes how I approach education.
- **Cultural wealth:** My father was extremely proud to be Puerto Rican and a *jíbaro* (akin to a country boy). In a sea of pastel polo shirts, he once visited me at college wearing a T-shirt with a big old rooster on the front and an equally large Puerto Rican flag on the back. He ensured we spoke Spanish at home and always visited every family member on the island. He taught us salsa and pushed us onto the dance floor. He counted every Puerto Rican on every baseball team roster and rooted for the Texas Rangers in the 1990s because of their high *Boricua* ratio. Our cultural identity gave us a sense of belonging and pride.
- **Work ethic wealth:** My sister Irene has been working in the food service industry since she was fifteen. One year she worked at an ice cream store and brought sundaes with all the toppings to my class. I was very popular that day. Formal schooling wasn't where she thrived, and instead she found her calling by building relationships, putting in long hours, and taking on whatever shifts were available. Over the years, she has built an impressive career as a trusted leader through her interpersonal skills, hard work, and hustle. She proves there are multiple

paths to success when you lean into your strengths. Her wealth of work experience and leadership is immensely valuable in the world.

- **Perseverance wealth:** Starting as a caretaker, my father was often overlooked and passed over for promotions. He was told his accent wasn't "management material." With a fighting spirit, he plastered index cards all over our 1980s pink-tile bathroom and made us drill him on English words and vocabulary. Through a wealth of sheer determination, every time he faced a rejection, he studied twice as hard to earn the next promotion.

Valuing every kind of wealth reflects Tara Yosso's cultural wealth model,[3] which identifies six forms of capital that students bring to educational spaces:

- **Aspirational capital:** the ability to maintain hopes and dreams despite barriers
- **Linguistic capital:** skills gained through communication in multiple languages
- **Familial capital:** cultural knowledge nurtured within families and communities
- **Social capital:** networks and relationships that provide support
- **Navigational capital:** the ability to maneuver through challenging institutions
- **Resistance capital:** skills developed through challenging inequality

When we acknowledge these multiple forms of wealth in ourselves and in our classrooms, something magical happens: Students who may have felt "poor" in traditional financial discussions recognize the strengths they possess. They aren't in deficit; they're looking to add financial knowledge to their existing portfolio.

Creating Space for Students' Wealth Stories

One of the most transformative exercises in my classroom is starting the course with a student survey. Asking intentional questions on an online or paper survey, we create space for students' wealth stories to emerge. I've watched them reflect deeply, saying:

- "I speak four languages; all my family does. I never thought about that as wealth before."
- "My grandma used to own a small store in Brooklyn. I didn't think of her as an entrepreneur until now."

- "In my culture, we have a community savings system called a susu where everyone contributes and takes turns receiving the pot. It's how my parents bought my brother his first car."

Another asset-based question I love to ask is, "Do you know anyone who is retired?" followed by "What did they do? How old are they? Where do they live?" Their responses illustrate the work ethic and familial wealth shaping their world.

- "My grandma. She worked the front desk in an office and is now sixty-four and lives in Florida."
- "My grandma is retired. She's in her sixties and she's in Mexico where my parents grew up."
- "My stepdad is retired from the military. He's sixty-something years old. He lives with us too now."
- "My grandma retired. She's in her seventies, and she was a maid her whole life."
- "My uncle. He worked in the postal office for his whole life."
- "My grandma used to own a restaurant in DR. I'm not sure how old she was when she retired; I have to ask her."
- "My grandma retired, and she just did everything to take care of her children and now they do everything to take care of her."

(Shout-out to the hustling grandmas who represent inspiring retirement role models!) These responses showcase the diversity of retirement experiences my students already bring to class. Questions like this help students see themselves reflected in financial conversations about retirement, a topic that can otherwise feel distant to young people.

PATHWAYS TO FINANCIAL BELONGING

Barriers to financial belonging aren't new, they're generational, systemic. But knowing that means you can work with awareness.

—SHANISHA DIXON-TYRELL,
CEO of Shanisha's Changing Lives Inc.

As we explored in chapter 2, inclusive financial education starts with understanding that financial spaces have been unwelcoming to many communities. When I teach about investing or homeownership, I always start with historical context, because financial concepts are deeply intertwined with larger systems. I want my students to know they belong in these spaces, even when challenges exist.

This approach didn't always come naturally to me. I'm wired to solve problems. I'm a great listener, but once I hear an issue, I want to fix it immediately. My partner has "joked" that sometimes he just wants to vent, not receive a five-step action plan. In college, when I first learned how financial systems were designed to exclude, I reflected on my own childhood and felt frustrated. My fix-it mindset transformed that anger into action: I became an ESL (English as a Second Language) teacher to help kids in my community.

Over time, I've learned that teaching financial education requires a balance: acknowledging systemic problems, giving space for reflection and providing actionable tools to create pathways forward. I'm naturally drawn to the tools—the strategies to navigate financial systems—because I know those frustrations firsthand and want to ease students' burdens as soon as possible. But slowing down to name the systems matters.

As Halle Amore Bauer, a New York City economics educator, explains, "When we're trying to be inclusive of students from marginalized identities, many have had negative interactions with our economic system. So if you put them in an econ or finance class that says, 'Look how great the American dream is,' they might think, 'That's not true for everyone.' For them, it can feel like a giant gaslighting campaign—unless the class addresses it."[4]

That's why I appreciate Shanisha Dixon-Tyrell, a community-based financial coach, and how she approaches history with empowerment. She told me how she enters the conversation: "I connect history to their lives. We talk about Tulsa or Black Wall Street, but then I show how redlining happened right here in the Bronx, in their neighborhoods. Their reaction? 'Whoa, that's my block!' I help them see: These systems were designed to limit you. But knowing that means you can work with awareness, not against yourself."[5]

Pretending these barriers don't exist while trying to teach "just save more" is one-dimensional. By sharing this honest history, Shanisha transforms frustration into agency. She creates a safe space where students can process their feelings about financial systems while learning how to move forward. And that's the first step to rewriting the rules and designing for belonging.

DESIGNING FOR BELONGING

My student population is usually left out, so if there's a movement towards inclusion, especially when it comes to personal finance, that's where I will be.

—CURT CRUZ, inclusion teacher-leader

So, how can we design welcoming spaces that build skill and confidence? As educators, we might not control the entire financial system, but learning spaces are our domain. It's where we create a vibe that makes everyone feel they belong in the money conversation. Our spaces are where we can nurture hope and possibility for learners' financial futures. These spaces may look different, but they all intentionally blend pedagogy with emotional connection. Belonging isn't accidental; it happens by design.

In my classroom, it's about building relationships over the course of a year, seeing the satisfaction on students' faces when they finally grasp concepts like interest or credit. Sometimes you see the seeds you plant in an aha moment in that unit or by the end of the semester. Other times, it's years later, when an alum emails you to say she's a business major and applying for a scholarship because of a book we read in class.

My friend who runs financial coaching sessions fosters belonging through deeply personal conversations about money fears and dreams. Another colleague leading community workshops builds trust by using examples specific to her neighborhood's economic realities. On her podcast, Arivee Vargas carefully selects guests with different financial journeys so listeners hear stories that mirror their own experiences. I've watched district administrators make belonging scalable by implementing policies that value diverse perspectives. Families have the greatest opportunity of all: They know their child the best and can weave financial lessons into everyday life.

For Curt Cruz, who teaches financial literacy to students with special needs in Maryland, fostering belonging starts with designing for access. He shared his approach with me: "These are concepts that I needed to break down, do major accommodations and modifications in terms of the goals, in terms of understanding, in terms of the reading level. So all of our lessons, when it comes to personal finance, we still align it to their IEP goals, not to limit them, but to make sure that it's like hitting two birds with one stone."[6]

By designing assignments that include families, Curt helps students build confidence in navigating financial spaces. "The projects that I usually work on with my students, some of whom are not verbal or very limited when it comes to their verbal abilities, sometimes require their parents to help them. And their parents text me later saying, 'Mr. Cruz, this is a unique subject that we didn't even know our child could do. We thought that at the beginning it was impossible for them. But we also recognize that it's a need.'" By making financial topics accessible to diverse learners, Curt helps his students build a foundation to tackle more complex financial challenges later. And with parent engagement, it becomes a multigenerational win.

Theoretical Frameworks That Center Inclusion

Creating financial spaces of belonging can be grounded in foundational educational theories centered on inclusion and transformation. Dr. Paulo Freire's Critical Pedagogy framework focuses on using education as a tool for social change. He focuses on empowering students from disenfranchised communities to transform their own circumstances. Instead of "banking" models of education—where we just feed them information—Freire highlights the importance of dialogue.[7] In financial education, this means encouraging students to critically engage with financial concepts instead of passively receiving them. This also means teaching students to navigate existing systems and helping them question and eventually reshape those systems.

Similarly, Dr. Geneva Gay's work in culturally responsive teaching is all about making classrooms that feel welcoming for everyone. She urges educators to validate students' identities and leverage their diverse backgrounds as assets. Her work asks us to create learning environments where students feel they truly belong.[8] In financial education, this means recognizing the wealth of knowledge, traditions, and practices students bring from their families and communities. Our students might describe communal saving approaches like susu circles or share how family obligations influence their budgets. Culturally responsive financial teaching respects and incorporates these diverse experiences.

Another framework that has transformed how I approach inclusive teaching comes from Dr. Chris Emdin's reality pedagogy and his "7 Cs" for effective teaching—co-generative dialogue, co-teaching, cosmopolitanism, context, content, competition, and curation.[9] Emdin's approach demonstrates how to connect authentically with students' lived realities, turning curriculum from something we deliver to something we cocreate. Here are two key principles and their connection to the financial education classroom:

- ★ **Co-generative dialogue:** Create intentional space for students and teachers to engage in conversations about improving the learning experience together. Ask students: "How can we make these money conversations matter to your life?" or "What from today's lesson connects to something happening in your life right now?" Ensure our curriculum incorporates genuine student feedback.
- ★ **Content:** Model what it looks like to engage with financial concepts as fellow learners rather than as experts with all the answers. Encourage students to explore trends alongside us, fostering a shared learning experience. Create a classroom culture that prioritizes curiosity and inquiry over immediate solutions.

These inclusive foundations from Freire, Gay, and Emdin reflect the Consumer Financial Protection Bureau's research on effective financial literacy education. Its five principles ask us to (1) know our students as individuals; (2) make information immediately relevant to their world; (3) focus on building practical financial skills; (4) connect learning to their personal motivation; and (5) create clear pathways for them to take action.[10] Financial education transforms lives when we put these principles into practice.

A modern framework that has reshaped how I think about creating inclusive learning spaces comes from financial activist Jasmine Rashid. Her approach encourages deeper engagement with financial topics in order to create change. We start by asking, "Why is this like this?" to examine why certain students may feel excluded and question traditional approaches to teaching money concepts. Then we check in with "How do I feel about this?" to acknowledge the emotional dimensions of financial learning. We inquire, "What's possible?" to envision environments where every student sees themselves reflected in financial success stories. Then, "What can I do right now?" prompts us to take immediate action toward more welcoming and culturally responsive teaching practices. Finally, we reach out to our community with "What can we do together?" to emphasize collective approaches that value everyone's input and create a sense of belonging. This intentional questioning helps ensure we're creating financial education spaces where every student feels at home, and they can connect with financial learning in ways that align with their values and experiences.[11] A sense of belonging isn't something we create once and check off a list. It's a continuous practice of asking questions, listening deeply, and adapting our spaces to honor every student's full financial story.

These frameworks of inclusion and belonging are not just theories. They have inspired work in real classrooms with real students. Through years of teaching, learning from other incredible educators, and constantly asking, "How can we make financial education inclusive?" I've developed what I call the RICH framework—an approach focused on Representation, Inquiry, Connection, and Holistic thinking.

The foundational pillars of this framework are applicable across many contexts. I've seen them inform one-on-one coaching, community workshops, district-wide curriculum planning, and even podcast content strategy. While the setting may change—from my classroom in Brooklyn to a workshop in Cleveland to a virtual training session—one truth remains constant: Financial education transforms lives when every student feels they truly belong in the conversation about money.

THE RICH FRAMEWORK: BELONGING AT THE MONEY TABLE

Creating true belonging in financial education requires intentionality in both our content and approach. Through years of teaching and collaborating with other educators, I've developed the RICH framework, a structured yet flexible approach to create spaces where all students feel they truly belong in financial conversations. (I tried not to make it a cheesy money acronym, but I couldn't help myself!) The framework emerged organically from the practices that most effectively fostered inclusion in my classroom. When I realized these elements spelled *RICH*, I was elated. After all, we're working to enrich students' understanding of wealth in all forms, while creating financially rich classroom experiences that honor every student's potential. And yes, financial knowledge can make us as rich as we want to be. Riches on riches!

The RICH framework consists of four essential pillars:

- **Representation:** ensuring diverse perspectives and identities are reflected
- **Inquiry:** fostering critical questioning and wonder
- **Connection:** making concepts accessible and relevant to students' lives
- **Holistic thinking:** embracing an asset-based mindset

Each pillar stands as a support for designing inclusive financial education, though some may need extra strengthening depending on your students' specific needs. Together, these pillars support a learning environment where everyone has a rightful place at the money table.

Representation: Featuring Diverse Perspectives

WHAT IT MEANS: Learners see their identities reflected in financial spaces through diverse representation. Students encounter a variety of perspectives on wealth and money management through texts, videos, scenarios, podcasts, and guests. A multicultural approach to financial education ensures that the curriculum and classroom environment honor the breadth of students' lived experiences while introducing alternative financial narratives that broaden their worldview. Educators also share their own authentic stories, bringing vulnerability and trust into the space.

WHY IT MATTERS: When students don't see people who look like them succeeding in financial spaces, they often believe that these spaces aren't for them. This invisible barrier keeps talented young people from pursuing financial opportunities and building wealth. Representation is about expanding students' sense of what's possible for their own lives. When my student Sherry told me, "I didn't know people like us did this stuff," she was experiencing a profound shift in her understanding of what was available to her.

Representation in Practice

- **Center diverse role models:** Highlight financial leaders across different genders, cultures, and socioeconomic experiences to illustrate multiple paths to success.
- **Use inclusive visual materials:** Put up posters and other visual materials that reflect the rich diversity of identities present in your classroom and in the financial world.
- **Embrace different cultural approaches to money:** Use examples that honor the various multicultural ways people understand and manage money.
- **Validate personal wealth narratives:** Encourage students to see their wealth stories as valuable contributions to their financial understanding.
- **Promote storytelling about money:** Create opportunities for students to share how their identities and lived experiences shape their views on money.
- **Share your own authentic financial stories:** Introduce concepts by including personal successes and setbacks.
- **Model financial vulnerability:** Discuss moments of learning and growth in your own journey.

Inquiry: Exploring the "Why?"

WHAT IT MEANS: Learners ask questions, challenge assumptions, and think critically about how financial systems work and who they serve. Students develop a sense of wonder that drives them to ask: *Why is it this way? What do I need to know to navigate it? How can it be different? How do others see this situation?* Exploring the why behind financial topics is encouraged. Educators also engage in inquiry and bring authentic questions from their lives into the classroom discourse.

WHY IT MATTERS: When students question financial systems, they gain agency and shift from being passive consumers to informed individuals. Instead of passively accepting the world around them as is, they start to understand that money rules can be understood, challenged, and even changed. This inquiry-based approach transforms learners into active shapers of the financial world.

Inquiry in Practice

- **Ask open-ended questions:** Encourage inquiry that explores multiple perspectives rather than focusing on a single "right" answer.
- **Demonstrate your own financial curiosity:** Share genuine questions from your financial life that you're still exploring.
- **Nurture curiosity:** Create a space where students feel comfortable asking why things work the way they do and support them in developing their own questions about money and wealth.
- **Embrace every question:** Foster a safe environment where every question is welcomed and students feel encouraged to take risks—there are no "dumb" questions.
- **Challenge financial norms:** Invite learners to rethink traditional financial rules and what is considered "normal" financial behavior.
- **Explore system design:** Prompt students to reflect on how financial systems are structured and what the impact is.

Connection: Making Finance Accessible and Relevant

WHAT IT MEANS: Financial concepts are connected to students' lived experiences, making abstract ideas concrete and applicable. This approach creates multiple entry points to financial knowledge that meet learners where they are, using tools and language they can access and understand. When we connect financial education to students' immediate lives and contexts, learning becomes meaningful and actionable. Accessibility means removing barriers so every student can benefit from the financial content that's offered.

WHY IT MATTERS: Financial concepts often remain hidden behind confusing jargon and abstract ideas. By connecting these concepts to students' everyday experiences and making them accessible, we open doors to powerful information that students deserve to understand. These connections empower students to navigate the world more confidently, with knowledge that feels relevant to their lives.

Connection in Practice

- **Simplify complex ideas:** Break down complex concepts into smaller, easy-to-understand pieces.
- **Mix up the presentation:** Present lessons using visuals, audio, text, and hands-on activities so everyone can engage.

- **Offer adaptable resources:** Provide materials that suit different reading and learning levels.
- **Avoid jargon:** Use clear language and explain important terms without unnecessary technical words.
- **Link to everyday life:** Connect abstract financial ideas to situations students experience daily, and design projects that tie classroom lessons to what's happening in the world.
- **Promote peer learning:** Create opportunities for students to learn from one another.
- **Explore local economies:** Develop assignments that let students investigate and understand their local economic environments.
- **Bring in community voices:** Invite local mentors, residents, and leaders to share their insights and experiences.
- **Build community partnerships:** Collaborate with local businesses and institutions to enhance the learning experience.
- **Host engaging events:** Organize workshops and events that feature external experts sharing their knowledge.

Holistic Thinking: Embracing an Asset-Based Mindset

WHAT IT MEANS: Holistic thinking honors the diversity that learners and educators bring to the table, including cultural, creative, familial, experiential, and community strengths. This approach also recognizes that financial wellness is closely tied to personal values. True financial wellness happens when our money practices align with what matters most, whether that's security, freedom, caring for family, community support, a connection with nature, or creative expression.

WHY IT MATTERS: When we celebrate the many forms of wealth, we create an environment where students can appreciate the assets they already possess instead of focusing on deficits. This asset-based approach validates the rich, diverse ways in which wealth can be expressed and empowers students to use their unique strengths to build financial well-being for themselves and their communities.

Holistic Thinking in Practice

- **Use language that emphasizes abundance:** Ask questions like, "What knowledge or resources do you already have around you?" and "What strengths can we build on?"
- **Encourage conversations about wealth:** Help students identify and reframe the unique forms of wealth they bring with them.

- **Highlight multigenerational financial practices:** Honor family financial traditions and recognize the value of financial knowledge that spans generations.
- **Affirm cultural and community assets:** Validate cultural wealth and community knowledge as real, legitimate financial resources.
- **Launch asset-focused projects:** Design projects that invite students to identify and expand on their personal and community strengths.
- **Integrate with existing structures:** Embed financial learning within family and community networks and promote shared, multigenerational learning.
- **Celebrate diversity:** Recognize and celebrate the many ways wealth shows up across different cultures and communities.

The RICH framework promotes an intentionality in how we teach financial literacy that goes beyond teaching isolated financial concepts. It empowers educators to continue making financial knowledge accessible, deeply personal, and transformative. When we prioritize **Representation** in our examples and role models, nurture student **Inquiry** about financial systems, create meaningful **Connections** to their lived experiences, and **think Holistically** about diverse forms of wealth, we build learning spaces where every student feels they belong. In RICH classrooms, students will see themselves in the curriculum and envision a future where they are active, confident contributors in an inclusive financial landscape.

What's remarkable is that the RICH framework's impact extends well beyond individual classrooms. As students gain both knowledge and confidence, they become ambassadors of financial empowerment in their families and communities. This is what happened to me. Learners challenge traditional notions of who "belongs" in financial spaces. Most importantly, they transform from passive observers of financial systems into active participants who can build wealth aligned with their values and create positive change.

PRACTICAL APPROACHES TO FINANCIAL INCLUSION

The RICH framework—centered on Representation, Inquiry, Connection, and Holistic thinking—provides an actionable road map for educators. Each pillar guides both content selection and pedagogy while creating a classroom atmosphere where every student feels included.

While this framework lays the foundation, the real impact comes from putting it into practice. Let me share some strategies that have transformed my classroom. These are not comprehensive; there are amazing educators like you with even more creative approaches to inclusion. Try focusing on one new practice at a time. I strive to incorporate these strategies regularly, but I can't use them all at once. Just choose one and give it a go.

Learning Environment

Your learning environment sends a powerful message about who belongs in financial spaces. It's reflected not just in major curricular choices but also in the smallest details, like what adorns your walls, the role models you highlight, and the ways students are showcased.

If you share a classroom or a space, take over a bulletin board and feature SMART goals, personal "whys," or nuggets of financial advice from your students. For instance, I begin my course with a Money Mindset $urvey and post the students' "whys" around the room. During Financial Literacy Month (April), I often make paper flowers and invite students to share their money tips. These visual cues affirm that everyone has a valued place in the conversation about money.

One critical member of your learning environment is . . . you! Sharing your own money stories—both triumphs and challenges—gives students permission to bring their authentic selves to financial conversations. Our vulnerability creates learning spaces of trust. Once, during a lesson on credit reports, I told my class about the time I cosigned a loan to help someone out. Let's just say I ended up with some ugly red blemishes on my credit report because of it. The room went completely silent after hearing about one of my failures. Seeing someone who they respect, and who has also made mistakes, makes success seem more attainable. When educators embrace vulnerability, learning shifts from a display of expertise to a shared, collaborative journey.

Relationship Building Through One-on-Ones

Often the most powerful moments happen in small conversations. Ask students about their weekends, what they spent money on, their siblings, or their parents. If they completed a survey at the beginning of the year, keep referring to the ideas they shared. These connections pay off in unexpected ways. One of my students always drinks a particular soda. Later, during our investing unit, I mentioned his drink preference and the parent company's stock, which started an engaging conversation. Or when students wear particular clothing or shoe brands, I can tie our discussion about stocks to companies they already know.

During the real estate unit, I might reference a student's grandparent living in another state to look up real estate prices there as an example. These small moments make students feel seen and valued, building trust that makes financial education more meaningful.

Abundant Language We Use

It's about the words we choose and how we respond to questions. If a student mentions their goal of having ten thousand dollars by graduation, and we say "Riiiight . . . good luck with that," we shut down their enthusiasm. "Let's break it down together and see what steps you can take this spring" validates the goal while helping them develop a realistic plan. We all know students can underestimate life costs. But the point isn't to discourage them; it's to give them tools to understand the path and break down the goal into measurable parts. If a student shares an interest in launching their own business or becoming an investor, engaging with questions like, "What would that journey look like for you?" or "How can we break it into actionable steps?" encourages abundant thinking and planning.

Mindfulness Moments and Entry Activities

Educator Halle Amore Bauer begins each class by grounding students: "I start every class with a five-minute mindfulness moment, which is sort of like my version of a warm-up. Sometimes the warm-up involves the content from class, but there's a secondary goal layered on top: Let's get all in the same space here. You're coming from different classes all over campus. Let's get in the same physical space and mental space so you can focus." Some ways to mindfully ground your class include:

- **Gratitude circles:** (I love these!) Begin class by inviting students to share one thing they're grateful for. This practice fosters a positive atmosphere and makes students feel seen.
- **Mood check-ins:** Have a brief round where each student shares a word or image that reflects their current mood, welcoming their emotional state into the learning.
- **Reflective journaling:** Allow a few minutes for students to write about a recent financial decision or a personal goal. This centers their minds and also sparks individual reflection before deeper discussions.
- **Visual grounding:** Display an inspiring image related to growth or stability and ask students to relate it to their own financial aspirations, aligning their focus for the day.

These moments create connection and psychological safety, which is particularly important when discussing sensitive topics like money.

Projects That Connect to Family

Curt Cruz uses entrepreneurship projects tied to students' cultural backgrounds. He explains: "We try to link [projects] to the culture of their families, of their communities. It's very interesting because the students bring out their creativity, marrying the culture of their families, their heritage. It builds diversity and appreciation for each other, plus the parents are involved. They're saying to me, not just for the students but for themselves, that they did not take this class before. They want to be involved because they want to learn as well, even as adults."

During our real estate unit, I have students research properties in New York and anywhere else in the country. They often look at properties in Atlanta, Georgia, and South Carolina, where they have family. One student chose Texas because she had a cousin that moved there, there's no income tax, and . . . Beyoncé was born there. I've had students ask about international options, where their families are from, so I expanded the project to include properties in the Dominican Republic and Mexico. This approach validates students' cultural wealth while teaching essential financial concepts.

By grounding our curriculum in family connections, we create financial education spaces that extend beyond the classroom. The personal insights they gain in our class spark conversations that ripple across generations. For instance, my student Adriana observed, "I didn't know living in a multifamily home was called 'house hacking' now. I talked to *Abuela* about it, and my family has been doing it for generations." Ryan added, "My aunt owns commercial property and rental property; I didn't know that. Now we're looking at her portfolio together." Isaiah reflected, "I spoke to my uncle about stocks; he is interested and already invests. We looked at his accounts together." And Sha said, "My cousin is always telling me about the S&P 500, and I was like 'OK, bro.' But now I understand what it is."

These reflections remind us that when learning is rooted in personal context, it ignites a broader dialogue that brings families together to collaborate on their financial futures. Family belongs, family contributes, and everyone benefits.

Diverse Role Models

Halle Amore Bauer uses Socratic seminars to engage students with diverse perspectives. She explains: "My favorite activity is the Socratic seminar. I assign a text which is another opportunity to be inclusive in the curriculum, like picking a text by a woman economist, or a person of color, someone who's not American or European. It can be a video, podcast, or reading. They all have the text in common. They fill out preparations, come ready to discuss, and run the discussion themselves. It empowers students to take ownership of their learning."

I use podcasts, books, videos, and social media accounts featuring diverse perspectives and identities. I remember reading a budgeting chapter in *Friends That Invest* by Simran Kaur where she discussed budgeting to care for parents or other older family members. That's something I have to account for in my own life, and I had never seen that perspective in a personal finance book before. It opened my eyes to how empowering it can be when your lived experience is reflected in financial spaces. I was thirty-seven at the time. Imagine how empowering it can be for young people to feel seen so much earlier in their lives.

Guest speakers

Invite professionals who reflect your students' cultures—real estate agents, investors, and financial sector experts—to share their journeys, including their successes and challenges. Guest speakers help students visualize themselves in financial spaces. Many professionals are excited to speak to our young people, but they're also nervous speaking in front of teenagers. I usually have a chatty student welcome them at the front to help them feel comfortable. Brainstorm a list of friends, family, or other associates, and ask away. Some possibilities include:

- **Financial professionals:** Financial planners, coaches, investment advisors, or loan officers from various backgrounds can discuss building credit, saving for future goals, or navigating financial challenges.
- **Community entrepreneurs:** Local business owners and start-up founders can share insights about risk-taking, financing, and vision. Their ups and downs help illustrate that financial success is built on planning and perseverance, which resonates for students interested in entrepreneurship.
- **Family members:** Retired grandparents, entrepreneurial cousins, or other relatives can bridge familiar voices with new financial insights. My personal teaching goal is to include more family members into our money conversations whenever possible.
- **Other professionals:** Professionals from insurance, accounting, or real estate can demystify specific financial topics, answer students' questions, and offer career advice. I've had experts Zoom in to discuss investing and career paths.

Real-World Applications

Curt Cruz creates practical financial experiences for his students with special needs. He explains: "I connect with local banks, and eventually they have their own personal bank accounts, both checking and savings. It's like a trophy for them. They say, 'Mr. Cruz, I didn't know I could actually have my own bank account.' I tell them, 'Yeah, nobody is stopping you. This is a life need, not just a requirement for our class.'" These real-world victories build the confidence students need to tackle more complex financial challenges.

What makes financial education the best is its endless real-world applications. I've had students research credit unions and compare them with traditional banks. While they can't open accounts until they are eighteen, they can explore student accounts, research saving rates, and share recommendations with their families. These hands-on experiences make abstract financial concepts tangible and accessible. The opportunities are endless, but here are a few other ideas for bringing financial learning into the real world:

- **Interactive simulations:** Use Next Gen Personal Finance's free, web-based Payback game to explore college financing, Jump$tart Coalition's Reality Check to show the real cost of living independently, or Intuit for Education's FinFutures to practice making spending decisions aligned with personal values.
- **Life scenarios:** Organize role-play budgeting exercises where students manage monthly expenses, handle unexpected costs, or even plan for a life event like going to college or starting a small business. These hands-on activities make abstract concepts tangible.
- **Philanthropy and community funding:** Create projects where students identify local or global communities in need. They can research a cause, plan a fundraiser, or coordinate a donation drive, showing first-hand how financial choices can create meaningful social impact.
- **Entrepreneurial ventures:** Have students design mini-business plans or social-impact projects that tackle real community challenges. The experience empowers them to apply financial skills creatively and see the tangible effects of their ideas.

Inclusive Grading Practices

Grades hold a lot of power. That's why I'm extremely intentional with the language I use when it comes to grading. I never say "failing," "getting a zero," or even "passing the class." I tell students from day one that they will do well in this class—90s or 100, whatever excellence looks like in numbers to them.

I don't want them orienting their mindset to "barely getting by." I tell them, "Whatever grade you want, pick that number now, and that's what you'll get. This isn't a visualization exercise. I'm serious. Just give me a number so we can get that out of the way, and you can start to learn it and earn it." Can you believe that actually works?

This is also why I don't spend time talking about grading policy and percentages, because let's be real—our grades are a lot less neutral than we think. We can all get a little red-pen happy; it's in our educator DNA. That's exactly the instinct we have to be conscious of if we want to use grades as a real tool to promote learning.

Halle Amore Bauer uses grading practices that promote continuous learning: "I have a really generous revision policy where students can revise anything and everything. They're incentivized to do so, and their grade is completely new. It's not like, 'You just get two points back.' We recreate the whole grade." I also see grading as an ongoing process rather than a fixed judgment. Financial education, to me, is one of the most important subjects they'll ever learn, so I leverage that and focus on the importance of that learning. If a student is behind, I'll say something like, "Here's what I want you to complete so you can understand [insert concept] for your life as a [insert life goal]," rather than tying their progress to fear or deficit.

Students still like real-time validation of their work. I use a "Paid" stamp on assignments, which they love. In the larger, most inclusive picture, they probably shouldn't need this kind of affirmation, but with teens, it makes a difference, so I keep doing it.

When grades aren't treated as a power tool of leverage, many of us feel a tiny panic. I did too. At first, I thought, *Will they just say, "Okay, I'm already getting a good grade, so I don't have to come or do anything"?* But it's the opposite. When we talk about their grades, students are thoughtful about their performance and, in actuality, harder on themselves than anyone else.

One way to hold students accountable in a meaningful way is through one-on-one grading conversations. While other students work independently on projects, I pull students aside individually. Sometimes it's mid-unit and formative in nature, and other times, it's for end-of-unit grading and reflections. During these conversations, I'll ask, "How would you grade yourself?" Their assessments are remarkably accurate, and they'll candidly admit, "I should participate more in discussions" or "I still need to submit that project." These moments create natural opportunities to set goals and highlight strengths they might not see in themselves: "You grasp these calculations quickly; have you considered accounting?" or "Your real estate analysis is excellent. Have you thought about being an agent or investor?" By treating assessment as a conversation rather than a verdict, we foster self-awareness and confidence in their progress.

Financial learning is a process, not a one-time achievement. It's about demonstrating growth over time, just as real financial journeys involve learning from mistakes and adjusting course. By treating grading as an ongoing conversation rather than a final verdict, we change assessment from something done *to* students into something done *with* them.

Classroom Currency and Incentives

In my classroom, we have an economic system of "bux," which is currency that used to feature my likeness as "Icey Bux" but now features my student leaders' faces. Our class economy has minted Lexi Loot, Chelsy Cash, and Lee Gouda. Students run the store, connecting currency to snacks with dollar amounts, and every other week or so, they can redeem bux.

This system organically sparks discussions about inflation (that's when printing too many bux floods the market), the durability of currency (that crumpled bill at the bottom of a book bag), and the process of minting (which involves my precious color ink). Supply and demand also come into play, as leaders raise snack prices when our inventory runs low.

Furthermore, I'm not above bribery. Anyone who teaches teenagers knows they'll learn almost anything for snacks. Of all my techniques, nothing quite motivates students to "fill out this 1040 to learn about taxes" better than gummy bears. I have heard some teachers say that they don't want to reward students for doing what they're supposed to do, which is valid. But I maintain my snack stash just in case. My truth is, aren't incentives what the economy is really all about?

PATHWAYS TO PRO$PERITY: THERE'S A SEAT AT THE FINANCIAL TABLE

Creating inclusive financial education benefits all students by creating spaces to share histories, lived experiences, and assets. When we expand our definition of wealth, acknowledge diverse financial experiences, and recognize multiple pathways to success, we create richer, more nuanced financial understandings for everyone.

As financial educator Michelle Samuels-Jones perfectly puts it: "While financial education alone is not a remedy for discrimination and bias in financial systems, effective financial education is essential in equipping marginalized and vulnerable populations to better navigate the financial landscape."[12]

By creating financial education spaces where everyone truly belongs, we're empowering the next generation to build a more equitable financial future for all.

SELF-REFLECTION

Self-reflection is at the heart of the RICH framework. Think of it as an ongoing practice that flows through all four pillars: Representation, Inquiry, Connection, and Holistic thinking. The answers to these questions won't be the same for every educator, and that's exactly the point. Just as there's no single "right way" to manage money, there's no single "right way" to create inclusive financial education spaces. What matters is the intentional effort to recognize and value the diverse experiences our students bring.

Consider these questions as you think about your inclusive approach to financial education.

Personal Reflection

- $ What personal experiences with money do you bring into the classroom?
- $ In what ways might your background influence how you view your students' financial behaviors or potential?
- $ What forms of wealth did your family prioritize?
- $ What are some examples of "good" financial decisions? Do these beliefs reflect your own cultural or socioeconomic background? How?
- $ When have you felt represented in financial spaces or conversations? When have you felt invisible?
- $ What aspects of the financial world do you question? What do you hope to change?
- $ What's a money idea that only made sense once you experienced it yourself?
- $ How does your identity, relationships, and community show up in your financial decisions?

Educator Reflection

- $ How might your students' financial realities differ from your own?
- $ In what ways do you make space for different experiences in your teaching?
- $ How can you add opportunities to honor their lived realities even more?
- $ After a lesson, reflect: What assumptions did you notice you had about your students' financial experiences?
- $ In what ways does your curriculum feature diverse financial role models and pathways to success?

$ Whose financial experiences do you typically use as examples? How might you expand those examples?

$ How do you create opportunities for students to share their own financial knowledge and experiences?

EDUCATOR RESOURCES

Student Discussion Questions

Quick prompts designed to ignite student conversation

- What financial habits or traditions exist in your family that might be different from others?
- When you picture someone "good with money," who comes to mind? Why?
- How do you think where you live affects your relationship with money?
- Have you ever felt out of place during a money conversation? What would have made you feel more welcome?
- When was a time you felt confident talking about money? What made that experience positive?
- Beyond dollars, what kinds of wealth does your family possess?
- What skills or knowledge do you have that could be valuable, even if they're not traditionally "financial"?
- How might your community's strengths be viewed as wealth?
- What matters most to you when it comes to how you use money?
- If money weren't a concern, how would you spend your time?
- How do you hope your relationship with money will be different from previous generations?

Standalone Activities (20–50 minutes)

Exercises that can fit into any lesson, with added discussion to extend learning

- **COMMUNITY WEALTH GALLERY**
  - **Purpose:** Help students visualize and celebrate the diverse forms of non-financial wealth they bring to the classroom.
  - **RICH Framework (Holistic thinking):** This activity guides students to recognize and honor their non-financial wealth, modeling asset-based thinking.
  - **Process:** Students create posters that showcase their cultural, linguistic, familial, and community strengths. Students identify three to four forms of non-

financial wealth they possess (cultural knowledge, languages, family traditions, skills, community connections). Educators can prompt students with questions about "Types of wealth in my family. . . " offering options such as love and support, resilience and perseverance, cooking/crafting/hands-on skills, humor and joy, caring for siblings or elders, faith or spiritual grounding, multilingualism, or entrepreneurship.

1. Students design visual storyboards using images, symbols, brief narratives, and concrete examples of how each wealth form shows up in their lives.
2. Students do a gallery walk, viewing each other's wealth stories and leaving appreciation notes highlighting strengths they recognize or shared connections.
3. The class participates in whole-group reflection, connecting these diverse wealth forms to potential financial opportunities and goal achievement.

FINANCIAL VOICES SHOWCASE

- **Purpose:** Expand students' vision of who belongs in financial spaces by highlighting diverse financial role models.
- **RICH Framework (Representation):** Expands students' understanding of "who belongs in financial spaces" through exposure to diverse financial experts and voices.
- **Process:** Students research and present financial experts who represent varied identities and perspectives.

1. Present students with a curated list of diverse financial experts across various platforms and backgrounds (social media, videos, podcasts). See the appendix for a starter list of diverse financial voices.
2. Students select one influencer and spend about five minutes exploring their content to understand their perspective and expertise.
3. Using Padlet or a similar platform, students post their findings including two to three key financial tips or insights, one memorable quote or piece of advice, and why this person's approach resonated with them. Time permitting, students explore a second influencer from a different background or area of expertise and add brief comparative insights.
4. Students conduct a digital gallery walk, reading classmates' posts, leaving thoughtful responses, and asking follow-up questions about different financial perspectives.
5. The class participates in whole-group discussion, sharing which expert they most connected with and what new perspectives they gained about

who can be a financial leader. Consider offering extra credit for students who follow one of these financial voices and share ongoing insights throughout the semester.

■ NEIGHBORHOOD MONEY MAP

- **Purpose:** Connect classroom learning to real community resources while identifying both strengths and gaps in students' neighborhoods.
- **RICH Framework (Connection):** Grounds abstract financial concepts in students' lived geography and real community resources.
- **Process:** Students collaboratively map financial resources available in their neighborhoods.

  1. Generate a comprehensive list of financial resources (banks, credit unions, financial counseling, community programs, informal networks) with teachers providing additional local resources from prior research.
  2. Small groups each focus on one type of financial resource, researching locations, services, accessibility, and community reputation through online investigation and brief interviews.
  3. Teams contribute findings to a shared physical or digital community map. Brainstorm realistic improvements or new resources that could strengthen the local financial ecosystem.

CHAPTER 4

THE EDUCATORS

Examining Our Own Money Stories

YOU'RE WORTH YOUR WEIGHT IN GOLD BARS

To start off my course, I always bring in a bunch of one-dollar bills, and have students examine the symbols, text, and design elements. We discuss what images like the thirteen stars, pyramid steps, arrows, and olive branch leaves might say about the country's values. During this analysis a few years ago, a student asked, "Miss, if these letters on the bill are the Federal Reserve, do they print it? What does the Federal Reserve do?"

Here I was, standing in front of thirty eager faces, supposedly the expert, and I genuinely wasn't sure. I could explain the basics: that there are twelve Federal Reserve Banks, that they issue the money, some things about monetary policy, yada yada. But the deeper mechanics of Federal Reserve's role were clear gaps in my own learning.

At that moment, I had two choices: Give them a cockamamie answer, or admit that I didn't know and needed to learn more. I chose the latter.

That night, I researched how money moves through the economy, the Federal Reserve's responsibilities, and the difference between physical currency and monetary policy. The next day, I shared with students not only what I found but also the process I used to find it. I shared how I read articles and then watched videos because I learn better when concepts are presented in multiple ways. You probably can tell by now that I spiraled into a macroeconomics learning wormhole for some time after.

Fast-forward some time, and that one question led to something bigger. After visiting the Federal Reserve Bank of Cleveland during a conference, I learned we could bring students to the Fed in our district. So this year, I took my current group of students to the Federal Reserve Bank of New York, eager to connect theory to reality. Unfortunately, we didn't get to see those shiny twenty-seven-pound gold bars, but the trip itself was a direct result of an authentic student question I once didn't know how to answer. Now I'm bursting with random Fed facts that I love to share: Did you know a one-dollar bill only lasts about 5.9 years before it's too worn to use? Or that $60 billion in New York bank money is actually stored in New Jersey—and handled by robots? And that the NY Fed holds gold bars worth $250 billion? The more you know.

That experience reinforced something crucial about our role as teachers: Education is not about having all the answers. It's about modeling curiosity, admitting gaps in knowledge, and showing students that learning is a lifelong journey. Curiosity, not absolute certainty, drives financial learning. And our authenticity as teachers matters far more than our expertise.

THE PERSONAL NATURE OF TEACHING MONEY

Teaching financial literacy feels fundamentally personal compared to other subjects. When I explain the Pythagorean theorem, I don't worry that students will judge my mathematical abilities based on my personal relationship with right triangles. But when I teach about budgeting, students naturally wonder: Does she follow her own advice? When I discuss investment strategies, they notice my "car"—aka the New York City MTA—my clothes, and many other choices I make.

Money intersects with our values, our fears, our family histories, and our deepest insecurities in ways that most academic subjects don't. It's difficult for financial educators to teach this subject from a position of detachment. And honestly, we shouldn't try. By acknowledging the personal side of money instead of pretending it doesn't exist, we become more effective teachers. Our students need to understand that financial wellness is a journey, not a destination, and that even their teachers are still walking that path.

The lively New Jersey educator Alex Lamon captures it beautifully: "The personal aspect is the whole entire point. If we were just teaching a finance class without the personal connection, it would be just another subject. But when students see you as a resource, when they know that you care and have had experiences that might be similar to theirs, then they're able to open up."[1]

Teaching Money While Navigating Your Own

Our ability to teach financial concepts effectively is deeply influenced by our own financial confidence. When we feel secure in our financial understanding, we can instruct with conviction. When our own money life feels messy, the corresponding stress doesn't magically disappear when we walk into our classrooms. When we're worried about our own student loans, credit card debt, or retirement savings, it can become harder to present financial concepts with the confidence and enthusiasm our students deserve.

Let's start with some truth-telling. If you're a teacher struggling with your own finances while teaching financial literacy, you're not alone. More than six in ten teachers have taken out student loans to support their education, and close to four in ten are still repaying them. These loans require many educators to take second jobs and result in high levels of loan-related stress.[2] In addition to student loans, many of us experience the same financial literacy gaps as the rest of the country, as described in chapter 2. When you're making monthly payments that exceed the national average while you're earning less than similarly educated professionals, that financial stress can be very real.

I've spoken to educators who describe the physical toll of financial stress—tension headaches when bills arrive, fear pangs when thinking about retirement, and even the urge to ignore money altogether. An article exploring teacher finances quotes financial literacy advocate Yanely Espinal: "Teachers' whole job is about serving students: coming in to work early, creating a safe space for students, grading papers at night, using their own money to buy supplies for students. It's very rare that you see a teacher pause and consider their own needs, asking themselves things like, 'How can I set myself up financially? Am I on track?'"[3]

Your own financial education is key to your professional growth in this field. Just as a chemistry teacher must be comfortable with the periodic table to teach it effectively, you need to be comfortable with your own financial understanding to teach financial literacy.

YOUR FINANCIAL EDUCATION AS PROFESSIONAL DEVELOPMENT

I already know that educators are eager to grow their financial skills. When *Education Week* surveyed teachers about professional development in personal finance, 66 percent expressed interest.[4] Take Christopher Jackson's story highlighted in this study. Jackson, a California high school teacher who pursued financial education training, "took several courses through Next Gen, originally to increase his knowledge of personal finance when teaching his students. But what he learned ended up changing his own life." He describes it as a wake-up call that helped him build a diversified investment portfolio, support his daughter's debt-free college graduation, and improve his credit score by over one hundred points. There are larger systemic forces at play, and becoming financially literate won't improve teachers' salaries, but it can improve their financial outlook. Jackson learned to leverage the unique benefits of teaching: "Our pensions, our summers, and even our structured pay increases can work in our favor. But too often, no one teaches us how money works."[5]

Start small and be patient with yourself. Your financial education journey doesn't need to be perfect or complete before you can effectively teach. Consider Daria Hall, an educator highlighted in the *Education Week* article. She "started taking courses in financial literacy to prepare to teach the new Economics and Personal Finance course" but continues learning "for herself and her family." She found that the knowledge creates "a ripple effect"—helping students navigate college costs, showing parents how to avoid predatory lending, and enabling her to diversify her portfolio and make values-based investment decisions.[6]

Your financial education is the call to adventure in this journey. As you build confidence in your own financial decisions, that confidence will naturally flow into your classroom, creating authentic, engaging learning environments.

The very personal reality of teaching personal finance creates both challenges and opportunities. The challenge is that we must examine our own money stories before we can effectively guide students through theirs. The opportunity is that when we approach financial education with vulnerability and authenticity, we create learning environments where real transformation can happen.

Understanding Our Money Stories

Every educator brings their own complex relationship with money into the classroom. These stories shape how we present financial concepts, which topics we emphasize, and how we respond to student questions and concerns.

Some teachers carry stories of financial struggle, growing up in households where money was scarce, watching parents argue about bills, or experiencing their own periods of financial stress. Others come from backgrounds of financial stability but lack practical money management experience. Some have developed strong personal finance skills through necessity or interest but worry about teaching concepts they're still mastering. And still others enter the classroom with a solid foundation in financial literacy, confident in their knowledge while working to understand the financial realities their students face.

Educator Alex Lamon shared his own formative money experience with me: "My parents had saved money for my college, but coming out of the

Great Recession in 2010, a bunch of that college money got lost. There was basically not enough time to recover. That caused a lot of fear of the unknown, a lack of control over money in this really weird way." This experience shaped his entire approach to teaching. He explains, "I didn't know what was happening, and they wouldn't talk to me about it. I felt this should be something that should be talked about. That was my motivation for even wanting to teach personal finance in the first place, wanting to erase any taboo about talking about money."

Notice how Alex's personal financial uncertainty became the foundation for his teaching philosophy. He didn't need to overcome his money story to become an effective educator; he needed to understand it and use it purposefully.

Understanding Our Money Scripts

Creating inclusive and trusting financial learning environments starts with understanding our own deeply held money beliefs, or what financial psychologist Dr. Brad Klontz calls money scripts. These unconscious beliefs, formed in childhood and reinforced over time, shape how we think about, use, and talk about money. Klontz identified four common money scripts many adults carry: money avoidance, money focus, money status, and money vigilance.[7]

You can explore your own patterns by taking the free Money Script Inventory at bradklontz.com/moneyscriptstest.

When I took the Money Script Inventory myself, my results revealed patterns I hadn't fully recognized. I scored high on money focus and money vigilance. My having a high money focus score means I tend to believe money is key to solving problems—though I also tend to feel like no amount is ever enough. My money vigilance score showed my cautious nature around financial decisions, valuing saving and being wary of unnecessary debt. Is this why I refuse to buy bottled water when we have perfectly good tap water and why I hate buying anything without a coupon?

Seeing these numbers on paper was both validating and eye-opening. It helped me understand why I felt a calling to teach financial literacy in the first place. That high money focus score revealed my deep-seated belief that financial knowledge could genuinely transform my students' lives and solve real problems they're facing. It also explained why I become uncomfortable about debt, especially when they're considering expensive colleges or researching credit cards. My money vigilance shows up in how I structure entire units around emergency funds and retirement planning, sometimes at the expense of teaching them it's okay to spend money on things that bring joy.

This awareness has made me a more intentional teacher. When a student excitedly shares their goal to start a business, I pause and ask myself: Am I immediately jumping to the risks and challenges, or can I first celebrate their entrepreneurial *Shark Tank* spirit? I still teach the importance of saving and planning, but I've learned to also invite guest speakers who can share different perspectives, like entrepreneurs who took calculated risks or financial advisors who help clients balance security with enjoying their money today. My students deserve to see the full spectrum of healthy financial relationships, not just the cautious, future-focused approach that feels most natural to me.

Consider these reflection questions adapted from Klontz's Money Script Inventory, and examine the ways these scripts might be showing up in your teaching:

Money Avoidance Scripts

- Did your family portray rich people as greedy?
- Were you taught that good people shouldn't care about money?
- Was money considered the "root of all evil" in your household?

HOW THIS MIGHT SHOW UP IN YOUR TEACHING: If you score high on money avoidance, you might unconsciously present wealth building as morally questionable or downplay the importance of financial success. For instance, when teaching about investing, you might focus heavily on the risks and ethical concerns of stock ownership while spending less time on the potential benefits of long-term wealth building. You may find yourself emphasizing that "money isn't everything" without adequately exploring how financial security can support students' deeper values and life goals.

Money Focus Scripts

- Do you believe money could solve all your problems?
- Were you led to think that your family's happiness depended on having more money?
- Do you feel that accumulating more money would make you a better person?

HOW THIS MIGHT SHOW UP IN YOUR TEACHING: Having a high money focus score might lead you to oversell financial success as the solution to life's challenges. When students share personal struggles, maybe they're stressed about family issues or academic pressure, you might instinctively pivot every conversation toward financial solutions. You could find yourself presenting high-income careers as automatically superior choices, even when students express genuine passion for lower paying but meaningful work.

Money Status Scripts

- Do you believe your self-worth equals your net worth?
- If you have money, do you feel like people will love you more?
- Do you buy things you cannot afford to impress other people?

HOW THIS MIGHT SHOW UP IN YOUR TEACHING: Money status beliefs might cause you to emphasize appearance and status symbols rather than promoting sound, practical financial planning. When discussing budgeting, you might unconsciously validate spending on designer clothes or expensive cars as worthwhile investments in a professional image, rather than helping students think critically about whether such purchases align with their actual values and long-term goals.

Money Vigilance Scripts

- Do you believe that money should be saved, not spent?
- In your family, was it wrong to spend money on yourself?
- Do you worry that there won't be enough money to take care of your needs?

HOW THIS MIGHT SHOW UP IN YOUR TEACHING: Extreme money vigilance might lead you to discourage all spending or present any financial risk as inherently dangerous. When a student excitedly talks about their dream of starting a food truck or opening an online business, your first instinct might be to immediately highlight all the ways entrepreneurship could fail, rather than first exploring how they could pursue their vision thoughtfully. You might spend so much time on emergency funds and conservative investing that students become too risk-averse, leaving them nervous about exploring any financial decision that isn't completely secure.

Identifying your money scripts isn't about self-judgment; it's about understanding how these beliefs influence our teaching. By becoming aware of our tendencies, we can present financial concepts more objectively and help learners build a balanced, authentic relationship with money.

THE TRANSFORMATIVE POWER OF VULNERABILITY

Research consistently shows that teacher authenticity enhances student learning; this is especially true in financial education. When teachers share appropriate aspects of their financial journeys, including the ups and the downs, they create psychological safety that encourages student engagement.

The teacher educator Alex Lamon describes his approach: "I'm open with my own students. I tell them, I show them credit card statements. I show them my student loan balance. I show them how much I've paid over time. I'm not afraid to tell them how much money I get paid, even though it's public knowledge, because there's not too many adults who are willing to share all that stuff with them." This openness creates natural teaching moments: "Even if it's like after class, a kid asking me, you know, like, 'Oh, I'm a senior. Should I have all my money in stocks? Is that bad?' Or I have kids telling me they're getting paid under minimum wage, and I realized they're just getting taken advantage of by their employer because their employer thinks they don't know any better."

Building on Alex Lamon's philosophy of transparency, New Jersey high school business teacher Delaney Roberts used the Rate My Finances activity to model vulnerability. In this exercise, she tells me, Delaney stands in front of her high school class and invites them to act as her financial advisors. Each student can ask her a question, which she answers honestly. As she explains, "My salary is public knowledge—they can see it online anyway!" Students then use worksheets to calculate her budget. Finally, they highlight the things she is doing well financially and propose a next step for her. By being willing to adopt Alex's idea and put herself in the spotlight, Delaney shows students that even teachers are still learning. Does she take the advice? She says playfully, "They give great advice . . . and I *should* take more of it."

Of course the name of the game is appropriate vulnerability. Sharing financial struggles doesn't mean overwhelming students with personal details or compromising professional boundaries. Instead, it means acknowledging that money management is an ongoing journey for everyone, including their teacher.

Here's what I've learned from connecting with hundreds of educators: Navigating your own money doesn't disqualify you from being an effective financial literacy teacher. In fact, it makes you more relatable and authentic. Students respond to genuine human connection. When you're honest about your own financial learning journey, including the mistakes, victories, and ongoing challenges, you create space for students to be honest about theirs. Students need to see that financial literacy is a skill that develops over time, not an innate talent that some people have and others don't.

When you share your process of learning about student loans or discovering the power of automatic savings, you're modeling lifelong learning, resilience, and the courage to tackle challenging topics. These are exactly the mindsets we want our students to develop around money. Remember too that it doesn't have to be a solitary journey. Connect with colleagues who are also building their financial knowledge. Share resources, celebrate small victories, and support each other through the inevitable confusion that comes with learning new concepts.

FROM FINANCIAL EXPERT TO LEARNING PARTNER

One of the most liberating realizations for financial educators is this: You don't need to be a certified financial expert to be an effective financial literacy teacher. You just need to stay curious about money topics and guide students through the same learning process you're experiencing.

The reality is that most teachers didn't receive financial literacy training in their preparation programs. Consider Utah, the first state to mandate financial literacy. In 2008, its students became the nation's first to graduate with mandatory financial literacy education. A year later, researchers at the University of Wisconsin found that most teachers had received little to no personal finance training during their own schooling or teacher preparation programs.[8] In those early years, Utah's pioneering students and teachers were learning financial literacy side by side.

But here's the encouraging part: Research from Montana State University shows that since 2009, teacher financial confidence has increased dramatically—from 9 percent to 70 percent.[9] Further research from the National Endowment for Financial Education and Champlain College highlights the benefits of investing in teacher financial training. In one study with Vermont teachers, educators received forty-five hours of graduate-level financial literacy training. The results were striking. First, teacher self-confidence skyrocketed by 139 percent. Next, students taught by these newly confident educators showed real improvements in their own financial knowledge and behaviors. Finally, the teachers themselves reported significant gains in managing their own finances.[10] These educators became better teachers *and* more financially empowered individuals—proof that you can teach and learn about money alongside your students while improving your own life. With the right support and professional development, teachers create a butterfly effect impacting thousands of lives.

Unlike subjects like mathematics or science, where teachers often have years of formal education in their content area, financial literacy educators are often learning as they teach. Beth Kobliner, author of *Get a Financial Life* and longtime financial education advocate, puts it this way: "You don't have to be a math person or a money person or a finance person to understand this. An art teacher is not teaching you how to paint only because they might have paintings in a museum. I have to have the basic understanding, but through teaching, I'm also growing as an artist."[11]

This perspective shifts the teaching dynamic from performance to partnership. Instead of pretending to have all the answers, we can model the curiosity, research skills, and critical thinking that characterize financially literate adults. When a student asks about cryptocurrency and you're not familiar with blockchain technology, you can say, "I'm still learning about this too. Let's research it together and figure out what reputable sources tell us about the risks and benefits."

This approach strengthens your credibility because it demonstrates intellectual honesty, which is a crucial skill for navigating the often confusing world of personal finance.

The Transformative Power of Learning Alongside Students

Becoming a teacher actually changed my whole life.

—COURTNEY POQUETTE, personal finance teacher, Winooski High School

You should follow Courtney Poquette on LinkedIn—her Financial Literacy Month outfits each April are hysterical. Courtney is an energetic twenty-year veteran educator who teaches personal finance in Vermont, and she embraces learning in partnership with her students. Despite holding a business degree, she openly admits, "I didn't have any experience with personal finance. I tell the students the only two things I learned in school about investing were when we played the stock market game in elementary school, and I came in last place. And learning about the stock market crash during the Great Depression."

Without the right context, those early experiences actually discouraged Courtney from investing. "I studied hard during the game," she explains. "I read the charts, put in the effort, and still ended up in last place. I lost money, and I thought, why would anyone want to invest?" The exercise was meant to teach percentages, but the unintended emphasis on losses, the impression that success came from pure luck, and the focus on market crashes convinced her she would never want to invest.

Courtney's transformation came through teaching itself. She reflects, "I often think, what would have happened if I didn't end up in personal finance?

If I didn't end up teaching this topic, if I didn't go to these conferences to learn more about this, I never would have been willing to invest."

Her willingness to learn alongside her students, participate in professional development, and admit her knowledge gaps has made her a powerhouse teacher. Today, she confidently and empathetically guides students through concepts she once found intimidating—all because she understands the learning process from the inside.

EDUCATORS' MONEY STORIES AND THE RICH FRAMEWORK

Once we recognize our own money narratives and let go of the need to be the expert, we can use that self-awareness to create more inclusive teaching practices. The RICH framework—Representation, Inquiry, Connection, and Holistic thinking—illustrates just how vital teacher introspection is for student success.

REPRESENTATION means seeking out diverse financial voices and perspectives, both similar and different to our own. Whether we grew up in financial stability, hardship, or somewhere in between, we can bring our authentic perspectives forward. At the same time, we must avoid assuming the lived realities of our students and instead give them opportunities to define their own experiences. Embracing vulnerability in your teaching demonstrates that financial educators come from all backgrounds and that financial struggles don't disqualify anyone from learning.

INQUIRY invites us to continuously question our assumptions about what students know, what they need, and what financial success looks like for them. Instead of projecting our own financial goals, we ask: What are their true aspirations? What values do their families hold about money? What obstacles do they face? What are collective ways forward?

CONNECTION challenges us to find ways to make financial concepts relevant to all students, not just those whose experiences mirror our own. This might mean using examples outside our personal comfort zones or inviting guest speakers who can share different financial perspectives, just as I once did.

HOLISTIC THINKING recognizes that our students bring many forms of wealth beyond financial assets, just as we do. When teachers acknowledge these diverse kinds of wealth, students feel valued for who they are rather than judged for what they lack.

By applying the RICH framework to our own development as financial educators, we create the foundation for authentic, inclusive learning spaces. Our classrooms can be a space where every learner, and every educator, is empowered by a richer, more diverse understanding of financial wellness.

PRACTICAL STEPS FOR TEACHER FINANCIAL GROWTH

START WITH SELF-ASSESSMENT: Take an honest inventory of your current financial knowledge and comfort level. What topics feel familiar? Which ones make you nervous? Where do you want to grow?

ADDRESS YOUR OWN MONEY SCRIPTS: Reflect on the messages about money you received growing up and how they might influence your teaching. Consider taking the Klontz Money Script Inventory to identify your unconscious beliefs.

INVEST IN YOUR FINANCIAL EDUCATION: Read reputable personal finance books, listen to educational podcasts, or take online courses. Treat this as professional development that enhances your teaching effectiveness. Check out Your Financial Learning Tool Kit (in this book's appendix and online) for resources that shaped my own personal finance journey.

PRACTICE FINANCIAL VULNERABILITY: Look for opportunities to share your learning journey with students in ways that normalize the ongoing nature of financial growth.

CONNECT WITH OTHER FINANCIAL EDUCATORS: Join professional learning communities where you can share experiences, ask questions, and learn from colleagues on similar journeys.

MODEL LIFELONG LEARNING: Let students see you researching questions, updating your knowledge, and adapting your understanding as you encounter new information.

PATHWAYS TO PRO$PERITY: FINANCIAL WELLNESS FOR EDUCATORS

Thank goodness teaching financial literacy isn't about being a financial guru. It's about embracing honesty, continuous learning, and creating classrooms where everybody is building a healthy relationship with money. Your personal money story, with all its twists and turns, is a strength, not a setback. It offers authentic insights that inspire and connect with students.

The goal is to become a confident learner who can guide others with empathy and hope. When you've navigated building an emergency fund, consistently investing, or tackling debt, you speak from real life. This makes your lessons both relatable and actionable. Financially confident teachers create more stable, inspiring learning environments. By investing in your own financial journey and acknowledging your students' realities, you pave the way for financial well-being for everyone in your learning space. Yas.

Next, we will take a closer look at teens and young adults, exploring how their relationship with money—shaped by technology, social media, and economic uncertainty—present unique challenges and opportunities for financial educators.

SELF-REFLECTION

Every educator brings different experiences and comfort levels to this work. Consider these questions as you think about your financial education journey.

Personal Reflection

- $ What financial topics do you feel confident teaching? Which ones make your palms sweat a little?
- $ How do you stay current with financial concepts and trends?
- $ How has your relationship with technology and digital information evolved?
- $ What's the last financial skill you learned? How did you learn it?
- $ Where do you go when you need reliable financial information?
- $ What financial knowledge gaps do you want to fill this year?
- $ What's one financial goal you're working toward right now? What emotions come up when you think about it?

Educator Reflection

- $ How do you respond when students ask financial questions you can't answer?
- $ What financial topics do you avoid teaching because you feel unprepared?
- $ What parts of your money journey could help students in their journeys?
- $ What professional development would boost your confidence as a financial educator?
- $ How do you model lifelong financial learning for your students?
- $ How do you want your students to feel about money when they leave your class? What would that require from you as their guide?

CHAPTER 5

THE FUTURE

How Youth Navigate Money

When I look around on the subway and see every human drowning in their phone, I get pangs of nostalgia. I think of walking with my friends to Sam Goody for the latest Boyz II Men single, or better yet, waiting by the radio to press record and tape over my dad's church sermons just to capture "On Bended Knee." I remember picking up that corded phone to eavesdrop on calls, watching the fancy kids page their crush "143," and dying of dysentery on *The Oregon Trail* (the MS-DOS one, thankfully).

Nostalgia hits hard sometimes, but ultimately, technology has made life easier. Now, any song from anywhere in the world streams instantly. Videos you once waited all day to catch on MTV are available on YouTube in seconds. Printing photos was always a gamble—you'd wait weeks only to find the film exposed and every picture black. Blockbuster Fridays were a thing, except when you disappointingly found *Clueless* was already rented. Back then, I waited until my mother was asleep to sneak online to talk to friends, but I couldn't quiet the dial-up screech. "Diana, you're talking to the computer *again*?" Yeah, I definitely don't miss that.

When I really think about it, I don't miss the old tech. I do miss the genuine, undistracted connection. The moments when conversations weren't interrupted by notifications. When we were more fully present with each other. That face-to-face human connection is what we're truly nostalgic about. But here's where a little perspective comes in handy.

I'm not a time traveler yet, but I know that older generations have always criticized the younger ones. Recently I went to the Council for Economic Education's annual conference and saw Alex Lamon's hilarious presentation, "No Cash, No Checks, No Clue: Teaching Gen Alpha Personal Finance."

His introduction featured a montage of headlines spanning decades, each one echoing the same anxiety: *This generation is ruining everything.*

- A 1976 *New York* magazine article titled "The 'Me' Decade" called out young boomers for being too focused on themselves and caring more about their own happiness than responsibility: "They discovered and started doting on *Me!* They've created the greatest age of individualism in American history! All rules are broken!"[1]
- *Time* magazine in 1990 described Generation X: "They have trouble making decisions. They would rather hike in the Himalayas than climb a corporate ladder . . . They crave entertainment, but their attention span is as short as one zap of a TV dial."[2]
- In a classic 2013 article titled "Millennials: The Me Me Me Generation," Joel Stein describes millennials as "lazy, entitled, selfish and shallow" and "stunted, having prolonged a life stage between teenager and adult."[3] Ouch!

Sound familiar? Even Socrates worried that the invention of writing would make young people forgetful. And the trend continues with Gen Z and Gen Alpha facing criticism for being too online, too sensitive, too distracted.

Here's what's clear: Every generation believes the next one is somehow deficient. But it's also clear that each generation has adapted, innovated, and moved society forward in ways the previous one couldn't imagine.

So, always the contrarian, instead of lamenting how "kids these days" are taking our society downhill, I am on a journey to rethink our perception of this generation. Honestly, we did questionable things too. We created dot-com bubbles, made a mess with mortgages in 2008, allowed discriminatory practices, and dealt with economic uncertainty that impacted millions. Our history is full of ups and downs. The difference is that today's young people are growing up with tools, awareness, and access to information we could only dream of at their age.

Today's young adults represent Generation Z, born between 1997 and 2012. Gen Zers, also called Zoomers, have never known a world without the internet, have lived through multiple economic crises, and possess digital characteristics that shape how they approach financial learning. Meanwhile, Generation Alpha, born between 2010 and 2024, are entering our high school classrooms, bringing even deeper digital integration to their learning experiences. Alphas have never known a world without smartphones. They lived through the pandemic during their formative years and grew up with online payment systems and financial apps. As one ninth grader recently told me, "I never use cash. Everything's just digital wallets and apps."

We are all adjusting to an era of change at breakneck speed. The point here isn't to compare or determine which generation is better or worse. At its core, each one is a response to the one before it, shaped by the world they inherit, carrying their own unique strengths and challenges. Clinging to the past while dismissing the present or future is shortsighted. Even iconic companies like Sears, Blockbuster, and Kodak remind us that failing to recognize the need for change has costly consequences.

The young people we're teaching today aren't broken. They're different. We don't have to fix this generation; we only have to be open to learning with them. Drawing on everything I've learned from teaching and working with young people, I want to share insights into how they approach money and life. More importantly, I want to emphasize the importance of creating real moments of connection, both in our classrooms and in our communities. Because meaningful learning is about adapting to change, while at the same time creating spaces where human connection thrives, no matter the generation.

To truly understand this generation's relationship with money, I talked to four remarkable Gen Z individuals: Ian Brock, cofounder of Dream Hustle Code and New Nerd, and three of my former financial literacy students—Lia, Jennalissa, and Rachel. Their insights throughout this chapter come from direct conversations about how they navigate money, what concerns them, and what they wish people understood about their generation.

AN EMPOWERED GENERATION

We want more out of life.

—IAN BROCK, cofounder, Dream Hustle Code and New Nerd

When Ian Brock was six years old, his parents taught him terms like *income*, *assets*, *liabilities*, and *profit*. By thirteen, he was learning about real estate and credit. At sixteen, he made fifty thousand dollars in three months through his coding company. Now, at twenty-one, he travels the country teaching financial literacy to middle school, high school, and college students as cofounder of Dream Hustle Code, an organization that helps young people build financial and tech skills.

Ian's story might seem exceptional, but it reveals something profound about today's young people: They're hungry for financial knowledge, and when they get it, they run with it in ways that surprise even seasoned educators. They also use that knowledge to empower themselves and their communities.

Lia, a student from my financial literacy course, captures this hunger perfectly: "I love money and therefore will try to save as much as possible." But her perspective goes deeper: "I have to be comfortable with sacrificing, because building wealth isn't easy, and it takes time and the right steps to execute it properly." Lia chose to spend her free periods studying for months, preparing for the Intuit Personal Finance Exam and became the first student to earn this credential in our school. I don't know about you, but at seventeen, I was trying to get to Taco Bell during lunch, not learn about tax brackets.

These aren't the actions of financially irresponsible digital zombies. These are the thoughtful reflections of young people who understand that money is a tool for creating the lives they want.

Growing Up Digital

Unlike previous generations who might have learned about money through physical transactions, this generation's relationship with money is fundamentally digital. My students have had constant access to the internet from a young age and are extremely comfortable with technology and social media. Research tells us that Gen Z spends 10.6 hours per day with media, with 95 percent having access to a smartphone.[4] What I see in my classroom is students who can efficiently move between learning platforms, fact-check information in real time, and create content that teaches others.

Jennalissa, another alum who took my course, demonstrates the potential of this technology integration. She explains, "After we observed stock markets in class, I had a cash app account where it allows you to invest in stocks. It may sound silly that I only invested one dollar. But the purpose of it is to see the process for myself of owning a stock and how it constantly goes up and down." Her one-dollar investment wasn't about making money. It was about understanding how to access investing using technology.

However, Ian talked to me about the challenges of this digital immersion: "Perception is reality, right? So, a lot of the stuff that they see on the internet is not necessarily true."[5] While Gen Z is comfortable with technology, they often struggle with information literacy, particularly in distinguishing credible sources from misleading content.[6]

Self-Directed Learners

What strikes me most about my students is how naturally they take ownership of their learning. Jennalissa didn't have a bank account at the start of my class, but she quickly recognized its importance and acted immediately, researching options, comparing features, and opening her own checking and savings accounts. This is how this generation operates.

Ian Brock's journey, from student to teacher, further illustrates self-driven learning. Instead of following a prescribed curriculum, he identified gaps in his knowledge, sought out mentors, and created his own path to understanding. From an early age, Gen Zers learned how to seek out answers independently, talk with others across the globe, and navigate digital networks that often confounded older generations.[7] They've grown up finding their own answers, and that independence becomes a superpower in financial education when we learn to work with it rather than against it.

Yet with this independence comes responsibility. Lia highlights her generation's strong sense of accountability: "We recognize when money isn't used the way it's supposed to be, and we quickly call out the people responsible." This critical awareness shapes how Gen Z evaluates financial information and makes decisions. They are motivated by the pursuit of truth and pragmatic about their financial choices.[8]

The Generation That Asks, "But Why?"

Generation Z isn't content with simply accepting the way things have always been. They want to understand the relevance of topics, driven by an inherent efficiency in their approach to information. While we are still seeing how this efficiency model unfolds, it presents an opportunity for educators to be intentional. We are constantly reevaluating the purpose behind each topic.

Ian highlights a defining trait of his generation: its willingness to challenge established norms. "In my generation, we're starting to question the rules. Well, *why* is that a rule? Why is this the case? Why don't we just do this instead of that?" This questioning mindset can sometimes create tension between current ways and alternate paths. But as time has told, questioning is also a force for innovation and positive change. My students tend to avoid labels and value individual expression, and they naturally challenge outdated financial advice and systems. Their curiosity isn't just about rebellion, it's about shaping a better, more thoughtful future. I make it a point to explain why certain systems function as they do and to present multiple perspectives on why they exist. So that if students choose to question existing systems, they do so with a more nuanced understanding of the full picture.

When we talked about non-fungible tokens (NFTs) and how they are a speculative asset in which many have made money, hands shot up: "Why would anyone spend thousands on that? Can't you just screenshot them?

What kind of benefits come with this?" At first, questions can feel like resistance. But I recognize it as exactly the critical thinking we want them to apply to financial decisions throughout their lives. Plus, these are the same questions being widely discussed in the NFT space, and there are no right answers.

Learning Collaboratively

While creating a social media video for New York City Public Schools with my students, I saw firsthand how deeply they collaborate. I provided a loose structure for the budgeting tips we wanted to convey, and then they took the lead, brainstorming skits, refining ideas, giving feedback, and reworking scripts until everything clicked. The final product was engaging for parents and students, and their ease in front of the camera made the concepts even more impactful.

Despite stereotypes about social media creating isolation, Gen Z is also highly collaborative and social.[9] They enjoy working together and value group problem-solving and teamwork.[10] That said, I've noticed that collaboration often requires a warm-up period. They don't instantly jump into conversations, especially before a class culture is established. But when provided with a meaningful task in a supportive environment, they naturally lean into teamwork.

Sometimes I discover the power of their collaborative nature by accident. During a real estate unit, students were independently researching houses in different Florida markets for imagined clients, when one student began walking around to rate others' properties. I instinctively turned it into a group activity, making him the "buyer" whom teams had to impress. The winning group—his chosen real estate agents—earned a reward. (Starbursts, of course. I told you, snacks are key.)

The energy shifted instantly, with students vying for him to choose their property's amenities. Knowing this generation, I rarely lecture for more than fifteen minutes; Gen Z prefers group work and peer learning over traditional lecture-style instruction. But honestly, it's not just young people. At this point, most of us struggle to sit through long periods of passive listening.

WHAT SUCCESS MEANS TO THEM

My dream goal is to have the money to spend and spoil my loved ones.

—RACHEL, twelfth-grade financial literacy student

Finding Meaning and Impact

Today's young people approach financial success through an entirely different lens than previous generations, literally. My millennial generation loves a boomerang that's perfectly executed, and a flawlessly curated fall pumpkin photo shoot. But Gen Z's "0.5 selfie" trend shows a shift in how they see the world and how they want to be seen. The lens deliberately distorts the image, stretches features, and creates a playful vibe. This willingness to be less concerned about perfection and embrace a more experimental style extends far beyond their photography. They are experimenting with traditional markers of money, success, and life itself.

Purposeful Work

For Gen Z, meaningful work isn't just a cute bonus; it's essential. According to Deloitte's *2025 Gen Z and Millennial Survey*, 89 percent of Gen Zers say that purpose is important to their job satisfaction and well-being. When evaluating a potential employer, more than half (54 percent) say meaningful work is very important to them.[11] This isn't just woo-woo idealism either; they're willing to act on these values. Forty-four percent have left a job because it lacked purpose, and 41 percent have rejected a potential employer based on their personal ethics or beliefs.

When asked what captures their attention, Ian is direct: "I mean money. That's the main one. But we also want more. This generation wants more out of life, and they want to find a way to get towards that higher calling or their higher purpose." For Gen Z, a fulfilling career means work that aligns with their values. They care a lot about social justice, environmental issues, and creating positive change in their communities. They want careers where they can see the tangible results of their efforts and feel that their daily work contributes to something larger than themselves.

Wanting financial security is not in contrast to their desire for purpose. Instead, Gen Z believes that financial security and purpose can go hand in hand. They're not choosing between money and meaning. They are seeking both. (OMG, me too!)

Impact Beyond Their Paychecks

Yet Gen Z also understands that purpose and impact extend beyond their nine-to-five. They're pragmatic enough to recognize that not every job will provide deep meaning, but they still want to have impact. They want their lives to matter. For many, financial stability itself becomes a tool for creating positive impact in their families and communities.

Rachel, who is in my girls' investment club, sees money through a lens of relationships and values: "My dream goal is to have the money to spend and spoil my loved ones." Her desire to use money to care for her family captures the vision of using money intentionally: "It is all about how you decide to use your money and spend it." She sees wealth building not as accumulation for its own sake, but as a tool for relationships and meaningful connection.

Jennalissa also describes how her financial education enabled her to become a resource for her family: "Knowing I have the knowledge and being able to be confident helps me to communicate with them." These students' financial goals prioritize obtaining money, not in and of itself, but as a means to care for their loved ones. Financial literacy becomes a form of community wealth that this generation will continue to share outward.

The Good Life Equation = Money + Meaning + Well-Being

Ultimately, this generation is seeking what Deloitte calls the trifecta: financial security, meaningful work, and well-being. When they can't find all three in their careers, they get creative. Some prioritize jobs with good work-life balance and higher salaries, which gives them the time and resources to create impact outside of working hours through volunteering, community organizing, or supporting causes they believe in. Others seek positions at mission-driven organizations even if it means accepting lower pay, believing their daily work can contribute directly to positive change.[12]

For Gen Zers, the question isn't whether to pursue purpose or financial stability. They are determined to find both. They're not choosing between caring for their families and doing meaningful work. They're seeking financial empowerment that allows them to live according to their values, support their communities, and create positive change through both their careers and their personal choices. This generation is distorting traditional definitions of financial success to create something more holistic and values driven.

THE ENTREPRENEURSHIP APPEAL

One consistent theme among young people is their interest in entrepreneurship. They want to create their own paths rather than follow traditional employment structures. Ian observes: "I don't know what's going on with this generation, but my generation just hates getting jobs for some reason. Everyone wants to start a business. They want to be entrepreneurs."

When we research careers, many of my students express interest in "being their own boss." Recent *Forbes* research supports this observation: "Gen Z's entrepreneurial spirit is remarkable, with 61 percent planning to start a business within the next four years." This entrepreneurial drive stems from multiple factors unique to their generation. The *Forbes* article explains, "Unlike previous generations, they grew up witnessing the gig economy, seeing social media influencers build businesses, and observing how technology can democratize entrepreneurship." Young entrepreneurs are motivated by the desire to create positive change, with 83 percent wanting to create a business that has social impact.[13]

However, Ian also brings a realistic perspective to the conversation, being an entrepreneur himself. He counsels patience and preparation: "Look, you might be working on this business for ten years and not make any profit, right? So I tell students to go work for somebody so that you can get paid to learn." The *Forbes* research confirms the need for further preparation: "While 76 percent of Gen Z believes entrepreneurship is achievable, many lack the foundational business knowledge needed to succeed."[14] This gap between aspiration and preparation is exactly what we can bring to our curriculum.

REAL TALK: HOW TO RELATE TO THEM

Authenticity over Authority

When I watch my students interact, I see how much they value authenticity in their friendships and learning experiences. They look for integrity in people, products, and relationships.[15] This has profound implications for financial educators. As described in chapter 4, when we tune in to our authentic selves, students appreciate it. I have seen all types of teachers connect with students—across personalities, backgrounds, cultures, and experiences. The one thing they had in common was being authentically themselves. They shared experiences with the class, and they genuinely cared about students. The caring looked different from teacher to teacher, but because they were genuine, students appreciated them for it. Gen Z learners value authenticity and transparency in their educators. Instead of viewing vulnerability as a weakness, they appreciate teachers who are willing to share both successes and failures. They see this as a sign of trustworthiness.

When I asked my student Lia about what financial educators should know, she made it clear that she prefers realness: "They should be 100 percent honest about everything related to finance. The media already covers up half of financial literacy, so educators being authentic and honest shows me that being involved in finance isn't easy and it takes specific steps to be successful."

Ian's advice to educators similarly reflects this need for authenticity: "Don't try too hard. You don't have to learn the latest trends, you don't have to learn about what latest dances they're doing on TikTok. You don't have to do this because if you empower them to speak, they will tell you what they need."

Instead of trying to be cool, effective educators focus on being genuine. Ian's success comes from his willingness to share both successes and failures: his cryptocurrency losses, his learning journey, and his honest assessment of challenges.

Appreciating Diverse Perspectives

Seeing women being successful in finance
makes me feel proud and inspired.

—LIA, twelfth-grade financial literacy student

Gen Z values honesty from educators and the authenticity of inclusive voices in financial education. A McKinsey study coined this generation the True Gen, highlighting their focus on authenticity, which gives them more freedom to express who they are and helps them better understand people who are different from them.[16]

One of the most valuable insights from Ian's experience is the importance of diverse mentorship. He describes learning from mentors of different backgrounds: "I have two mentors—Mr. C, an African American man, and Mr. B, a white man." His perspective challenges simplistic assumptions about representation: "I think you need to have a mix of both. I can relate to Mr. C. I see myself in him. I also learn a lot from Mr. B and get experiences that maybe people in my own community may not have." The takeaway for educators is powerful. Ian says, "You can never really tell how much impact somebody's going to have on kids. It may just be the information or just showing them something that they didn't even know was possible."

This perspective aligns with Gen Z's pragmatic approach to learning. They value authentic knowledge, real connection, and genuine support. Students benefit from different approaches to financial literacy, hearing voices that resonate with their lived experiences while also encountering other perspectives that challenge and expand their thinking.

Lia echoed this sentiment in her reflections on representation in finance: "Seeing women specifically being successful in finance makes me feel proud and inspired because it shows me that we can be successful too despite stereotypes and expectations from society." She later cited Vivian Tu, an author and influencer featured in our class, as someone she looks up to, explaining, "Not only does she share where she first started, but she informs people how hard it is to get into the industry and provides the steps it takes to get into it." The value of authenticity value surfaces again when she says of Tu, "She's 100 percent honest—and her book explains everything about finance." Lia's words underscore why diverse perspectives matter so much to this generation, both for exposure and empowerment. A mix of voices encourages creative thinking and helps students rethink long-standing assumptions, showing them that financial success is not limited by background, identity, or preconceived expectations.

Making It Relevant

Youth engage most deeply with financial topics that connect to their world. This has always been true, but increasingly more so today. During our crypto and blockchain unit, I wanted students to grasp the concept behind non-fungible tokens (NFTs), the digital one-of-a-kind items that belong only to their owner. So I asked if they played *Roblox*, the popular online game where players buy virtual gear and accessories. About half looked up surprised, and nodded. I explained that fungible tokens are like standard *Roblox* accessories, and many people can own the same item. But non-fungible items are like rare, exclusive swords that only one player can have. That comparison sparked an aha moment. Thanks to my constant exposure to *Roblox* through my kids, I was able to connect NFTs to students' everyday experiences and make the concept of fungibility easier to understand. (Look for more about NFTs and Web3 in chapter 11.)

According to McKinsey research on Gen Z consumers, they look for authenticity and integrity in the brands they support and they can quickly spot when a company is just paying lip service to values.[17] Last year, when explaining credit inquiries, Ian compared it to dating: "I relate asking for credit and compare it to dating or something relatable like that. If you have too many inquiries on your credit report from the banks, they might look at you as riskier. So I asked the teens: Have you ever had a person that's always blowing up your phone? That's suspicious. Same thing with credit inquiries: Too many requests makes you look suspicious." These analogies translate financial concepts into familiar emotional territory.

Beyond relatability, Gen Z wants clear, practical connections between what they are learning and how it applies to their everyday lives. A recurring concern I hear from my students is whether traditional education will truly prepare them for real-world success. Ian echoes this sentiment: "The main issue I've had with students, especially in high school, is they feel like what they're learning in schools is not going to help them in the real world." Our youth are less willing to settle for vague promises about future benefits when the relevance isn't immediately apparent. They want to know why something matters now.

This sense of urgency pushes educators to be more intentional in explaining why topics matter. Lucky for us, financial education is beautifully positioned to provide immediate connections to their lives. As Ian puts it, "Financial education offers a solution because the connection to real life is immediate. It's a direct link; there's no workaround—you need to understand how money works. You need to know how to make money because it will help you when you graduate no matter what you do. It's clear as day. Because you need money to live."

Interactive Learning

The need for relatability is tied to Gen Z's preference for visual and interactive learning. Jennalissa explains, "I would say teaching more about saving, budgeting, etc., using technology (apps, social media) and making it visual." She also recommends teaching approaches that emphasize interactivity, sharing, "In my experience, my generation also learns better through hands-on activities. Like that Junior Achievement trip we did where we used an iPad to manage a hypothetical identity, budget our life from our pets, our kids, and our expenses, and see the outcome of our decisions. That trip was gold." (Shout-out to Junior Achievement of New York for their engaging Finance Park field trip! If you get a chance to partner with them, you should.) This preference for interactive learning reflects broader generational characteristics that highlight their collaborative nature.

WHAT THEY'RE WORRIED ABOUT

Sorting Through the Digital Noise

Alongside the vast amounts of helpful content online is an equally massive dose of useless or even harmful material. While Gen Z excels at finding information, they often face challenges when it comes to evaluating its quality. With an endless stream of digital content vying for our clicks, it can be tough to distinguish valuable insights from the attention-seeking noise. Despite their comfort with technology, they still need guidance to navigate online information.

Whenever you scroll through social media, it is easy to find hundreds of "finfluencers"—influencers offering financial advice online—advocating quick pump and dump schemes or a guaranteed way to make a million. Last year, a student shared a video of a young man in front of a Maserati, holding a stack of cash to his ear like a phone, and jokingly asked, "Miss, you gonna help me get that this year?"

Ian Brock addresses this issue directly with his students, emphasizing the importance of research and verification "If you're going to enter a field or invest, you have to spend a minimum of one hundred hours practicing it, and then you have to practice it more."

Their digital fluency must be paired with strong digital literacy skills. While Gen Z is highly adept at navigating online spaces, we cannot assume they know how to differentiate valid information from misinformation. If we don't explicitly teach them how to evaluate sources and identify scams, they risk costly consequences.

During our scams and frauds lesson, one example focused on the puppy scam, where scammers pose as dog breeders, using fake listings and stolen photos to trick buyers into sending money for nonexistent puppies. When one student got to this example during the group work, he shared that he was a victim of this scam. Until then, he didn't know how widespread it was. He bravely shared that he and his mother had lost two thousand dollars. Thousands of examples like this reinforce the urgency of teaching students how to verify and evaluate online content.

Why Financial Security Feels So Important

I'm determined not to live paycheck to paycheck.

—JENNALISSA, student, University of Connecticut

Economic factors—rising inflation, tariffs, disrupted supply chains, emerging cryptocurrencies, increasing student loan debt, AI's impact on jobs, and market volatility—are reshaping Gen Z's relationship with money. Having witnessed the 2008 financial crisis as children and coming of age during the COVID-19 pandemic, this generation approaches finances with heightened awareness and pragmatism. Being digitally plugged in since birth, they have been exposed to these messages all day, every day—far more than any generation before them.

Being hyperaware of these challenges have sharpened their financial Spidey senses. According to Deloitte's *2025 Gen Z and Millennial Survey*, nearly half of Gen Zers (48 percent) report not feeling financially secure—up from 30 percent in 2024. More than half (52 percent) are living paycheck to paycheck, and 37 percent struggle to cover monthly living expenses. For the fourth year in a row, the cost of living tops their list of concerns.[18]

Rachel captured this generational feeling: "My generation has grown up watching prices go up on everything. Like, my mom talks about when gas was under two dollars, and now it's over four dollars. We've seen how inflation affects everything—food, housing, even our college costs. It makes you realize you have to be smart about money because everything just keeps getting more expensive."

This shared sense of insecurity has driven many Gen Zers to seek financial stability. Jennalissa's journey—from impulsive spending to intentional living—exemplifies this shift: "I used to spend every penny I made from small jobs without saving any. Now, I'm determined not to live paycheck to paycheck. I want to live comfortably." These mindset shifts come from facing economic challenges and having the knowledge and skills to make informed financial decisions.

Understanding Gen Z's characteristics and concerns allows us to create meaningful learning spaces for them to build these skills. Their mix of financial awareness, entrepreneurial drive, and values-based decision-making offers a unique opportunity for financial educators. Instead of a simple checklist for teaching this generation, the following strategies are about a mindset shift, helping us leverage Gen Z's strengths while supporting their unique challenges.

PRACTICAL APPROACHES FOR SUPPORTING AN EMPOWERED GENERATION

Sometimes giving students independent, focused time to form and refine their own opinions and ideas is the best move. At the same time, financial education thrives when students talk, engage, and learn together. Gen Z naturally gravitates toward collaborative learning, as they value interactive discussions and shared problem-solving. By creating opportunities for teamwork and real-world application, educators can tap into these strengths and help students navigate complex financial concepts. I am still working on giving students more opportunities to talk and collaborate, because the results are always intriguing.

Rather than positioning ourselves as the sole source of financial wisdom, we can cultivate classrooms where knowledge flows in multiple directions. After learning about credit scores, students discuss scenarios where different decisions impact credit, deciding together if outcomes are positive or negative on their score. There isn't always a single right answer; they have to explore the nuances together. During tax lessons, students collaborate to file taxes for different demographics, navigating challenges together, offering support, and managing frustration as they build real-world financial skills.

These collaborative structures reflect how this generation naturally deals with complex information. Financial problem-solving teams tackle real-world scenarios together: "Your friend is eighteen and wants to build credit. They're considering three different credit card offers. What questions should they ask, and which would you recommend?" Using tools like Bankrate, students compare options, present their reasoning, and learn not just about credit cards but also how to evaluate financial products critically.

Knowledge-exchange circles create regular opportunities for students to share financial discoveries. What banking apps have they tried? What interest rates have they found? What new digital tools are emerging? These discussions often introduce me to financial innovations I haven't encountered yet—students become teachers, sharing insights about everything from high-yield savings accounts to investment platforms designed for their generation. This peer-to-peer learning acknowledges that financial literacy also requires collective knowledge to stay current with an evolving financial landscape.

PRACTICAL APPROACHES FOR PURPOSE-CENTERED FINANCIAL EDUCATION

Gen Z seeks meaning in everything they do, and financial education becomes most powerful when we help students discover their personal why. Rather than starting with budgeting categories or investment types, I begin each unit by asking students to define their financial goals through the lens of their values. Rachel's desire to "spoil my loved ones" isn't just a sweet sentiment; it becomes the foundation for understanding saving strategies, budgeting priorities, and long-term wealth building. When students can connect compound interest to their dream of supporting family members, or relate emergency funds to their desire for independence, abstract concepts transform into personal tools for achieving what matters most. Values-based financial planning becomes our anchor, helping students understand that every financial decision—from daily spending to long-term investing—can be grounded in their aspirations.

Fostering this agency requires us to step back from our instinct to provide immediate answers and allow students to explore. Although Gen Z has the ability to find any piece of information, if I sense their hesitation to begin, my first impulse is to look it up and provide the answer to keep the class moving. This is something I constantly challenge myself to improve. I'm continuously working on shifting that dynamic, encouraging students to take a more active role in their learning. So, when a student asks, "How is cryptocurrency taxed?" I resist the urge to launch into an explanation and instead turn it into a collaborative research opportunity: "That's a great question. Let's look at that together and see what credible sources tell us." These spontaneous questions become doorways to deeper learning, empowering students to find answers together, building both financial knowledge and research skills that will serve them for life.

When the class faces complex financial questions without clear-cut answers, it's important to model the problem-solving process rather than offering oversimplified solutions. For example, you might say, "This is a situation where the math matters, but so do your personal values. Let's work through both." This approach helps students appreciate that uncertainty is a natural part of financial decision-making.

Encouraging students to use their autonomy to find answers—and teaching them to evaluate information—is supported by modern technology and is an absolute necessity. Rather than dismissing financial content on social media entirely, we can encourage students to analyze it critically. We no longer need to be the sole guardians of financial wisdom. Instead, we can guide students through a vast landscape of financial information, which definitely includes its fair share of questionable content. This investigative approach honors their natural curiosity while building critical evaluation skills they'll need to sift through misleading information throughout their lives. The key is recognizing that autonomy doesn't mean abandoning structure. It isn't just about assigning a task and saying, "See ya Friday!" Instead, it's about creating flexible frameworks and timelines where students can exercise choice within guidelines.

PRACTICAL APPROACHES FOR RELEVANT FINANCIAL LEARNING

Impactful financial education bridges the gap between abstract theory and lived experience, using relevant references to make concepts stick. When I explain NFTs, I connect them to gaming platforms students already understand. Variable expenses become more concrete when linked to streaming subscriptions they manage, and stock market concepts feel immediate when we discuss companies whose brands they wear, use, or follow online.

Visual and interactive learning strategies cater to this generation's preference for experiential over passive learning. Whether through formal programs like Junior Achievement Finance Park or classroom simulations, students consistently engage more with hands-on experiences. Infographics and charts help make concepts like compound interest or debt payoff easier to grasp, while platforms like Napkin Finance and Visual Capitalist provide engaging content that sparks meaningful conversations and writing prompts. Technology further enhances experiential learning, especially when we use tools and apps like Moomoo to track market trends, interactive Yahoo Finance charts to explore company performance, and educational calculators to run real-world financial scenarios.

Perhaps most importantly, this generation values realness above being super polished. They can sense when educators are genuine versus performing a role. Sharing real financial questions from my own life, discussing complex topics honestly, and modeling thoughtful problem-solving creates a classroom environment where students feel safe to ask their own questions. By embracing our roles as fellow learners rather than all-knowing financial experts, we create spaces for genuine financial growth. This means not shying away from real consequences. Gen Z prefers honest conversations about issues like student loan debt, rising housing costs, and economic uncertainty, topics that directly affect their futures. Addressing these realities head-on helps students see that every financial decision is nuanced, with benefits and costs.

This approach supports a generation that values truth, collaboration, and purpose in building financial lives that align with their deepest values and highest aspirations. When we meet Gen Z where they are rather than where we think they should be, financial education becomes a powerful tool for both individual growth and collective financial empowerment.

YOUTH VALUES AND THE RICH FRAMEWORK

Young people today naturally relate to the values that make the RICH framework powerful. When I watch my students engage with financial concepts, I see these connections everywhere.

REPRESENTATION takes on new meaning when students see young financial leaders alongside traditional experts. They need to know that financial success isn't limited by age or following one prescribed path. At the same time, they benefit from seeing what long-term financial journeys look like for people who took more traditional routes.

INQUIRY matches perfectly with their instinct to question everything. Instead of accepting "that's just how it is," they want to understand why financial systems operate the way they do. Their questioning feels like rebellion, and it just might be. But it's exactly the critical thinking we want to encourage.

CONNECTION speaks to their need for relevance. Every financial concept has to connect clearly to their actual lives and future dreams.

HOLISTIC THINKING aligns with how they approach life. Their finances can't be separated from their values, relationships, and desire to make a positive impact. They want their money choices to reflect who they are and what they care about.

This generation doesn't compartmentalize the way previous generations might have. Their financial wellness has to integrate with their purpose-driven approach to life, and that's a strength we can build on.

PATHWAYS TO PRO$PERITY: MEETING THEM WHERE THEY ARE

Our challenge isn't to turn back the hands of time or change this generation's traits. Instead, the goal is to leverage their preferences to educate them while addressing their real concerns about economic uncertainty.

Gen Z's strengths—digital fluency, autonomy, collaboration, and purpose-seeking—make financial education a powerful tool for their values-driven lives. The speed of technology means they are active participants in their future right now. Ian's journey, from learning financial terms at six to teaching thousands of peers at twenty-one, and Jennalissa's transformation into an informed family financial planner, illustrate how this generation leverages resources and shares knowledge within their networks. Their drive for truth and practicality means they quickly spot financial education that feels outdated or disconnected from their realities. Their autonomy and collaboration also mean they supplement learning through peers and digital tools, regardless of classroom instruction. The best financial education embraces these traits, using money as a relatable tool to provide knowledge while supporting students in building lives that align with their purpose and values.

In the next chapter, we tackle the emotional big kahuna of all financial education: money mindset. We'll explore how understanding our beliefs about money transforms every financial topic.

SELF-REFLECTION

Take a moment to unwind and set a reflection mood with your favorite music, whether you're streaming a playlist, playing a CD, have records spinning, or are dusting off an old 8-track. Take a trip through time as you reflect on your experiences—as a young person, as an educator, or as that ever-learning "young educator" we all still are. Consider these questions.

Personal Reflection

- $ What did money conversations look like when you were a teenager? How might that be different from your students' experiences?
- $ What motivated you to learn as a young person? What bored you to tears?
- $ When young people know more than you about apps, trends, or digital tools, how does that feel?
- $ What do you genuinely admire about today's young people? What worries you?
- $ How has your relationship with technology changed over time?

Educator Reflection

- $ Where do you give students choice in your classroom? Where could you give more autonomy?
- $ How do you balance collaboration with individual work?
- $ When students question traditional financial advice, do you see it as curiosity or challenge?
- $ How do you connect money concepts to what students care about right now?
- $ How do you show up authentically and build trust with students?
- $ How do you help students navigate the gap between financial influencers and legit financial advice?
- $ When was the last time a student taught you something? How did that change your teaching?

EDUCATOR RESOURCES

Student Discussion Questions

Quick prompts designed to ignite student conversation

- How do you talk about money at school, at home, and with your friend groups?
- What financial goals excite you most, and how do you see money helping you achieve them?
- When you think about successful people in finance or business, who comes to mind and why?
- How has technology changed the way you think about or interact with money?
- What financial topics do you wish were taught differently or more thoroughly?
- How do you evaluate financial information you encounter on social media or online?

- What questions about money do you wish you could ask without judgment?
- How important is it to you that financial advice comes from people who share your background versus people with expertise?

Standalone Activities (20–50 minutes)

Exercises that can fit into any lesson, with added discussion to extend learning

MY MONEY STORY TIMELINE

- **Purpose:** Discover how student experiences influence their deeper values and aspirations.
- **RICH Framework (Holistic thinking):** Integrates money decisions with past, present, and future life purpose.
- **Process:** Students create personal timelines of significant money moments and lessons learned in their lives.

1. Students brainstorm financial moments from early childhood to present (first money memory, personal money decisions, challenges, influential people).
2. Students create illustrated digital or physical timelines highlighting key learning moments throughout the years.
3. In small groups of three to four, students share their timelines, identifying common similarities and differences in experiences.
4. Students discuss how past experiences influence current money attitudes, fears, and strengths.
5. Students add projected positive financial milestones and goals, connecting past lessons to future aspirations.

GEN Z FINANCIAL INNOVATORS SHOWCASE

- **Purpose:** Highlight young people who are creating financial solutions and businesses.
- **RICH Framework (Representation):** Shows financial success isn't limited by age or traditional paths.
- **Process:** Students research and present on young entrepreneurs and financial innovators from diverse backgrounds.

1. Students research young business owners, financial educators, or innovators from various backgrounds.
2. Students create presentations highlighting their journeys, challenges, and lessons learned.

3. Students present findings and peers discuss what makes their approaches unique to their generation.
4. Students identify specific lessons that apply to their own financial goals and aspirations.

■ "QUESTION EVERYTHING" FINANCIAL PROJECT

- **Purpose:** Encourage students to critically examine financial rules and systems.
- **RICH Framework (Inquiry):** Develops critical thinking about why financial systems work the way they do.
- **Process:** Students choose a financial "rule" to investigate, question, and analyze from multiple perspectives. Students select common financial advice—"Buy a house," "Avoid debt," "Never lease a car"—to investigate thoroughly.

1. Students research historical context, cultural perspectives, and alternative viewpoints on their chosen financial rule.
2. Students interview people from different generations and backgrounds about their perspectives on this financial advice.
3. Students present findings that demonstrate understanding of nuanced financial decision-making and when rules might not apply.

■ DIGITAL FINANCIAL LITERACY LAB

- **Purpose:** Leverage students' digital fluency to explore, evaluate, and create credible financial content.
- **RICH Framework (Connection and Inquiry):** Uses their digital skills while developing critical thinking about financial information they encounter daily.
- **Process:** Students investigate financial content online and create their own reliable financial education materials.

1. Students evaluate financial content in their social media feeds or examples you provide for validity. To help them fact-check, they apply a simple three-question test to analyze finfluencers: a) What are they trying to sell you? b) How do they make their money? c) What might be missing from the story (risks, losses, time involved)?
2. Teams create fact-check reports comparing misleading versus credible content, identify red flags in online financial advice, and examine patterns in misleading content.
3. Students develop accurate financial education materials (videos, infographics, posts) focusing on misinformation they uncovered.
4. Students evaluate each other's work, reflect on how creating content shifted their perspective, and discuss responsible financial information sharing.

SECTION II

TEACHING FINANCIAL LITERACIES

CHAPTER 6

EXPLORING MONEY MINDSET

Teaching about money mindset feels vastly different from teaching more cut-and-dry topics like paycheck deductions or credit scores. Money mindset learning goes deeper to explore the invisible forces that influence our everyday decisions. These forces are inherited from family, culture, and society. They shape both our everyday financial decisions and the larger beliefs that guide our lives. They show up in small moments, like deciding whether to spend $3 more for organic strawberries (isn't it wasteful to pay more on that?). They also influence bigger questions about what it means to have enough (Once I have a million, then I'll finally feel secure . . . right?).

Before we get to teaching money mindset, we must first understand our own relationship with money. What has money been saying to us our whole lives? What kinds of stories has it been telling us? This application chapter invites you to explore your financial beliefs, and just like Planet Fitness, this is a no-judgment zone. We're not looking to tear ourselves apart, but we do need to understand where our beliefs originate. When we are aware of our own money stories, we are less likely to pass on limiting beliefs unintentionally to others. That awareness enables us to build trusting spaces for our students to explore their own deeper beliefs with curiosity and empathy.

DEFINING MONEY MINDSET

Put simply, our money mindset is how our beliefs affect our thoughts, feelings, and behaviors when it comes to money. Our thoughts and emotions, both consciously and unconsciously, influence how we view and handle our finances. Everyone has a unique perspective on money based on their personal experiences. These perspectives shape our financial decisions, often in ways we don't realize. The summation of our experiences, feelings, and actions creates the type of money mindset we have.

Money and Emotions

The word *money* elicits strong emotions and deep-seated beliefs in all humans. There's no two ways about it: When you ask someone their thoughts on money, they will usually have an emotionally charged answer.

Emotions are not random. They are deeply connected to how we think and act. The BTFAR (Beliefs, Thoughts, Feelings, Actions, Results) framework shows us how these connections work. Our internal emotional state can directly lead to many different financial results. Let's break it down to see what happens internally—and how the framework connects to our emotions around money.

From the get-go, we have deep beliefs about what money is, what it can do for us, and if we even deserve it. A lot of those beliefs come from what we heard growing up in our families, what we saw during tough times, and the stories our communities shared about money and value. Often these beliefs sit beneath the surface, subconsciously shaping our choices before we even realize they're pulling the strings.

These beliefs create our thoughts about specific money situations. When one of my students sees a designer purse, her belief that "my family doesn't waste money on pricey things" instantly creates the thought "I shouldn't want this." Or vice versa. Maybe her family belief is that "I should buy things when I work hard," so the thought is "I deserve this pricey bag." When my teenage self considered college, her belief that "education is the only way out" created thoughts of possibility mixed with pressure, "I have this opportunity so I must make sure I'm the first to graduate."

Our thoughts then spark feelings of excitement, shame, fear, hope, and guilt. I see this happen when I discuss financial goals with people. Some of them light up with anticipation while others are more worrisome. Those feelings aren't accidental. They are the emotional response to thoughts rooted in our beliefs. You might have positive emotions about money because you have good associations with having money in your life, or you have hope that you will achieve financial freedom. You also might have negative emotions associated with money due to past financial hardships, societal pressures from those around you, or a sense of insecurity when comparing yourself to others.

Then come our actions. Maybe they enable us to balance our savings, investing and spending joyfully. Or we might impulse buy workout clothes late at night, keep an Amazon cart always ready to go, and say yes to brunches we can't afford. Or we deprive ourselves, avoid financial conversations, or sabotage opportunities when our money-related feelings become overwhelming and hiding seems easier. Sometimes we perform all these actions within one week.

Finally . . . drumroll . . . we get our results. Our positive mindset beliefs of "I can learn to manage money well" lead to thoughts like "I should research this investment opportunity," which generate feelings of excitement and curiosity. Alternatively, results can reinforce our original limiting beliefs. When someone with a "money is scarce" belief makes fear-based financial choices that keep them struggling, it feels like proof that they were right about money all along.

When we identify our BTFAR responses to money, we can start peeling back the layers to understand what's shaping our emotions and our results. Humans are messy. Sometimes we will experience all of these beliefs, thoughts, feelings, actions, and results simultaneously. The important thing is to notice what is happening internally so if we are getting results we don't want, we can dig deeper and adjust to get the results we do want.

Money wellness expert Shannah Game captured the emotions of money in a recent newsletter: "The real story isn't in your net worth! It's in the $4.75 cupcake you bought when you were sick of saying no to yourself. It's in the Amazon cart you filled at 2 a.m. It's in the money you spent to leave your life, your marriage, your friendship, your family, your career. Or stay. Or numb out. Or finally feel something. Money isn't just math. It's memory. Identity. Desire. Shame. Joy. Power. It's everything we were told to manage quietly."[1]

Money is never just about money. It's about everything we've experienced, everything we've been taught, and everything we're still learning about ourselves.

Influences That Shape Your Money Mindset

Just like Riley in the movie *Inside Out*, we can build a healthier mindset by unlocking the core memories that have shaped our attitudes toward money. The conversations I've had with myself, other teachers, and students highlight several key factors that helped form our financial mindsets. Some influences nurture positivity and abundance while others contribute to more negative mindsets of scarcity. This is a time to think back and do an inventory of what sorts of influences we were exposed to so we can figure out if they are healthy for us or not. Our money mindsets are often influenced by factors like:

- **Family messages:** A household where every financial discussion ended in arguments and constantly hearing, "We'll never be able to afford that" vs. having a grandmother who quietly showed you her envelope budgeting system and how she managed to send money back home while raising five kids

- **Cultural background:** Collective saving practices in some cultures vs. individual wealth accumulation in others
- **Societal narratives:** "Pull yourself up by your bootstraps" vs. "It takes a village"
- **Personal experiences:** That time you couldn't afford to go on the field trip vs. when someone gave you an unexpected gift that changed everything
- **Social circles:** Friends who talk openly about their side hustles and investment strategies and who normalize conversations about money vs. those who roll their eyes at saving or investing as "bougie" or unrealistic and dismiss financial planning as pointless because "something always comes up anyway"

STARTING WITH GRACE AND UNDERSTANDING

When you start reflecting on your own money story, it's natural for feelings to bubble up—frustration, regret, the classic shoulda, coulda, woulda. That's normal. It's important to remember that most of the time, the people who influenced us were doing the best they could with the information they had. They were reacting to what they were taught, like all the generations before them.

So the goal of reflecting on your mindset influences isn't to find someone to blame for your past money decisions. Instead, it's a time to gain understanding, to think about where your beliefs came from, who shaped them, how they show up in your life today, and which ones you want to keep or let go of.

It also includes being kind to yourself. We are so hard on ourselves. ("How could I have been so stupid?" "Why didn't I know better?") Please have grace for the decisions you made with the mindset you had back then, and offer yourself forgiveness as you reflect on who you are now. Doing this frees up positive energy to focus on who you want to become.

Reframing My Negative Money Mindset

The good news is we know that money mindsets can be changed. If you find yourself with more of a negative money mindset, or constant deficit thinking, it's not just you.

Before I got this swanky abundant mindset, I had a major case of the deficits. When I was growing up, my family counted every penny and money talk was always about stretching what little we had. I remember when we picked our clothes from garbage bags that others donated to us, or got our furniture by driving up the street to see what other people threw out. When we couldn't afford the Timberlands everyone in Queens was wearing, my sweet mother splurged twenty-five dollars on a pair of boots called Big Macs. They were from JCPenney and had a tractor on the side instead of the iconic tree. If you know anything about kids in New York City in the 1990s, wearing an off-brand logo was the social kiss of death.

For a long time, I defined my identity by comparing myself to those who seemed to have more. In my mind, there were clear lines between people with money and people without it—and we definitely fell into the "without" category. Those feelings sometimes seeped into my self-worth. I wondered if I was only deserving of picking through garbage bags. I always imagined having more, but did not think it was possible for people like me. To this day, I feel a wave of discomfort before I check my account balances, even though the numbers are healthy. Certain aspects of childhood can have lasting effects on our emotional relationship with money.

You Say Broke, I Say Thrifty

These can be heavy topics. But after reading countless finance and self-growth books, being surrounded by amazing people with growth mindsets, traveling, and more maturity, I have a totally different perspective on my upbringing.

New Abundance Me now realizes that we were actually ahead of our time. I love buying secondhand clothes, now called *thrifting*, from places like ThredUp. Getting hand-me-downs from my more fashionable friends is now celebrated as *sustainability*. Picking up a gently used lamp on the street is now an act of *upcycling*. And reveling in fewer possessions is now called *minimalism*. I am proud to look back at our scrappy old way of salvaging items and helping others with what we had. We were financial trendsetters.

Techniques to Reframe Our Money Thoughts

We don't have to become positive money mindset cheerleaders overnight. Adjusting our money mindset is about becoming curious about our own financial stories. When I started examining my beliefs about money, I unlocked memories and influences that I didn't know existed. While some stories were helpful, others were holding me back both financially and emotionally. I've still got a few scarcity beliefs I need to let go of, but I'm getting there.

Once you can identify factors that have contributed to your money mindset, you can work to change your thoughts around them. In her book *Wealth Warrior*, Linda García introduces the concept of "money wounds," which are deeply ingrained limiting beliefs that block our path to wealth. She urges us to peel back the layers and free ourselves from these false beliefs. For instance, she reframes "I'm not good with money" as a mindset that becomes a self-fulfilling prophecy. When we tell ourselves we're bad with money, we avoid learning about it, which keeps us stuck in patterns that don't serve us. Instead, she proposes we use the phrase "I am more than capable of understanding money."[2] The reframe here is about recognizing that financial skills can be learned and developed over time.

Another limiting belief we can reframe is the popular "wealthy people are greedy." This mindset often arises in communities where wealth has long been linked with exploitation or corruption. García helps us understand that wealth itself is merely a tool. It isn't inherently good or bad. We can utilize money as a tool to make a positive impact on the world as well. She emphasizes that becoming financially educated allows us to use money in positive ways that align with our values.

As educators in our meta-cognitive era, when we catch ourselves expressing limiting thoughts, we can practice reframing them. Instead of saying "I'll never understand investing," we might say, "I'm building my financial knowledge step-by-step." The more we understand our own financial beliefs, the more effective we will be at creating inclusive spaces where our learners can develop positive money mindsets and confidently engage with financial topics.

Why We Teach Money Mindset

So we are getting in touch with our own money mindset. But will students really understand this topic? Isn't it a little woo-woo? Can't we just jump into fun topics with concrete answers, like compound interest and mortgages?

If you understand what money mindset is, you realize that it isn't really its own separate topic. Technically, I teach about mindsets first, but I continue to spiral back to them throughout all subsequent units. It's a topic that lives inside every single other topic. As you teach topics like budgeting, investing, and credit, you will see direct connections between our money beliefs and our actions in these areas. Teaching money mindset is not just a financial literacy unit, it is about empowerment, critical thinking, and breaking cycles.

There are powerful benefits to teaching money mindset as both a distinct unit and a recurring guest star throughout our curriculum: (1) interest and engagement; (2) financial benefits; and (3) student empowerment. Teaching financial skills without addressing the psychology behind money decisions sets us all up for a cycle of continual frustration. We get confused about why we are "bad" at saving, why we can't stick to budgets, and why the thought of investing makes us break out in a cold sweat. When we teach money mindset alongside practical skills, we create a foundation for financial education that sticks.

Money Mindsets Spark Engagement

Teenagers are mostly interested in one topic . . . themselves! That's what makes money mindset content particularly engaging for our students. It's about who they are as humans: their thoughts, their beliefs, their emotions, their experiences, their goals. Money mindset work gives students space to explore their inner selves. Their personal beliefs are validated in a learning space, which is unusual for most academic subjects. Students are pleasantly surprised to be talking about money and relationships or their spending habits in a classroom setting. When Abby realizes her money personality comes from wanting to make sure her future family doesn't struggle or when Donna wants to invest so she can own a home because no one in her family has done that before, they are really learning about themselves.

What makes this content powerful is how they can make connections between their personal experiences to the larger world around them. From an early age, we observe how money impacts our families, communities, and society. Yet, we are not always conscious of why we make the decisions we do. Money mindset activities give students the academic language to explore their financial beliefs and attitudes in the larger context of the world.

At the start of my course, I give my students a Money Mindset $urvey and one of my questions is: What is a money-related question you have that you have always wanted to ask someone? Student responses highlight how they already are thinking critically about financial topics:

- "Why does the world revolve around money?" (Elizabeth, tenth grade)
- "Money grows on trees and the government prints it with the snap of a finger. There are so many ways to make money, so why should we save it and be scared of losing it?" (Noah, eleventh grade)
- "Does creating accounts with apps such as Klarna, Afterpay, and PayPal actually save you money?" (Kisha, twelfth grade)
- "How much money is too much?" (Kayla, tenth grade)

A student's firsthand experience with money makes it a powerful entry point for teaching broader economic concepts. Elizabeth's question shows us how she is already challenging systems she sees around her. Noah's inquiry opens the door to fiscal policy and inflation. Kisha's question is an analysis of buy-now-pay-later apps she sees every time she purchases an item. And Kayla asks a lifelong wonder for many of us: What does it mean to actually have enough money?

What continues to hook them is that money touches everything they care about. As our students transition into financial adulthood, they face numerous money-related decisions. This real-world applicability makes talking about money and decision-making especially impactful for this age group. The topic has the perfect combination of being emotional and relatable, which makes it particularly engaging for young adults. When we talk about money mindset, we are discussing their career dreams, relationships, and vision of a good life. Money becomes the lens through which they can examine every one of life's questions.

Money Mindsets Drive Financial Success

On a purely dollars and cents level, our mentality around money has the power to propel our financial goals or to keep them dormant. Negative mindsets, also referred to as scarcity mindsets, involve beliefs and attitudes that hamper our ability to manage finances effectively and often lead to self-limiting behaviors. For instance, a person with a negative money mindset might associate wealth with guilt or believe that they are inherently bad with money. If that's our mental belief, we tend to perform self-sabotaging behaviors such as overspending or avoiding dealing with money altogether.

Over time, negative beliefs and behaviors can perpetuate a cycle of financial distress and defer the motivation to set and achieve long-term financial goals. In other words, when we feel negatively about money, it can turn into a nasty loop where we feel hopeless and stop caring about planning for the future. On the *I Will Teach You to Be Rich* podcast, financial advisor and author Ramit Sethi helps his guests identify psychological barriers that are hurting their finances. The majority of his advice encourages people to overcome the mental blocks and negative beliefs about money that contribute to their financial struggles. The financial impact of negative mental models is why it is imperative to facilitate these conversations in the financial literacy classroom. Money mindset discussions can help improve students' awareness to prevent them from making financial decisions based on scarcity, fear, or false self-narratives.

In the classroom, we can orient students toward abundant ways of thinking about their lives. In *The Financial Activist Playbook*, financial activist and writer Jasmine Rashid explains that financial activism is all about shifting from a mindset of scarcity to one of abundance. As we know from chapter 2, our money beliefs don't exist in a bubble; they are affected by larger systemic forces in society. What's exciting about being an educator is that we can answer Rashid's call to action when we repurpose, modify, or create new strategies to tackle complex conditions our students face. In our classrooms, we have the unique opportunity to resist and undo systems that don't serve our students and design and build ones that do. As Rashid reminds us, "We have no choice but to navigate contradictions," and as educators, we're positioned to help students navigate these contradictions with both optimism and critical awareness.[3] What an amazing opportunity to help students navigate existing systems—and maybe prepare them to transform those systems for the better. Woohoo!

When I was speaking with Ian Brock, founder of Dream Hustle Code, he made a great point about changing money mindsets. He said, "What I've learned is that money isn't like a god. It's just a tool. My mindset shifted from 'Okay, I've got to go get money' to 'How do I use this money to accomplish my goals?'" Learning about our money mindset can cause powerful shifts like this from scarcity thinking to purposeful financial planning.

Money Mindsets Build Empowerment

Discovering that we have control over our mindset is empowering at any age. When we reflect on our beliefs and behaviors, we realize that we can change what we've always assumed was true. A healthy money mindset empowers us to make informed decisions in all aspects of our lives.

As educators, we are in a unique position to challenge limiting mental models. By guiding our students to reframe their thinking, we are helping them approach financial choices with more confidence. This newfound "I've got this" attitude can shape how students pursue extracurriculars, follow postsecondary paths, or envision their future self.

When students replace deficit narratives with intentional habits, they begin practicing values-aligned saving, spending, and investing. These choices continue into adulthood, reinforcing a sense of control over their financial futures. Cultivating a more positive mindset can empower our students to:

- overcome limiting beliefs like "Money is the root of all evil" or "I'll never be rich"
- feel in control and confident about managing finances
- align spending with personal values and goals
- adopt a long-term perspective on building wealth

I've seen these effects happen firsthand. Early financial education helps students see money as a tool to build the life they want.

Finding Your Why

Students with a positive money mindset are also poised to spread the wealth. Being able to help their families, friends, and communities is a huge motivator for students to become financial change agents. In last spring's Money Mindset $urvey, I asked them the following questions: What short-term goals or long-term financial goals do you have? Why do you want the goals you listed? And why is that? (I repeat "why" so they can move past the superficial to uncover their core values.)

Their responses demonstrate how community serves as a major motivator for them:

- "To be a millionaire. So I can support myself and my mother to have anything we want." (Jade, tenth grade)
- "Make enough to retire and die giving my money to my family. Me giving the money to the family is important since I want to repay them for what they have done for me." (Chris, eleventh grade)
- "Right now, I want to at least save up to five hundred dollars by the end of this school year, because I want to learn how to save in general with the money I get. Also, long-term, I want to be a millionaire, or at least just make a lot of money by doing things I enjoy. I want to be just wealthy because I know the life I want to live is expensive. And give back to my mom." (Jen, ninth grade)
- "To help my family as they get older. The goal is important to me because my parents are not going to be able to pay the house rent for much longer." (Elias, twelfth grade)
- "Be a millionaire by the time I'm eighteen. This is important to me because I feel like I could help my family out." (Anthony, tenth grade)
- "To be financially free. In order to be supportive for my family and others in need." (Liam, twelfth grade)

These answers are real tearjerkers, right? The financial goal of being a millionaire is always at the top of their minds. But being a millionaire is simply what we have learned to associate with wealth in this country. The deeper insight is the *why* behind that number. They want the money to help their families, give back to their community, and have financial freedom. In my opinion, the why is far more important than the number. Financial goals can shift and adjust as they move through life. Their why is the driver of life fulfillment.

Once students realize how impactful positive money mindsets are, they are eager to pass the empowerment on to their loved ones. Their motivations remind us why it's so important to center their "why" in financial education. Teaching money mindset concepts is essential for helping students define what wealth truly means to them.

The Ultimate Goal: Financial Well-Being

The ultimate goal of financial education isn't money itself—it's peace of mind about money. Money doesn't just affect our bank accounts. It affects our minds. According to a Bankrate study, money affects more Americans' mental health than work, health, or current events, with 47 percent of Gen Zers, 50 percent of millennials, and 54 percent of Gen Xers reporting negative impacts.[4] Working on our money mindset has tremendous upsides for our mental wealth.

When my students talk about wanting to help their families or achieve financial freedom to support their family, they're describing what financial wellness means to them. For them, financial well-being is the sense of security and the freedom of choice that money can provide. Financial well-being isn't even tied to a specific income. According to research from the Consumer Financial Protection Bureau (CFPB), financial well-being is about having control over day-to-day finances, being able to absorb financial shocks, staying on track to meet financial goals, and having the freedom to make choices to enjoy life.[5] What I love about this definition is that it's not about a specific dollar amount. It's about how money makes you feel.

From personal experience, I've learned that financial well-being isn't just about the numbers in your account. It's about the security of knowing I can handle an emergency, help others in need, sleep soundly without money stress, and say yes to the things that matter to me. CFPB research shares that people with modest incomes can feel financially secure, while those with much higher incomes may not feel this way, regardless of how much they make.

Financial well-being shows up differently for each student. For Jade, it's knowing she can support herself and her mother. For Elias, it's helping his family as they get older. For Chris, it's being able to "repay" his family for what they've done for him. It's striking how often their definitions center on caring for others. The beautiful thing is that positive money mindsets create the foundation for whatever financial well-being looks like in their lives. I'm with the CFPB on this: Financial well-being is the real end goal of financial literacy. And the best part is your money mindset isn't set in stone. It's something we can work on. And for the rest of us still figuring out our money mindset, the path to that well-being begins with something we can all work on—our mindset.

SELF-REFLECTION: YOUR MONEY MINDSET

Before taking our students through their own financial journeys, we need to turn inward to examine the stories we each carry about money. Our unchecked beliefs and biases show up in countless classroom moments, from our reaction to a student mentioning their family's financial struggles to the assumptions we make about what is possible for different learners.

Some of these reflection questions might be uncomfortable. And others might remind you of money stories you'd rather not remember. But I've learned from personal experience that the way to become a more confident and compassionate financial educator is by remembering our messy money stories. We can't authentically empower our students if we have hidden chrometophobia, otherwise known as money fears. (See? It is a real thing!)

Approach these reflection questions with the same empathy you'd offer a friend sharing something vulnerable. Take your time. Find a quiet space free of distractions. Maybe grab your favorite notebook or open a document where you can really think through your responses. I've organized the questions with personal reflections first, then educator reflections, because understanding ourselves as humans comes before understanding ourselves as teachers.

Personal Reflection

- $ Was having money seen as a positive thing in your family?
- $ What did your family value when it came to money?
- $ Was money scarce or abundant growing up?
- $ How do you talk about money with your friends and family?
- $ What is the purpose of money in your life?
- $ What is your relationship with money now?
- $ What types of advice do you give others about money based on your experience?
- $ What financial choices have you made that you are proud of?
- $ Do you have any lingering regrets about your money decisions?
- $ If you could go back in time, what top pieces of advice would you give your teenage self?

Educator Reflection

- $ Do you think money mindset is the best way to start financial education?
- $ When your students talk about money, do you sense they have a fear of money? A reverence? A hopeful tone?
- $ What types of lifestyles do you think your students can achieve?

- $ How do your financial experiences play into your financial literacy teaching?
- $ Do you hold any biases about your students based on your own experiences?
- $ What do your students share about their families and money?
- $ What do you believe about your students' family money values?
- $ What ideas do you have to build an abundant money mindset in your students?
- $ Do you anticipate any money conversations becoming uncomfortable in the classroom? Which ones?
- $ How can you enter uncomfortable classroom conversations with curiosity?

That mix of introspection, maybe some discomfort, definitely some insights is exactly what we want our students to feel when we approach money mindset work. It's personal. It's revelatory. It's revolutionary. And it connects us to financial topics in a deeper way than spreadsheets and calculators alone can.

This self-reflection work transforms us from educators who teach about money to educators who understand money as a deeply human experience. Once we've explored and honored our own money stories, we can guide students through their own reframing process, with authenticity and compassion that comes only from having done the work ourselves.

TEACHING APPLICATIONS: MONEY MINDSET

Unit Overview

In my classroom, I've found that students need to *experience* money mindset, not just hear someone talk about it. It requires us to go deeper than surface-level financial concepts in order to empower them through self-awareness. There's no single "right" way to teach this topic—that's part of the fun. Much of the learning should be flexible, shifting based on student curiosity and discussion.

Throughout this unit, I apply the RICH framework to ensure money mindset teaching feels personally meaningful rather than technical. **Representation** means featuring diverse voices sharing how cultural backgrounds shape money beliefs. **Inquiry** encourages students to question inherited assumptions about wealth and success. **Connection** links mindset concepts to students' actual family experiences and personal goals. **Holistic thinking** recognizes that students bring diverse cultural approaches to money and various definitions of financial success to their learning.

This exploration connects to the National Standards for Personal Financial Education, particularly the Spending standards, as students examine the beliefs that drive their spending decisions.

I usually spend around two weeks on this unit, anchored in four major topics.

- **Defining Money Mindset:** Understanding beliefs, scarcity vs. abundance thinking, and unconscious biases
- **The Influence of Culture and Society:** Recognizing how family, community, and media shape our money beliefs
- **How Mindset Shapes Financial Behaviors:** Connecting internal beliefs to external actions and outcomes
- **Developing a Growth Mindset for Finances:** Building confidence and self-efficacy around money decisions

Empowering Educator Talk

Suggestions for trust-building language to explore money beliefs

- "You can change how you think about money. Your current beliefs aren't set in stone."
- "Everyone has a unique money story. Your experiences and ideas are valuable here."
- "There's no single 'right' way to think about money. We'll explore different ideas to find what works for you."
- "It's okay to question inherited ideas about money—that's how you learn and grow."
- "It's normal to feel uncomfortable talking about money. That feeling can mean you're learning something important."
- "Your family's money situation doesn't decide your future. You have the power to write your own money story."

Student Discussion Questions

Quick prompts designed to ignite student conversation

- What's the first money memory you have? How do you think it shaped your current beliefs?
- If money is just cotton and linen, what makes it so valuable to us?
- Is money scarce or abundant in the world? What makes you think that?
- What does it mean to be "rich" versus "wealthy"? Are they the same thing?
- How much money do you think can buy happiness? What's the tipping point?
- What money advice did you grow up hearing? Do you still believe it's true?
- How do you feel when you spend money on something expensive? What about when you buy something cheap?
- What would you do differently if you knew money was unlimited?

- Who in your life has the healthiest relationship with money? What makes it healthy?
- What money-related question have you always wanted to ask but felt too embarrassed to?

Quick Activities (5–15 minutes)

Perfect activities for warm-ups, transitions, or when you have extra time

- **Money Word Association:** Students write the first five words that come to mind when they hear the word *money*. Share patterns and discuss emotional connections.
- **Scarcity vs. Abundance Statements:** Read statements like "There's not enough good jobs for everyone," "Money can grow and create more opportunities," or "It's hard to get ahead if you didn't start with a lot of money." Have students move to corners labeled "Scarcity Thinking" or "Abundance Thinking" based on how they interpret each statement, and ask them to explain their thinking.
- **Money Personality Quick Sort:** Students pick a card for the money personality that suits them best (Saver, Spender, Investor, Giver) and explain their choice.
- **Family Money Messages:** Students write one message about money they heard growing up, then discuss which messages serve them and which might need updating.
- **Rich Life Vision:** Students sketch or describe in thirty seconds what a rich life looks like to them, emphasizing it doesn't have to be about money.

Standalone Activities (20–50 minutes)

Exercises that can fit into any lesson, with added discussion to extend learning

- **Would You Rather? Money Mindset Edition:** Students choose between scenarios that reveal their money beliefs and priorities, then explain their choice and discuss what it reveals about their money mindset.
  - Have $1 million now or $50,000 every year for life?
  - Be broke but everyone thinks you're rich or be rich but everyone thinks you're broke?
  - Have financial security or financial freedom?
  - Give away half your money or keep it all but never earn more?
  - Win the lottery or earn the same amount your whole career?
  - Earn $100,000 doing work you hate or $50,000 doing work you love?
  - Overspend on someone or have someone overspend on you?

- **Money Mindset Journal Challenge:** Students complete daily reflection prompts over a week to build self-awareness.
    - Day 1: What do I believe about money?
    - Day 2: How do I feel when I spend money?
    - Day 3: What money fears do I have?
    - Day 4: What would I do with unlimited money?
    - Day 5: How has my money mindset changed this week?
- **Does Money Make You Happy?** Pair students to answer "Millionaire True or False?" on Quizlet, and then watch the TED-Ed video "Would Winning the Lottery Make You Happier?" Then discuss the question: What are your thoughts about money and happiness?

EDUCATOR RESOURCES

Curriculum Resources

Free, ready-to-use lesson plans and activities to ground your money mindset unit

- **Intuit for Education:** The Importance of Financial Literacy and Money Mindsets Units
- **Next Gen Personal Finance (NGPF):** Unit 1 (Behavioral Economics)

Classroom Book Resources

A curated selection of books students can read to enrich their understanding of money mindset

- ***Cultura and Cash: Lessons from the First Gen Mentor for Managing Finances and Cultural Expectations*** by Giovanna González (chapter 1)
- ***Get Good with Money: Ten Simple Steps to Becoming Financially Whole*** by Tiffany Aliche (introduction and chapter 1)
- ***I Want More Pizza: Real World Money Skills for High School, College, and Beyond*** by Steve Burkholder (introduction)
- ***I Will Teach You to Be Rich: No Guilt. No Excuses. Just a 6-Week Program That Works*** by Ramit Sethi (introduction)
- ***Mind Your Money: Insightful Stories and Strategies to Help You Reach Your #MoneyGoals*** by Yanely Espinal (chapter 1)
- ***Money Out Loud: All the Financial Stuff No One Taught Us*** by Berna Anat (chapter 1)
- ***Rich AF: The Winning Money Mindset That Will Change Your Life*** by Vivian Tu (introduction and chapter 1)

CHAPTER 7

CREATING VALUES-BASED BUDGETS

What I discovered on my own financial journey is that saving and budgeting topics aren't really about spreadsheets and numbers. Sure, tools like the 50/30/20 rule give clean percentages to follow, but like the weight of grades in the gradebook, numbers are only part of the story. Budgets are about something deeper: our values, our dreams, and our understanding of what truly matters.

When people ask me to help with their budgets, I try to focus on the core reasons they want to manage money better. Their answers often reveal motivations: "So my mother doesn't have to worry," "To start my own business someday," or "To travel more and see the world." Learning to budget isn't just about plugging numbers into cell A1 or knowing how to sort expenses into fixed and variable categories. Money management is about how we express values like love, ambition, and hope.

Before we can guide our students in creating budgets that reflect their values and dreams, we need to be clear on our own financial priorities. Let's begin by exploring your personal budgeting story, then we'll move on to helping students craft theirs.

DEFINING BUDGETING AND SAVING

Budgeting is simply having a plan for your money. A good budget helps you spend the money you have on what matters most to you. Some people call it a spending plan or a money management system. The goal of a budget is to make each dollar work for your priorities and about setting money aside for future needs, wants, and dreams.

I teach saving and budgeting together because we tend to save more when it's part of the plan from the start. Budgeting and saving together hit the sweet spot, like having a field trip the day before vacation. When saving is part of the budget, reaching our money goals feels more achievable and even enjoyable. Both are essential for creating the future we want, which is why I always cover them together.

The Emotions of Budgeting

Once, while leading financial literacy professional development on budgeting, I wanted to get to know the educators as people first. We asked them about their own budgeting practices, and the shift was immediate in tone and body language. Several teachers shared feelings of helplessness.

- "I don't even know where my money goes honestly."
- "It just comes in and goes right back out."
- "I don't even bother budgeting; there's no point."
- "I should probably be better, but I'm not."

I'm sure many of us can relate to these feelings. There is an overwhelming sentiment in our society that money comes in only to go out. With so many costs, expenses, and temptations in our modern world, budgeting can sometimes feel pointless. I mean, who among us hasn't seen that "As Seen On TV" ad and thought, *Maybe I do need to build a waterproof boat out of duct tape.*

It's hard not to spend money. We're bombarded with thousands of advertisements every day, encouraging us to buy, many more than those urging us to save money. Have you ever seen an ad that said, "Skip the impulse buys and save toward your values"? Exactly. So instead of beating ourselves up for spending, let's focus on budgeting with intention.

Values-Based Budgeting

Traditional budgets fail for a reason: They're built on restriction rather than intention. When budgets are too rigid, with no room for life's surprises or joys, they become unsustainable. It's like a diet that bans your favorite carbs. You might stick to it for a week, but eventually, you'll rebel and eat three bowls of pesto pasta in one sitting. That's why flexible, values-based spending plans work better than rigid budgets.

Remember how I said that money mindset topics show up in every unit? Well, here it is again. I've learned to teach saving and budgeting as interconnected practices rooted in personal values. When we're clear on what matters most to us, we can make more intentional spending choices. Budgets actually become fun—as crazy as that sounds—when our spending aligns with our biggest dreams.

Let's connect budgeting to the BTFAR model from chapter 6. When we are unhappy with our budgeting, it might be because our BTFAR responses look like this:

- **Beliefs:** "I'm bad with money" or "Budgets are restrictive"
- **Thoughts:** "I'll never be able to save" or "This is too hard"
- **Feelings:** Shame, anxiety, and hopelessness about finances
- **Actions:** Avoiding budgeting, overspending, or giving up
- **Results:** Financial stress and unmet goals

When we shift to values-based budgeting, our results are more favorable. Our BTFAR responses might look like this:

- **Beliefs:** "My money can reflect my values" or "I have control over my finances"
- **Thoughts:** "I'm learning and growing" or "This budget serves my dreams"
- **Feelings:** Empowered, curious, and hopeful
- **Actions:** Tracking with compassion, adjusting as needed, celebrating progress
- **Results:** Financial clarity and movement toward goals (fun!)

The key to making this shift lies in asking ourselves the deeper why behind our financial choices. Instead of focusing solely on the "what" or "how much," values-based budgeting asks: What does this purchase represent? What values am I expressing through this choice? What future am I building toward?

Budgeting is where your mindset turns into your actions. It's the practical expression of what we explored in chapter 6. When you align your budget with your values, budgeting shifts from feeling like a restrictive exercise to becoming a powerful tool for achieving what matters most to you. But what does this look like in practice? How do we make financial decisions based on our values rather than struggling to stick to rigid budgeting rules?

Ugly and Blue—and Built to Last

When I spoke to Tiffany "the Budgetnista" Aliche, she shared a childhood memory about budgeting toward values. "I distinctly remember wanting a bike for my birthday when I was about eight or nine," she told me. "I'm one of five girls, and my sister had gotten a bike when she was ten, so naturally I wanted one too."[1]

When her father took her to buy a bike, he gave her a choice. "There was this Barbie bike that I wanted with the baskets, tassels, the whole nine yards—or there was this ugly blue bike from Sears." She remembers being surprised to have a choice at all: "[But] he wasn't really that kind of traditional parent where you get what you get and you don't get upset. He was trying to teach me a financial lesson."

Instead of simply saying no to the prettier bike, her father tied the decision to something she'd experienced recently. "I remember last week you were upset about your sister getting your favorite dress when you grew out of it," he reminded her, referencing their family's hand-me-down system. He was helping his daughter see the pattern: "You get that bike, you're going to grow out of it."

This is where values-based thinking kicked in. Aliche explained, "I just remember thinking, wait—I could always get another bike. But then I remembered when my sister turned eleven, she got a camera, and I wanted a camera too when I turned eleven." She found herself weighing the trade-offs: "Do I get a bike that I ride for like a year or so, or do I get a bike that can last me?" She chose the "big, blue, ugly bike" and rode it all the way through college. "It was my first financial lesson that even small choices are big choices," she reflected. "Look how far into the future that blue bike took me."

Her father wasn't restricting her choice; he was helping her understand the trade-offs and connect her decision to her deeper values, like longevity and getting the most use out of her bike. "He was very good at—it's the way I teach now—very good at: Here are the facts. Make your decision." This is values-based budgeting in practice: understanding what matters most to you and making informed choices that align with those priorities.

SAYING YES TO ALMOND CROISSANTS

When I was saving up for my trip to the Paris Olympics, every time I passed the home decor aisle, I'd think: "Adorable knickknack or beach volleyball in France?" I love a good summer-vibes mason jar, but France won every time, so I kept pushing my shopping cart. Not because I was depriving myself but because I was excited to say yes to something that mattered more, like eating almond croissants every day for two weeks straight.

Budgeting is about choices. The best budgeting results come from being clear on what you value most. This is different for everyone; there is no "right" answer to what you should value. In her book *Get Good with Money*, Tiffany Aliche builds on the beliefs she learned as a child to extend this values-based philosophy. Budgeting becomes a tool for saying yes to your dreams and goals, rather than just restricting your spending.[2] This is why addressing our money mindset here is crucial—our beliefs about budgeting directly impact our results.

Ask yourself which savings goals inspire a yes rather than leaving you feeling deprived when you have to say no. This is where the magic of focused savings goals comes in. When you're excited about something specific—dinner out with your family, a down payment on your first home, an emergency fund that spares you stress about popping a tire on a pothole—saying no to smaller purchases becomes easier.

Our young people experience this same shift. One of my students was frustrated by how fast her money disappeared each week, and she came to me for help. When we tracked her spending, she realized she was dropping a lot of money every day on food after work. We dug deeper into her goals—saving for college decor and books—and why those goals mattered. She valued independence and supporting her family. That summer, she reframed her spending around those priorities. Suddenly, the chicken tenders and fries weren't as appealing. "I realized I was spending like thirty dollars a day on random food," she told me. "But if I skip that for the summer, I can afford all the things for my dorm and be more independent." She even sent me pictures—her dorm room was an adorable pink fuzzy explosion that made her excited and ready to start college.

A tangible, exciting goal weakens the pull of daily temptations. When you budget, you're taking care of your future self. Keeping your values front and center allows you to make intentional choices with your money. You're not saying no to everything; you're saying yes to what matters most.

Our Backgrounds and Budgeting

Every family has money wisdom, even when it does not look like traditional financial advice. I think about my students who understand community savings circles, who've watched grandparents spend every dollar with intention, or who've learned that supporting family is sometimes the highest form of wealth building.

I think back to how my mother could take one poor chicken and turn it into three meals: chicken salad, *pollo empanizado*, and a pot of *sopa de pollo*. She was—and still is—a chicken magician. Funny how these days, when she shops on my dime, she stocks up on organic free-range chicken and pasture-raised eggs.

But Mom taught me more than magic in the kitchen. She taught me how to cook healthy on a budget, shop for unit prices, and honor what we had. I learned how to stretch, savor, and save. In our house, I once looked at frugality negatively, but I've since reframed my mindset. Now I view budgeting not as restriction, but as something creative, communal, and sustainable. My upbringing shaped the way I think about money—as a source of possibility and resourcefulness.

There are so many financial gems of wisdom our families pass down. Values-based saving and budgeting honors these diverse approaches. Financial wellness isn't about following someone else's formula. Budgeting and saving for financial wellness are about creating systems that reflect your unique background, priorities, and dreams.

STRATEGIES TO BUDGET WITH PURPOSE

Paying Yourself First

Saving often triggers strong visceral emotions. Most people I meet intrinsically want to save more, are saving something, or feel they should be saving. Savings is a popular, albeit emotionally charged, financial topic.

We want to save, but it's nearly impossible if (1) your savings goals aren't deeply aligned with your values, and (2) you wait until the end of the month to save.

That was me. Every month I'd tell myself, "With that extra one hundred dollars at the end of the week, I'll save for a down payment." Do you know how much I saved with that method? Nada. I needed a way to take the temptation out of my savings goals.

Pop quiz! Question: When you get your paycheck (before you pay Netflix or click "Buy now") who should get paid first? Answer: You!

Many of the books I read talk about a little mind trick called "pay yourself first." This principle isn't new. George Clason's 1926 classic *The Richest Man in Babylon* advises setting aside at least 10 percent of your earnings for savings or investments before anything else. It's a simple but radical mindset shift: Instead of spending first and saving what's left, protect your goals up front.

Automate It

Simple? Yes. Easy? Not always. The game changer for me was automation. For each paycheck, a set amount vanished into my emergency fund before I even saw it. At first, I begrudged losing that spending power. I was nervous I wouldn't be able to buy another bodycon dress if I wanted to. It felt like my money was disappearing into a savings abyss.

But as that emergency fund grew, so did my excitement and confidence. This small, automated step was empowering. Soon, I became comfortable saying no to things I didn't really care about anyway. I felt confident that I was building toward goals like emergency savings and travel funds.

By paying yourself first, you're literally putting your money where your values are and ensuring your goals get funded before anything else. When we pay ourselves first through automatic savings, we're literally putting our money where our values are, immediately and without question.

TRACKING THOSE PENNIES

Do you want to keep your tab open? No. No, you do not.

One turning point in my financial journey came in my twenties, the morning after a night out with friends, sitting in my kitchen, biting into some leftover fried chicken. I sat there wondering why I left my card open at the bar the night before. There went $146 down the drain. I was at the point in my life where I started to really hate the idea of spending foolishly on things that had no value to me after.

Sometime later, inspired by a budgeting book I'd read, I took a small but meaningful step: I tracked every penny I spent for a week. One adventurous weekend, I hopped on a one-dollar Bolt Bus to Boston to visit college friends, tracked that. Went to a Celtics game, tracked every penny there. Ate sushi and a seaweed salad and tracked those pennies too. When my sister-in-law saw me typing my 7–Eleven purchase into my Notes app, she asked, "Girl, are you really tracking every penny?" Yes, I assured her, it was a new experiment, and I began to explain what values-based budgeting was . . . and she completely lost interest. But that week, I tracked every coffee, every MetroCard swipe, every pack of gum. I was determined to solve my money mystery through sheer pain and documentation.

And it worked. For the first time, I saw exactly where my money was going. The financial fog lifted, and I felt a surge of control. It may seem silly to track every penny, but your spending is a mirror of your values. Tracking my money transformed budgeting from a restrictive exercise into a tool for intentional living. Granted, after one week of following my pennies, I was exhausted, but it was an excellent exercise in mindful spending that taught me a lot.

THE COURAGE TO LOOK AT YOUR SPENDING

You can track your spending in different ways—in real time like I did or by reviewing your past spending. If you want to truly see if your money is reflecting your values, look at your bank statements. For many people I've worked with, this step is uncomfortable as they would rather hide from their spending.

You know when you ask the class a question and students look away, thinking if they don't make eye contact with you, that you won't see them? It's the same thing here. If you don't look at your past spending, you'll keep spending the same—until you take out that highlighter and stare your purchases in the face. Pull up bank statements and look at your spending for the last week, month, three months, or even year. I find two to three months is the most telling. Highlight trends like dinners out or subscriptions in different colors. Are there patterns in the days or weeks you spend? Have you been taking rideshares more often than usual? Do you find yourself eating out every weeknight?

Remember to be nice to yourself and nonjudgmental as you analyze your past spending. Tracking your money is about awareness, seeing where it goes so you can realign it toward your saving goals.

Creating Speed Bumps: Thinking Before Buying

When I spoke to Karen Holland, creator of the financial education organization Gifting Sense, she described mindful spending as creating a "speed bump" in our purchasing decisions. Her decision-making framework asks students to slow down and evaluate purchases by considering factors like cost per use, alternatives, and whether the item aligns with their values. As Karen explains, "Speed bumps don't stop you from getting anywhere you really want to go, but they help you get there safely." Her approach transforms impulsive spending into intentional choices that reflect what students truly value. Educators, parents, and students can access her free DIMS SCORE Decision Tool and other resources at giftingsense.org.

Making Sense of Your Spending Patterns

Once you have tracked your spending, analyze whether your money is going where you truly want it to. Are your rideshares for safety or more because you don't feel like climbing down the stairs and bake in that humid subway? Are you eating out to connect with others or because you don't feel like heating up that Trader Joe's chicken shawarma? This isn't about judgment; it's about awareness.

The popular 50/30/20 budgeting rule—spend 50 percent of your money on needs, 30 percent on wants, and 20 percent on savings—can be a helpful starting point. But remember: It's a guideline, not a hard rule. Your percentages might look different based on your income, location, and circumstances. What matters more is that you make intentional choices with your money. See these categories to analyze your spending:

- **Fixed expenses:** Housing and transportation typically take the biggest bite out of your budget. Since big-ticket items are consistent and high-impact, give extra attention to aligning these costs with your values—downsizing, carpooling, or refinancing are options.
- **Variable expenses:** These fluctuate month to month. Look for areas you can trim to fund higher-priority goals. For example, does your personal care budget align with your values, or would you rather use that money for your travel fund? Only you know the answer.
- **Miscellaneous expenses:** Analyze your purchases:
  1. Rate each purchase on a 1–5 scale, with 1 = momentary pleasure or even regret (you no longer have it or wish you hadn't bought it) and 5 = lasting satisfaction or significant life improvement.
  2. Review recent transactions and assign scores.
  3. Identify low-scoring purchases and make adjustments. Going forward, swap impulse buys for experiences or goals that score higher on life satisfaction.

Remember that this is a flexible practice. You will likely revisit your tracking when life shifts or you feel your spending drifting from your intentions.

Reframing Negative Budget Thoughts

This might be the most important lesson I can share about budgeting: Your inner voice matters, so be kind to yourself. When I first started tracking my spending, I was my own harshest critic. Every "mistake" was proof that I was terrible with money. The internal dialogue went like this: *Why did I need to spend $146 to buy everyone multiple rounds of drinks? Who do I think I am? I could have saved that. I'll never control my money. I'll never be able to move out.* (Then I take a frustrated bite of fried chicken!)

When you start analyzing your money habits and spending, you might catch yourself starting sentences with:

✘ I'm such a failure, I can't believe I . . .
✘ Yup, I've always been bad with money . . .
✘ That decision was so dumb because . . .
✘ Only an idiot would . . .

Hard stop. Screeching-brakes hard stop. Then reframe your thinking. Negative self-talk doesn't motivate change—it actually paralyzes us with shame. Social worker and researcher Brené Brown emphasizes that shame is harmful, often leading to destructive behaviors rather than solutions. In her article "Shame vs. Guilt," Brown says, "I define shame as the intensely painful feeling or experience of believing that we are flawed and therefore unworthy."[3] When it comes to money mistakes, we already struggle with the decision itself—and then we pile shame on top. Beating ourselves up won't improve our financial situation.

So let's muzzle the shame and practice reframing our negative budgeting thoughts. Change "I'm so dumb, I can't believe I spent $100 on pillows and soy candles," to "That spending didn't align with my values. This month instead of going to HomeGoods, I'm putting that money into my emergency fund." Reframe "I suck. Why did I spend $160 on takeout last week?" to "Last week is the past. This week, I'm going to meal prep, eat out twice, and put $80 toward my trip to Machu Picchu."

The shift from judgment to curiosity, from shame to intention, transforms everything. When we speak to ourselves with compassion, we take away negative emotions that hold us back from achieving our goals.

Being Flexible When Life Happens

As I became more comfortable with my spending patterns and financial goals, I learned to relax my grip on penny obsession. I still track my money, but with more compassion instead of judgment. A good values-based budget is meant to be flexible.

Budgets became more enjoyable when I shifted from asking "Did I stick to my budget?" to "Is my spending aligned with my values this month?" Some months, that meant putting more money toward travel or pricier experiences. Other months, it meant doing low-cost activities like putting a hammock up in the park or sneaking candy into movies on five-dollar Wednesdays. In her book *Deeper Than Money*, Chloe Elise says, "As you create your spend plan, know that it is your guide, not a ball and chain keeping you to this one path. It is your road map that you will update and change to ebb and flow along with you."[4] The numbers can change, but the intention on our values-based goals remains constant.

Now, in the real world, budgets must be flexible. I teach my students that some months, certain categories will spike. Maybe it's June of senior year and you need a suit for graduation that will make your grandpa proud. Maybe you started a new job and need a few professional outfits. That's not budget failure; that's just life. Other months, you'll naturally spend less. Maybe you're too busy with exams to eat out, or you're perfectly happy shopping your own closet. Sometimes we can plan ahead for big financial events like a quinceañera, a summer trip to the old country, or holiday shopping. Other times, life happens—like someone slashing your tires—and you didn't anticipate the expense of new ones. And that's okay. Try your best to think ahead and plan for events and emergencies. But ultimately, your budget will ebb and flow with your life's rhythms. If you overspend and it wasn't worth it, take time to analyze why it happened—and get back to your values-based budgeting as soon as you can.

Rethinking the Word *Budget*

To many, the word *budget* feels like a punishment. One of the first things I learned in my financial journey was how much language shapes mindset. Budgets felt intimidating, like something that would judge me and leave no room for joy. That's when I started exploring other terms like *money tracker* or *money management system*. Author Chloe Elise says, "I stopped using the word 'budget' at the beginning of my financial journey because everything I had ever been exposed to surrounding budgets sounded restrictive and like zero fun was allowed." Instead, she uses the term *spend plan*, which involves laying out what you plan to spend your income on and figuring out what, if anything, is left over after expenses.[5]

For our educational purposes, since it's familiar to students, I continue to use the term *budget*. But it's worth revisiting what feelings and associations the word brings up for us and our students.

WHY TEACH VALUES-BASED BUDGETING

Budgets and savings are pillars of most financial literacy curricula—that's fairly universal. But teaching how saving and budgeting are emotional acts rooted in core values is not as common. Traditional approaches often focus heavily on calculations and budgeting rules, overlooking the emotional aspects of money. Encouraging our students to explore the importance of their goals and dreams makes saving and budgeting far more meaningful.

Teaching saving and budgeting with a values-based approach means recognizing that our financial choices are influenced by our personal values, which are shaped by our unique cultural experiences and family traditions. This is why there's no one-size-fits-all strategy for managing money. Instead, we can help students create financial plans that reflect their individual values, identities, and cultural backgrounds.

Students Already Understand the Why

When we frame saving and budgeting as tools for achieving their personal why, students immediately connect. One of the questions I ask on my Money Mindset $urvey is: Do you budget your money? Their words reveal they're already thinking about budgeting in values-based ways.

Students who budget describe their approaches:

- "I save cash and only use it when I need to or have to."
- "With the money gifted every week, I have to determine how much money to use per day in a way where I can save at least 20 percent by the end of the week."
- "I try to think about how much I'll spend in a week on food to know how much extra I'll have to spend freely on other things that I want."

Students struggling with budgeting express their desires:

- "I struggle to budget my money at times, but I know I need to."
- "I don't budget, but I write out the things I need at the time under the need category then put the prices of the various things and the wants would be on the other side."
- "No. I tried to budget my money by putting it to the side and getting what I need not want."

Notice how even students who say they don't budget are actually describing values-based decision-making. They're already prioritizing. We just need to teach them the tools and language to do it more effectively. Teaching budgeting through their why is not a foreign concept, it is just building on a vision they already have.

Striking the Balance Between Now and Later

One of the biggest balances I strive for in teaching is acknowledging my students' immediate money needs while still planting seeds for their financial futures. I've lived it; back in high school I flipped burgers for $5.15 an hour, proudly smelling like fry grease because I urgently needed the money to help my family. The good news is we don't have to choose between short-term money moves or long-term planning. Immediate needs can be the perfect entry point to teach everything else.

When I asked Tiffany Aliche about this, she shared her "peas with pizza" approach: First we give them the pizza (immediate, relevant financial learning) and then we add the peas (long-term planning) to their plate. For students with urgent financial needs, we can spend 80 percent of our time teaching them immediate money-making strategies and 20 percent of our time connecting those skills to long-term wealth building. These urgent needs are very real—nearly 24 percent of US households are living paycheck to paycheck.[6] Budgeting can't solve poverty or wage stagnation, but it can help people make the most intentional choices possible within their constraints.

Aliche even designed a classroom challenge to bring it all to life: "Can we raise six thousand dollars in six months?" In week one, students brainstorm micro-business ideas; week two brings young entrepreneurs to share real-world tips; week three is all about drafting simple business plans; and by week four, students are pitching for start-up funds. "By the end," Aliche explains, "you've made actual money together, opened savings accounts, and everybody got money deposited. Now it's not just talking—they experienced it." This approach teaches budgeting, saving, investing, and entrepreneurship through lived experience rather than theoretical scenarios.

Whether you launch a deep-dive project like this or start small, begin with students' lived experiences. Rather than lecturing about retirement savings to a student who needs gas money for work, acknowledge the importance of having money now. Then use those immediate money solutions as a bridge to broader wealth-building concepts. This approach honors where students are in their financial journeys today as a way to expand their horizons in the future.

Budgeting Can Be Liberating

When students learn to align their spending with their personal values they begin to feel a new level of confidence. Instead of feeling restricted by budgets, they start to see how budgets can empower them. Take Naiymah, an eleventh grader who explains, "Financial education gave me more confidence to budget, save, and make smarter financial decisions, and not just spend impulsively."

This confidence comes from understanding the why behind financial choices. When students connect their daily spending decisions to their deeper dreams—whether saving for college decor, supporting family with groceries, traveling to Instagram-worthy destinations, or starting an online business—budgeting shifts from a restrictive exercise into a purposeful tool for achieving what matters most.

Most importantly, this approach teaches students they have power over their financial futures. In a world where young people often feel overwhelmed by economic uncertainty, learning to manage money in alignment with their values gives them a real sense of agency. They can't control inflation or job markets, but they can control how they respond to their financial circumstances. When my alum Ryan shared that our course "changed my mindset completely from being someone who always thought about what the next purchase was to what the next investment is," he was describing this shift from reactive spending to intentional money management.

Many students grow up in homes where money is a source of tension. Some come into our spaces feeling powerless over their financial futures. Teaching values-based budgeting and saving equips them with strategies to make intentional financial decisions. In doing so, budgeting stops being a source of stress and becomes a tool for empowerment. Budgeting gives students agency over their financial lives and even becomes emotionally liberating.

Budgeting Builds Lifelong Habits

Students who learn to budget based on their values are more likely to stick with their financial plans over time. Values-based budgeting is more sustainable because it's based on personal motivation rather than external rules. Students are not just blindly following someone else's formula that doesn't make sense for their life. Instead, they're creating the life they want to build, using values-based budgeting to support that vision.

As life happens, this mindful approach to budgeting also gives students the tools to pivot. Circumstances in their lives will change. They will get new jobs, relationships will start and end, and life goals will shift. But with these skills, they'll know how to adjust their budgets while staying true to their core values.

Budgeting is a lifelong habit, and teenagers can capitalize on their gift of time to build skills. They have years to practice before facing major financial decisions like student loans, car purchases, or housing costs. The earlier students learn to align their money with their values, the more time they have to build habits that reflect who they are and what they care about.

Starting early also allows students to make financial mistakes while the stakes are low. It's better to learn about impulse spending with babysitting money than with a credit card. And it's easier to build the budgeting habit on a part-time paycheck than when you're juggling a full salary alongside rent and car payments. Their small decisions now become practice for the bigger ones ahead.

Every conversation I've had with someone who's found their financial footing in life follows a similar pattern: They figured out how to make their money reflect what mattered most to them, whether that was traveling, supporting their family, starting a business, or buying a home. It all began with money management personalized to them.

Budgets Honor Diverse Perspectives

Values-based budgeting recognizes the diverse ways students bring money to life—whether allocating funds for a big family reunion cookout, planning a sweet sixteen to honor family traditions, saving for a gap-year service trip abroad, or setting aside money to become the first in their family to graduate college. In each case, the unique core values—community, legacy, service, and education—drive every financial decision.

SELF-REFLECTION: YOUR BELIEFS ON BUDGETING

In order to teach financial education,
you don't have to be financially perfect.

—TIFFANY ALICHE,
founder of The Budgetnista

Teaching budgeting is deeply personal work, though many don't think of it that way. Every time we talk about priorities, trade-offs, or financial goals, we're asking students to examine their values and dreams. This is why we should do that vulnerable work with our own finances, so that our teaching has the authenticity required to connect with our students.

I learned this lesson sitting in my kitchen after that unnecessarily expensive night out. Seeing the gap between where my money actually went and what I claimed to value was uncomfortable to face. But we're all better for being honest and making small changes in the right direction.

These reflection questions can help you uncover your own budgeting beliefs and biases. You might tackle them now, or after trying some hands-on budgeting practices. The key is examining our own relationship with money, just as we ask students to examine theirs.

Personal Reflection

- $ What emotions do you experience when you think about saving money? Why do you feel these ways?
- $ What was your first experience trying to budget your money? How did it feel?
- $ How has your upbringing influenced your attitudes toward saving and budgeting?
- $ Are there any recurring expenses in your budget that don't truly align with your values or priorities?

- $ What is the last purchase you made that you were proud of? Why did you feel that way?
- $ How do you envision your financial future, and what action can you take today to move closer to that vision?

Educator Reflection

- $ What aspects of your budget practice can you share with students?
- $ What savings or budgeting topics are you excited to teach?
- $ How do the socioeconomic backgrounds of students influence your approach to teaching saving and budgeting?
- $ Are there any biases or assumptions you hold about money management that might be affecting your teaching?
- $ What hooks, methods, or topics would make saving and budgeting more relevant and engaging for your students?

TEACHING APPLICATIONS: BUDGETING AND SAVING

Unit Overview

Teaching budgeting through a values lens requires us to flip the traditional approach. Instead of leading with categories and percentages, we start with what drives students: their goals, values, and motivations. We teach frameworks for financial decision-making instead of strict rules. This method empowers students to understand *why* budgeting matters to their life vision and then how to budget for that vision.

Throughout this unit, I apply the RICH framework to make budgeting feel personally meaningful rather than restrictive. **Representation** means featuring diverse voices sharing how they align money with their values. **Inquiry** encourages students to question traditional budgeting advice and explore what works for their unique circumstances. **Connection** links budgeting concepts to students' actual goals and family experiences. **Holistic thinking** recognizes that students bring different cultural approaches to money management and various definitions of financial success.

This unit aligns with both the Spending and Saving standards from the National Standards for Personal Financial Education, teaching students to create budgets that allocate income to necessary and desired spending while building savings for future goals and emergencies.

With the fundamentals under our belt, it's time to get into hands-on application. I usually spend two to three weeks on this unit. Here are the core topics I highlight in this unit, followed by hands-on applications:

- **Defining Values-Based Budgeting:** Understanding how personal values should drive financial decisions, moving beyond restrictive budgeting to purposeful spending, and creating budgets that feel empowering rather than limiting
- **Understanding the Psychology of Money Management:** Exploring emotional triggers around spending and saving, recognizing family money messages and cultural influences, and developing healthy money mindsets that support long-term financial well-being
- **Practical Budgeting Strategies:** Implementing "pay yourself first" methodology, tracking expenses that align with values, creating emergency funds that provide real security, and building sustainable systems for managing money that work with your lifestyle
- **Aligning Spending with Personal Values and Goals:** Using frameworks for conscious spending decisions, connecting present choices to future aspirations, and creating accountability systems that help maintain values-driven financial habits

Empowering Educator Talk

Suggestions for confidence-building language around budgeting and saving

- "Your spending shows your values. Every dollar is a vote for what matters to you."
- "Budgeting isn't about limitations, it's actually about freedom. Align your spending with your goals."
- "Think of your budget like GPS. It guides you to your goals, and you can reroute your path when needed."
- "Your family taught you about money. You get to decide what to keep and what to change."
- "Everyone does impulsive things sometimes. Learn from that and get back to your values."
- "Saving isn't about saying no to everything. It's about saying yes to your future self."
- "All financial goals matter. If it matters to you, it's important."
- "Small wins count. Even saving five dollars a week now builds the habits you need later."
- "Your budget will change as your life changes. Having flexibility in moving toward your goals is totally fine."

Student Discussion Questions

Quick prompts designed to ignite student conversation

- You get $100. Should you save it or spend it? How do you decide?
- How do you know if something is worth your money?
- What's something you love to spend money on that makes you happy?
- Have you ever regretted spending money on something? What happened?
- What's one thing you spend money on that your friends might think is weird, but it's totally worth it to you, and why?
- Your family thinks you waste money on something you love. How do you explain why it matters?
- You get money for graduation. Your parent suggests you save it, but you really want new clothes for college. How do you decide what to do?
- Your friend wants you to go to a movie, but you're saving for something special. What do you do?
- When you see someone driving an expensive car, what's your first reaction? Why is this?
- What's one thing you want to be able to buy without worrying about paying for?

Quick Activities (5–15 minutes)

Perfect activities for warm-ups, transitions, or when you have extra time

- **Reality Check Activity:** Jump$tart's Reality Check online tool helps students see the relationship between their dream lifestyle and the income required to support it. Students answer questions about their ideal life, including housing, transportation, and lifestyle choices, and discover what level of education and career they'll need to afford it. Perfect for opening conversations about aligning dreams with financial planning. See *jumpstart.org/education/reality-check/*.
- **Budget Personality Quiz:** Help students identify their natural money management style (Spender, Balancer, Saver, or Investor) and then teach strategies that work with that style. Khan Academy has a simple money personality quiz in their Financial Literacy Unit 4 (Lesson 1).
- **Who Gets Paid When You Get Paid?** List examples of owners or CEOs that we pay: a landlord, the Netflix CEO, the Shake Shack CEO, a corner store owner, and the credit card company. Use companies and products they—and you—use to make it relevant. Then ask, "Who's missing from this list?" The revelation that they should be first on their own payroll is an aha moment.

- **Future Headlines:** Imagine it's five, ten, twenty, or even fifty years from now. Students write financial headlines celebrating a major financial success, then draft a short article explaining how they achieved it, highlighting the budget decisions they made, the money habits they built, and the challenges they overcame.
- **Values Speed Dating:** Students identity their core values, then rotate through stations representing different financial goals, such as buying a car, paying for college or training, starting a business, travel and experiences, financial independence, supporting family or community, buying a home, building an emergency fund, debt-free living, and investing. They spend three minutes at each station identifying which goals resonate most with their values.

Standalone Activities (20–50 minutes)

Exercises that can fit into any lesson, with added discussion to extend learning

- **The Why Behind the Want:** Students list four to five things they're saving or shopping for, then ask "Why?" three times for each item to move from surface desire to core value. Example: "I want a car." → "Why?" → "Independence" → "Why?" → "Freedom to travel" → "Why?" → "Control over my life." Students label the deepest value, like autonomy, security, or recognition, and brainstorm budget-friendly ways to honor that value without derailing their financial plan.
- **Purposeful Purchases:** Students identify their top five values from Brené Brown's *Dare to Lead* List of Values, then use the DIMS SCORE Decision Tool at giftingsense.org to evaluate a purchase they're considering. They work through four key questions: What does this purchase represent to me? Which of my values am I expressing? What future am I building toward? Will this matter in a week, month, or year? Students then review recent purchases and discuss how each reflects—or doesn't reflect—their core values.

EDUCATOR RESOURCES

Curriculum Resources

Free, ready-to-use lesson plans and activities to ground your budgeting unit

- **Banzai:** Budgeting Topic
- **Econedlink:** Classroom Resources—Personal Finance—Search "Budget/Money Management."

- **Jump$tart Clearinghouse:** Search "Budget"
- **Intuit for Education:** Budgeting Unit
- **Khan Academy:** Personal Finance Unit 2 (Saving and Budgeting)
- **Next Gen Personal Finance (NGPF):** Unit 10 (Budgeting)

Classroom Book Resources

A curated selection of books students can read to enrich their understanding of budgeting

- ***Cultura and Cash: Lessons from the First Gen Mentor for Managing Finances and Cultural Expectations*** by Giovanna González (chapter 4)
- ***Get Good with Money: Ten Simple Steps to Becoming Financially Whole*** by Tiffany Aliche (chapter 2)
- ***I Want More Pizza: Real World Money Skills for High School, College, and Beyond*** by Steve Burkholder (chapter 2)
- ***I Will Teach You to Be Rich: No Guilt. No Excuses. Just a 6-Week Program That Works*** by Ramit Sethi (chapter 4)
- ***Mind Your Money: Insightful Stories and Strategies to Help You Reach Your #MoneyGoals*** by Yanely Espinal (chapter 2)
- ***Money Out Loud: All the Financial Stuff No One Taught Us*** by Berna Anat (chapter 2)
- ***Rich AF: The Winning Money Mindset That Will Change Your Life*** by Vivian Tu (chapters 2, 3, and 4)

CHAPTER 8

DEVELOPING CREDIT CONFIDENCE

My father and I used to go to Mets games at Shea Stadium in the 1990s. It was a magical time in Queens, New York, when tickets were cheap and the games kept us on the edge of our seats because we didn't know if they'd be the "Amazin'" Mets or absolutely terrible that night. Good times. Before we headed to our seats, there used to be vendors lined up to give you free Mets items—if you signed up for their credit cards.

Given his financial situation, my father would walk right up and sign up for every card. Why, you ask? His credit was so bad after a bankruptcy that he knew he'd get denied every time, but we could still score tons of Mets swag. And score we did: stadium cushions, fleece blankets, trucker hats, a Bobby Bonilla T-shirt, wooden bats, and collector pins.

So you're thinking this story is both funny and sad. (Yeah, for real.) But here's the uplifting part: One warm April game at the beginning of the season, my dad approached a credit card booth expecting the usual denial and a Mr. Met bobblehead. Only this time, he got approved—no more free swag because Papi's credit was improving.

The amazing (or Amazin') part of Papi's story is that he rebuilt his credit. He made some poor financial decisions, but over time, he paid his bills back, spent within his means, and avoided carrying debt anymore. When my students ask about my credit score, I tell them that you don't have to come from a family that was good with credit to have good credit yourself. You can learn from their positive and not-so-positive choices and write your own excellent credit story. I'm inspired by how my father improved his decisions over time without a strong financial background. I still have one of those Mets wooden bats, a reminder of his wild credit journey.

DEFINING CREDIT IN HUMAN TERMS

In this country, credit is one of money's loudest conversations. It speaks about trust, reliability, and future possibilities. When someone extends credit to you, they're essentially saying, "I believe in your future self's ability to honor this commitment. Make sure you pay me back." Debt becomes the responsibility that comes with that trust.

Your credit is your financial reputation. Just as your reputation with friends builds over time through reliable actions, your credit reputation is based on your financial behaviors. Every on-time payment strengthens that reputation and every late payment weakens it. The beautiful thing is that reputations can be rebuilt, as my father discovered at Shea Stadium.

CREDIT IS A FINANCIAL RELATIONSHIP

At its core, credit represents the relationship between you and a lender. It reflects patterns of past behavior which make you worthy of future credit. Your credit score, ranging from 300 to 850, is a snapshot of how you've managed borrowed money over time. Together, these credit score factors reveal how dependable you are as a borrower:

1. **Payment history:** Do you pay on time?
2. **Amounts owed:** Do you use credit responsibly?
3. **Length of credit history:** How long have you been proving yourself?
4. **New credit:** Are you taking on too much at once?
5. **Types of credit:** Can you manage different kinds of financial relationships?

When I teach about credit scores, I compare them to everyday trust in our daily relationships. If you consistently show up when you say you will, then your friends begin to count on you. But if you are one of those people who say, "I'll try to make it" and never do, you are known as a flake and people stop inviting you to things. If you borrow earphones and return them in perfect shape, people will lend to you again. But if you lose those earphones or return them with the wires hanging out, no one's lending you anything anymore. Credit works the same way, except the "friends" are banks, credit card companies, and other lenders keeping track of your financial promises. Your credit score reflects your history of paying money back when you borrowed it.

Behind the scenes, three major credit bureaus—Equifax, Experian, and TransUnion—are the financial report cards keepers. They collect information from your lenders and create your credit report, which is basically a lot of your financial relationships told through data.

It's also important for our students to understand credit is not free money; it's money you owe someone. As Beth Kobliner, author of *Get a Financial Life* explains, "I know some people who thought, 'Hey, I have a bank account. I have a checking account, and then I have a credit account like it's my credit account.' But that's not right. That's borrowing. That's a loan. So just the very concept that a credit card is a loan is fundamental to credit literacy."[1]

Once students grasp this concept, I focus on the most important habit they need to develop: paying the bill on time. Payment history is the biggest factor in your credit score. I emphasize this repeatedly: Pay on time and ideally, pay in full each month, but always pay on time.

Credit Cards as Financial Tools

Credit cards are one of the most contentious financial tools in our culture. They're just neutral pieces of plastic stamped with numbers. But like most tools, they can be used to build or destroy, open doors or create barriers, depending on the skill and intention of the person using them.

Many of us experienced their destructive potential right on our college campuses. There were credit card booths on the quad giving out school-branded shirts and Frisbees if you signed up. I received preapprovals for cards sent right to my dorm room. My mother was strongly against credit cards and wouldn't let me get one, even though I was an adult on paper. I really wanted one, but I respected—and healthily feared—her too much to open one on my own. Many of my peers were targeted this way and opened credit cards before they had the knowledge to make informed decisions.

Beth Kobliner has similar memories of easy credit: "If you look back to the eighties when I was in college, they would literally hand out credit cards on the main green. All you had to do was sign your name. You didn't have to show you had a job. You didn't have to prove you have an income. Basically, you sign your name, you get a credit card. And a lot of people I knew got pretty deep into debt pretty quickly. You just put it on the card."

New credit cards feel like found money. Need groceries? Put it on the card. Want to grab burritos with friends? Card. Outfits for the winter ball? Card. It is easy to confuse available credit with available money. Unlike cash, which creates immediate awareness of spending, credit cards create psychological distance from our purchases. We spend more when using cards because the transaction doesn't feel real at the moment. After the adrenaline from the purchase fades, the pain of payment comes later. And with compounding interest charges, those payments get bigger and badder as time goes on.

The result was predictable: Many students graduated with crushing credit card debt alongside their student loans. I know many people who maxed out credit cards in their youth and spent years digging themselves out of debt. Some are still paying those cards down. If that's your story too, know that you're far from alone. And the fact that you're here, helping students learn about credit? That's pretty amazing.

Thankfully, this type of college marketing was curbed thanks to the Credit Card Accountability Responsibility and Disclosure Act of 2009 (CARD Act). This legislation changed how credit cards could be marketed to young people. Now, borrowers under twenty-one must either have a parent cosigner or demonstrate sufficient income to qualify for their first credit card. Additionally, companies offering gifts for card applications must stay at least one thousand feet away from college and university campuses.[2] These protections matter deeply for the students we teach. We know from personal experience and from working with young people that they need time to develop financial judgment before taking on the responsibility of a credit card.

Yet I believe that as educators, we need to show students both sides of the coin. Credit cards can be useful when used responsibly. I frame credit cards as convenience tools rather than substitutes for your income. Cards have benefits, but *the money to pay for purchases should already exist in your checking account*, particularly when students are starting to build credit. Those first years with a card are like training wheels for learning not to overextend yourself. For example, I tell students that when I buy groceries, I charge them, but I already have the money set aside to pay the bill. I'm not borrowing money I don't have. When used strategically, credit cards offer benefits that cash cannot, like fraud protection when shopping online, spending records for budgeting, the ability to dispute charges, and rewards for spending what you would anyway.

For students, highlighting both sides of the coin matters. Many come from families where credit cards represent financial stress or desperation. They've heard only negative things about credit card debt or watched parents struggle with minimum payments. Teaching them about responsible credit card use helps them consider how these tools might fit their vision and goals.

Even experts can disagree about when to use credit cards. Some say it's fine to charge unexpected car repairs or emergencies, others argue these expenses should come from a cash emergency fund. What matters most is teaching students to be informed users of credit—understanding both the benefits and the drawbacks—so they can make smart decisions knowing all of the facts.

Understanding the Credit Reporting System

Papi's journey shows that credit bureaus actually reflect your growth over time. Equifax, Experian, and TransUnion are simply record keepers, compiling information on your credit-related behaviors. Their credit reports are the detailed story of how you've managed borrowed money. The lenders in your relationship will send them monthly updates on your payment habits. Students often ask me, "Who decides my credit score?" The answer: mathematical formulas created by companies like FICO, using the data these bureaus collect. But the empowering part is, you control the story they're sharing.

Credit as Reparable

Credit scores aren't permanent labels. We definitely want to do the best we can to avoid damaging our credit, *and* credit can always be rebuilt. Sure, we'd rather not be in a situation where we are digging ourselves out of a hole for years. That's why we teach our students about responsible credit and debt use. However, it is just as important for them to know that our credit score is reparable and changes based on our behaviors. Beth emphasizes the stakes clearly: "I feel very strongly that credit card debt can be a very insidious thing, and could really be disabling for someone." Yet she also provides hope: "If you have it, there are ways of paying it off in a sensible way."

Additionally, credit is not inherited. The student whose parents filed bankruptcy when they were twelve doesn't inherit that financial reality. They get to write their own credit story, decision by decision, month by month. I learned this lesson the day Papi's credit card application got approved instead of denied. He had taken steps to control his spending and live within his means. It took years, but his credit steadily improved.

I've watched students' energy shift when they learn credit bureaus don't consider their family's credit history, childhood neighborhood, or socioeconomic background. They care more about paying bills on time and managing borrowed money responsibly. Knowing that they can control their credit is incredibly liberating.

When Someone Asks You to Co-Sign

As your students develop strong credit — thanks to everything they've learned in your class—they may find themselves to be the person in their family and friends with the good credit. And with that positive financial reputation comes something no one usually warns them about: People will ask them for help.

Co-signing a loan for a family member or friend feels like an act of love and loyalty. But when you co-sign, you're equally responsible for that debt. If they miss a payment, it shows up on your credit report.

This doesn't mean never co-sign—it means going in with eyes wide open. Can you afford to make those payments if they can't? Are you prepared for this to affect your relationship if things go wrong? I know firsthand that co-signing can get messy, especially when relationships and money collide. Situations like this are a good reminder that debt is rarely black and white.

THE NUANCES OF DEBT

I talk a lot with my students about student loan debt. These conversations reveal how emotions and numbers interact when making financial decisions. Some students come to me terrified about taking on any debt at all, shaped by family stories about the financial stress or parents struggling with their own student loans. For them, debt is the enemy. Others come to me eager to attend their dream school regardless of cost. Already swept up in the excitement of living on campus and football tailgating, they might not be considering the long-term implications of that large student loan.

These are deeply personal family decisions with no universal right answer, and they deserve to be made with full information rather than pure fear or excitement. Both reactions make sense emotionally, but my job is to ground those feelings in facts. These conversations matter because framing debt as something to avoid can accidentally shame families who've used it strategically or out of necessity.

For many people worldwide, debt carries a heavy emotional weight. I'm focusing on debt held over time, not short-term charges you pay off right away. Many, like my mother, are uncomfortable with debt, which makes sense given how serious it can become if we aren't informed and careful. We often view debt in moral terms, making nuanced conversations tricky. But I love nuanced conversations, much to the irritation of the more impassioned people around me. So let's talk about when debt serves us and when it doesn't.

GOOD DEBT VERSUS BAD DEBT

Many experts categorize debt into the classic "good" versus "bad."

"GOOD DEBT" typically helps you build wealth or increase your earning potential over time. Student loans for education, mortgages for homes, and business loans for entrepreneurship usually fall into this category. This is because education leads to higher earning potential for graduates, homes can appreciate in value, and businesses can generate revenue. These debts also often come with relatively low interest rates as well as tax benefits.

"BAD DEBT" refers to high-interest credit card purchases, payday loans, and sometimes car loans as new cars generally lose value quickly. This debt costs more and doesn't typically build wealth, though it's not always avoidable. We might need reliable transportation for work and emergencies require immediate attention.

NUANCE ALERT: Some experts argue that any debt can become "bad" if not managed responsibly, regardless of its initial purpose. A "good" student loan can become a burden if the degree doesn't lead to higher income and a mortgage can be a problem if property values fall or interest rates rise significantly. Everyone agrees that unmanaged, high-cost debt is "bad." Yet the role of debt in personal finance and the best strategies for managing it are largely dependent on the individual and their values.

The Student Loan Conversation I Wish I'd Had

My teaching strategy focuses on providing students with the tools to make informed decisions about any debt, regardless of whether it's deemed good or bad. Many students approach me in their junior and senior years to think through their student loan options. Our conversations are about not only figuring out how they are going to fund college just to get through the doors but also how that loan impacts their quality of life after graduation. We work through calculations together, like this common one—if you take out federal loans each year totaling $25K at 6 percent interest, your monthly payment after graduation will be about $277. Whether that number feels manageable or overwhelming depends on their anticipated career path, family circumstances, and personal values.

Students need permission to have complicated feelings about debt. The student terrified of any loans might be missing out on life-changing educational opportunities. That fear-inducing $277 payment might actually be entirely doable given their career goals. On the other hand, the student ready to borrow $100K for any degree might need help understanding how a $1,110 monthly payment could limit their choices—or their family's—for decades.

Values and goals should drive these conversations. A student who values adventure might choose a debt-free lifestyle to maintain that flexibility to work abroad after they graduate. Another student, prioritizing carrying on the family business, might take on more debt, confident about future earnings. I've worked with students passionate about nonprofit work who want to avoid high monthly payments, and with STEM-minded students headed to medical school, where larger loans might make more sense.

I can't decide for them, but I can help them understand the numbers and the values behind their decisions. We have a responsibility to teach students to evaluate debt based on its purpose, its terms, and how it aligns with their circumstances and dreams.

The Responsibility of Debt

Being responsible with debt requires an honest assessment of our ability to repay and the true cost of borrowing. When my brother Dave was deciding between a speedy good-looking car and a dad van to get to his job, we calculated not just the monthly payment but the total cost over the life of the loan. He compared financing options and considered how different down payment amounts would affect his monthly budget. This process helped him make an informed decision rather than an emotional one. He kept his speedy dreams alive with an e-bike first, then eventually embraced his destiny with a sensible vehicle that fits eight comfortably.

For students, understanding debt as both responsibility and opportunity means learning to ask thoughtful questions like:

- What will this debt help me achieve?
- Can I afford the payments without sacrificing other important goals?
- Are there less expensive ways to meet this need?
- What happens if my financial situation changes?

Debt Payoff Strategies

Sometimes the most responsible thing we can do is acknowledge when debt has become unmanageable and create a plan to address it. We should do our best to teach students how to avoid getting into debt, but if it happens—or if they know others who have stressful debt—we need to broach this topic as well. I've watched students transform their family's financial trajectory by sharing strategies like these with them:

DEBT SNOWBALL METHOD: This approach has an emotional lens. You pay off your smallest debt first, then roll that payment into the next smallest. The idea is to build motivation and a sense of accomplishment through "quick wins," even if it means paying more interest overall.

DEBT AVALANCHE METHOD: This strategy makes more mathematical sense. It prioritizes paying off debts with the highest interest rates first. This approach saves the most money on interest in the long term, though it might take longer to see individual debts disappear.

NUANCE ALERT: There's no single right way to manage debt; the best method often depends on your personal financial psychology and goals. For more support, explore resources from the Consumer Financial Protection Bureau or the National Foundation for Credit Counseling.

WHY TEACH CREDIT LITERACY

Whether we like it or not, credit in this country plays a big role in our ability to live our lives. Credit affects our ability to buy or rent a home, purchase a car, pay for education, or start a business. We might also need credit for other expenses like medical costs or home renovations.

Given how widespread it is in our lives, it's essential for students to have the tools to navigate credit with knowledge, not fear or blind trust. By understanding how credit works, they can take advantage of financial opportunities while avoiding pitfalls that could derail their plans.

Credit, Employment, and Housing

Students should know that even when they just are starting out, their credit history can affect opportunities like getting a job or renting an apartment. For roles involving finances such as accounting, retail, or banking, employers may review credit reports to see whether applicants manage money well. While they cannot see credit scores, they can see credit reports, including payment history, account balances, and any bankruptcies or collections.[3] If an employer uses credit information in hiring decisions, they must get written permission first and notify them if credit issues influence their decision. Several states, including California, Colorado, and Connecticut, restrict when employers can use credit checks. They recognize that financial struggles don't necessarily reflect job performance capabilities.

Most landlords run credit checks when you apply for an apartment, to see if you'll pay rent on time. Unlike employers, landlords don't typically need special permission for credit checks. Students with a limited credit history might need a cosigner, a larger security deposit, or additional income documentation.

Understanding the connection between credit, employment, and housing makes credit literacy immediately relevant to students' future independence.

Credit Tricks and Traps

Today's students face different but equally complex challenges. For example, students face new forms of credit marketing. Although laws like the CARD Act created protections, there are always new ways to be hypnotized into credit card debt. Beth Kobliner observes that "this generation is much more scared of debt" having heard cautionary stories from previous generations. However, new deceptive practices have emerged: "There are just a huge number of these buy now pay later (BNPL) plans. It feels very high tech. And they're like, 'Look how great this is. You don't have to pay interest.' But the problem is that it makes people feel like, even though it's a hundred-dollar thing, it only costs me twenty dollars . . . So I can buy more things." As educators, we can help them recognize tricky practices like BNPL.

Students also have to guard against avoid fraudsters whose tricks can ruin their credit. (Case in point: While minding my own business in New York City, someone in Europe used my credit to rack up thousands of dollars in swimwear purchases at stores in Brazil.) Identity theft and fraud are real and constantly evolving. That's why every student must know how to protect their credit story before damage is done. Here are key protections students should know:

- **Right to a free credit freeze or fraud alert:** Both are free and block new fraudulent accounts from being opened in your name. Set them up at IdentityTheft.gov.
- **Right to a free annual credit report:** Everyone's entitled to one free annual credit report from each bureau at AnnualCreditReport.com.
- **Right to dispute errors:** Everyone can file disputes online with each credit bureau if they see something suspicious:

  1. Equifax *equifax.com/personal/credit-report-services/credit-dispute/*
  2. Experian *experian.com/acrdispute*
  3. TransUnion *dispute.transunion.com*

Credit as Empowerment

Credit knowledge can change our students' lives. When we teach credit with nuance—acknowledging the good and the bad—we give students tools that shape the quality of their futures. Credit can either block your path or open doors, and understanding it ensures it works for you, not against you. This knowledge doesn't just affect our students but lives for generations to come. Teaching credit as a responsibility and an opportunity is one of the most empowering gifts we can offer.

It's also empowering for students to know that while credit and debt are powerful tools, they don't reflect their worth as a person. They simply reflect past decisions and circumstances, things that can be fixed with knowledge and intentional actions. That old wooden Mets bat reminds me that we can grow from our most challenging financial experiences.

Students should know that struggling with credit is often a structural issue. Credit access hasn't been equally available to all communities. Women and people of color have continually faced barriers like outright denials and predatory lending. Some families inherit barriers to fair credit while others inherit generational advantages. With that awareness, students can make informed choices for their lives and advocate for financial systems that work for everyone.

SELF-REFLECTION: YOUR CREDIT CONFIDENCE

Teaching credit requires honest examination of our own attitudes and experiences. Credit conversations often trigger strong emotions because they connect to our deepest values about responsibility, risk, and self-worth. Before we can guide students through these nuanced topics, we need to understand our own biases.

This reflection work helps us recognize that credit education is deeply personal. As Beth Kobliner notes, once we understand our own relationship with credit, we can discuss debt-related shame and fear with the authenticity and compassion our students need.

Personal Reflection

- $ What's your earliest memory of learning about credit? How has it shaped your current views?
- $ Can you recall a positive experience you've had with credit? What about a negative one?
- $ How do you feel when you use credit? Excited, anxious, or indifferent?

- $ What beliefs do you hold about credit? Where do these beliefs come from?
- $ What did your family say about credit? How did they act with credit?
- $ What role does credit play in your long-term financial goals?
- $ Are you a "credit card maximizer" who uses rewards strategically, or do you prefer cash-only approaches?

Educator Reflection

- $ How comfortable do you feel teaching about credit? What areas make you most confident? Most uncertain?
- $ Does your cultural background influence how you teach about credit?
- $ What emotions arise when you think about your own credit score or debt? How might these feelings impact your classroom discussions?
- $ Have you ever experienced credit denial or credit rebuilding? How does that experience inform your empathy for students facing similar challenges?
- $ What assumptions do you hold about your students' relationship with credit?
- $ Are there aspects of credit education that you find yourself avoiding or rushing through? What drives those choices?
- $ What language do you use when discussing debt, and how might that language impact students?
- $ How do you navigate credit conversations with students whose families might be struggling with debt?

TEACHING APPLICATIONS: CREDIT AND DEBT

Unit Overview

Credit education requires balancing multiple truths simultaneously: Credit can be both necessary and risky. Our job is to equip students with the knowledge to make informed decisions that align with their values and circumstances.

We approach credit by first exploring what financial freedom and responsibility mean to each student's unique circumstances, then building toward technical understanding. Throughout this unit, I apply the RICH framework to ensure credit education feels accessible to all students.

Representation means featuring diverse voices sharing credit rebuilding success stories. **Inquiry** encourages students to question assumptions about debt and creditworthiness. **Connection** links credit concepts to students' real family experiences and future goals. **Holistic thinking** recognizes that students bring different cultural values and financial circumstances to credit decisions.

This unit directly addresses the Managing Credit standard from the National Standards for Personal Financial Education, teaching students how credit allows people to purchase goods and services today while agreeing to pay for them in the future, usually with interest.

I spend about one to two weeks on this unit, structured around these core topics:

- **Understanding Credit as a Tool for Financial Opportunity:** Exploring how credit works and its real-world impact on housing, employment, and life opportunities and viewing credit building as an investment in future possibilities
- **Credit Scores and Strategic Credit Building:** Identifying factors that influence credit scores, creating actionable plans for building credit history responsibly, and developing habits that strengthen creditworthiness over time
- **Navigating Credit Cards and Consumer Debt:** Evaluating credit card offers critically, understanding interest rates and fees, and developing strategies for responsible use while avoiding common debt traps
- **Credit, Debt, and Community Impact:** Recognizing how credit access affects wealth-building goals, understanding systemic barriers for different communities, and developing strategies for supporting family and community financial health

Empowering Educator Talk

Suggestions for trust-building language around borrowing and debt

Our students, like us, have varied experiences with credit and debt. Compassionate language helps create classroom environments where students feel safe discussing money topics without shame or judgment. Consider using phrases like these to frame credit and debt conversations with students:

- "Your credit future is in your hands. You get to decide what that story looks like."
- "It's normal to have mixed feelings about credit and debt. These topics are really personal."
- "Think of credit as a tool—a hammer or a smartphone. It's useful, but you need to know how to use it safely and wisely."
- "Your family's money experiences, wins or struggles, are valuable lessons. You can use what they've learned to make your own smart choices."
- "Lots of people face challenges with credit, but it's not a dead end. With the right info and a little time, you can definitely turn things around."
- "Sometimes, getting fair access to credit has been harder for certain communities. So, if someone struggles with credit, it's not a reflection of their worth or who they are as a person."
- "Everyone's money journey is unique. There's no shame in asking questions or reaching out for help when you need it."

Student Discussion Questions

Quick prompts designed to ignite student conversation

- How do you think you'd feel making your first major credit decision? What support would you want?
- When might borrowing money align with your values? When might it conflict?
- Imagine you're helping a friend who's struggling with credit card debt. How would you support them while respecting their dignity?
- You get preapproved for your first credit card. Should you apply or wait? How do you decide?
- Describe a time when using credit might help you achieve something really important to you. What would that look like?
- If you could teach one thing about credit to someone you care about, what would it be, and why?
- Different families have different relationships with debt and credit. What wisdom does your family have about borrowing money?
- What credit advice do you think you'd give to the next generation? What do you hope will be different about their credit journey?
- How do you want to be known for the way you handle borrowed money? What would that look like in practice?

Quick Activities (5–15 minutes)

Perfect activities for warm-ups, transitions, or when you have extra time

- **Credit Score Bump or Drop:** Provide students with examples of actions. Students decide if the actions help or hurt the person's credit score. Action examples: Eva sets up autopay for the full statement balance each month, Elias applies for three new credit cards in one week, or Ellie carries a $900 balance on a card with a $1,000 credit limit.
- **The Path to Good Credit (Intuit for Education):** An interactive, game-based simulation where students make real-world decisions and see how their choices affect their credit score over time.
- **Values-Based Credit Framework:** Students create personal decision-making frameworks by completing these sentence starters: "I would consider using credit when . . ." and "I would avoid using credit when . . ."
- **Credit Stories Circle:** Students share (anonymously if preferred) family stories about credit, both positive experiences and challenges. Focus on lessons learned rather than judgments.

- **Credit Advisor to Future Self:** Students write letters to themselves five years from now, giving advice on the best credit decisions to make and why those choices matter to their goals.
- **Community Credit Research:** Students investigate local credit unions, banks, and financial counseling services, and share with others how to access these resources.
- **Credit Reality Checks:** Provide students different beliefs about credit on slips of paper. Have them research the reality and the nuances of the belief. Belief examples: "You must carry a balance to build credit," "Checking my own credit score will ding me," or "All debt is bad debt."

Standalone Activities (20–50 minutes)

Exercises that can fit into any lesson, with added discussion to extend learning

- **Diana's Decisions Activity:** Students link real credit behaviors like making payments, utilization levels, and credit applications, and explain how actions will make Diana's credit score go up ↑ or down ↓. Students discuss any nuanced impact that these choices can have:
    - Diana sets up autopay for the full statement balance each month (score ↑)
    - Diana autopays only the minimum due (score ↑)
    - Diana misses her credit card payment by five days (score ↓)
    - Diana applies for three new credit cards within two weeks (score ↓)
    - Diana closes her oldest credit card right after opening a new one (score ↓)
    - Diana takes out a $2,000 personal loan to buy a laptop (score ↓)
    - Diana becomes an authorized user on her parent's long-held card (score ↑)
    - Diana becomes an authorized user on her parent's card. Parent has fair credit. (score likely ↓)

- **Credit Tool Analysis:** Present credit cards, student loans, and car loans as financial tools. In small groups, students will:
    - List each tool's ideal use (when it supports someone's goals and values)
    - Identify potential downsides (when it could derail those same goals)
    - Build two mini case studies per tool
        - Success scenario: Define a borrower (age, job, income, credit score, and purpose) who uses the tool wisely to meet a clear goal
        - Cautionary scenario: Define a borrower profile whose situation or objectives make that tool a poor fit

- **Credit Report Decoder:** List key events such as late payment, paid collection, unpaid collection, Chapter 7 and 13 bankruptcies, soft vs. hard inquiries, and closed accounts in good standing. In pairs, students will:
  - Match each event to its official duration (seven years, ten years, two years) using the Equifax article "How Long Does Information Stay on My Equifax Credit Report?"
  - Students compare durations and discuss why more serious events (like bankruptcy) stay longer than minor ones (like inquiries).
  - Discussion prompt: Share one insight on why some items expire sooner than others and how that might impact someone's credit journey.

EDUCATOR RESOURCES

Curriculum Resources

Free, ready-to-use lesson plans and activities to ground your credit unit

- **Banzai:** Borrowing and Credit Topic and FICO's Score a Better Future Fundamentals Curriculum
- **Jump$tart Clearinghouse:** Search "Credit"
- **Intuit for Education:** Credit Unit
- **Khan Academy:** Personal Finance Unit 3 (Interest and Debt)
- **Next Gen Personal Finance (NGPF):** Unit 4 (Types of Credit) and Unit 5 (Managing Credit)

Classroom Book Resources

A curated selection of books students can read to enrich their understanding of credit and debt

- ***Cultura and Cash: Lessons from the First Gen Mentor for Managing Finances and Cultural Expectations*** by Giovanna González (chapter 6)
- ***Get Good with Money: Ten Simple Steps to Becoming Financially Whole*** by Tiffany Aliche (chapters 4 and 5)
- ***I Want More Pizza: Real World Money Skills for High School, College, and Beyond*** by Steve Burkholder (chapter 4)
- ***I Will Teach You to Be Rich: No Guilt. No Excuses. Just a 6-Week Program That Works*** by Ramit Sethi (chapter 1)
- ***Mind Your Money: Insightful Stories and Strategies to Help You Reach Your #MoneyGoals*** by Yanely Espinal (chapter 5)
- ***Money Out Loud: All the Financial Stuff No One Taught Us*** by Berna Anat (chapter 5)

CHAPTER 9

ACCESSING THE STOCK MARKET

Two older people with shiny silver hair, hand in hand, looking out at Alaskan glaciers from a cruise ship deck. I saw that vision of financial success in the pages of a *Money* magazine sometime in the aughts. I said to myself, *This looks like a nice life. I want this. I should figure out what they do.*

In that same magazine, I flipped to a full-page maroon ad for a company called Vanguard. It said something like, "If you want to be an investor, we can take you there." I thought, *Being an investor feels like something responsible adults do. (Maybe they can take me* there*!)* So instead of spending my entire tax return on sneakers and bottle service, I decided I'd invest it.

Although this was back in the early days of internet research, I found a website that recommended something called index funds. I didn't even know what funds were. I was so nervous to invest, it took me around four months to actually do it. But then I got a surge of YOLO and clicked the "Buy" button. Boom, suddenly, I was an investor.

I was surprised about six months later to see I had made around $120. Of course I didn't contribute any more, as I already had put the most I had at one time into this invisible machine. At the time, I knew very little. I thought investing was gambling for fancy people. I didn't know anyone who knew anything about investing—and definitely didn't know anyone who could explain it to me.

Yet that simple realization—that money could grow passively—planted possibilities in my mind. It made me challenge the assumptions I had of myself that investing was inaccessible and not for people like me.

Like I said, I didn't know what investing really was, and I took that money right out within a year because I needed it to move into a different apartment.

But that's not the point. For someone who had never seen money grow on its own, earning interest was a small miracle. Years later, standing in my classroom when we start the investment unit, I see that same nervous excitement in my students' eyes. They ask many of the same questions I had for years. They are eager to access a world that feels so full of promise and, simultaneously, so distant. My simple $120 gain made me ask a question that many of us have. Why did it take me so long to start?

IMPORTANCE OF ACCESS TO INVESTING

The answer isn't complicated. The knowledge gaps and confidence barriers that kept many of us waiting on the bench are the same ones that students face today—shaped by systems that were never rooting for them. Thankfully, amazing educators like you and leaders in the finance field are changing the game. Together, we are fueling an accessibility campaign that invites our students to see investing as understandable, actionable, and for them.

Redefining What's Possible

Physical proximity meant nothing,
because it was such a foreign concept to me.

—YANELY ESPINAL,
director of educational outreach,
Next Gen Personal Finance

Yanely Espinal's story shows the impact of breaking through financial barriers and aligning with purpose. Once a New York City teacher with $20,000 of credit card debt, she's now the director of educational outreach for NGPF, a best-selling author of *Mind Your Money*, and a national educator whose Instagram content (@missbehelpful) has generated over 4.5 million views. She's also helped shape financial education policy across multiple states.

When we spoke, Yanely described the irony of living in the financial capital of the world yet feeling miles away from it: "Despite living just twenty minutes from Wall Street on the J train, it was actually so far from me in terms of connecting to it, understanding it, and feeling relatable. Physical proximity meant nothing, because it was such a foreign concept to me."[1]

Early on, Yanely believed investing wasn't for her: "In my mind, I'm like, oh, this is for millionaires and millionaire men. Certainly not for everyday people. And definitely not for women." Even when a friend explained how mutual funds could build wealth, the message didn't connect. She says, "It went in one ear and out the other. I never felt like it was worthwhile to be curious, because it was so clearly not for me. So in my mind, I just wrote it off completely and put this wall up between me and anything related to that world."

This psychological barrier of self-doubt and disconnection is what we can help students overcome. As Yanely put it, "We create these barriers in our mind. When you believe that world isn't for you, you manifest that separation. The biggest barrier was simply believing someone like me could learn about Wall Street and actually grow money in an investment account."

It wasn't until Yanely read *The Money Book for the Young, Fabulous & Broke* by Suze Orman and *The Simple Path to Wealth* by J. L. Collins that the wall came all the way down. It finally clicked that "regular, everyday people can do this. Which means that I could do it." Today, Yanely is fully invested in making financial education not just available, but deeply relatable.

Seeing Yourself in the Market

I believe in your upward trajectory.

—TREVOR ROZIER-BYRD,
founder and CEO, Stackwell Capital

Technology both scares and intrigues us, but what's most exciting is its potential to break down long-standing investment barriers. Leaders like Trevor Rozier-Byrd are driven by their experiences to make investing more accessible. As CEO of Stackwell Capital, Trevor is reimagining how financial tools serve everyday people. Their platform is easy to use, the financial education is free, and the focus is on long-term wealth building—intentionally designed for communities that Wall Street has overlooked.

Like Yanely, Trevor grew up close to global finance yet it felt worlds away. At his New Jersey high school, most classmates had parents who were investment managers and traders. "These kids knew they were going to college for business to work on Wall Street. There was no question," Trevor recalls. But for him, that path felt out of reach. "I didn't think I was smart enough or capable enough. So I never even considered it." That gap in confidence and knowledge followed him into college. Even after he earned a degree from Boston College, investing still seemed off-limits.[2]

After graduating, he finally tried investing for himself: "I bought a couple of shares of Mastercard and Bank of America stock. These were companies I was already interacting with as a consumer." When his portfolio grew $300 in a single day, he couldn't believe it. His Apple stock purchase at $68 per share eventually paid for a year of school tuition.

These early wins built his confidence, but it was representation that truly shifted Trevor's mindset. When he worked on an IPO (initial public offering) involving BET founder Bob Johnson, everything changed. "It was the first time I'd ever seen an all-Black management team. I felt a sense of representation." In that moment, entrepreneurship felt possible: "I can start a company one day. I can do exactly what he is doing."

"The wealth gap isn't just about lack of capital. It's about confidence, knowledge, and trust in financial institutions," Trevor told me. He believes Stackwell's mission is to meet people with empathy and belief: "I see you. I understand your challenges. And I believe in your upward trajectory." Access alone isn't enough, he says. "It has to be paired with education and delivered in culturally competent ways—so people feel seen, represented, and empowered."

Trevor's story reminds us that financial empowerment begins when people gain knowledge, build confidence, and see themselves in the investing world. When students feel represented and supported, they start to believe that investing is possible, and that they belong in the conversation.

THE HUMAN SIDE OF INVESTING

So how do we bring that message to life for our students? We can start by showing them how close the investing world really is. To bring the stock market into the classroom, I start the unit with a simple question: "How many of you have used a product from a publicly traded company today?" Hands stay down until I start listing: "Did you check Instagram? Brush your teeth with Crest? Eat some Kellogg's Frosted Flakes? Wear Nike socks?" By the end, every hand is up.

The stock market isn't that mysterious. It's an exchange or marketplace where we can own pieces of the companies that shape our daily lives. When my students realize they could buy the latest AirPods *and* own a piece of Apple itself, their interest is piqued because they understand what it means to own stock in something that is relevant to them.

Investing Terms for the People

Now that we know the stock market is all around us, let's break down the basics with relatable language that will help us explore investing with our students confidently.

Stocks Versus Shares

- **Stock:** Ownership in a publicly traded company. You can use this term to refer to owning a piece of one company or many. For example, you might say, "I own stock in several different companies" or "I own stock in Crocs (CROX)."
- **Share:** A single unit of ownership of a company's stock. You might say, "I have enough workout leggings, so instead I bought ten shares of Lululemon (LULU)."
- **Ticker:** A short unique set of letters, like a nickname, used to identify a company's stock on a stock exchange. You might say, "Funny, the ticker for Harley-Davidson is HOG."
- **Company:** A business that makes products or offers services. To invest in a company, it must be publicly traded, meaning its stock is available on exchanges like the New York Stock Exchange (NYSE) or Nasdaq. A familiar example of a publicly traded company is Shake Shack (SHAK).
- **Parent company:** A larger company that owns most of another company, or a subsidiary. For example, if you love chalupas and want to invest in the Taco Bell company, you'd have to invest in Yum! Brands (YUM), its parent company, which also owns KFC and Pizza Hut.
- **Brand:** A product name, logo, or identity created by a company. For example, in many Latin households, we use Vicks VapoRub to cure all illnesses. Vicks is a brand name, though, so if you want to invest in it, you'd buy shares of its parent company, Procter & Gamble (PG).

WHY IT MATTERS: These terms are used interchangeably, but they are slightly different. Students need to understand stocks aren't just abstract tickers with red and green numbers scrolling on a screen. When you buy shares, you're purchasing actual ownership in a real company. Knowing the difference between a company, its brands, and a parent company helps you understand exactly what you're investing in.

RESOURCE: I like the YouTube videos from @TheStockMarketGameProgram. Even if you don't end up doing the game, they have some good intro videos. Moomoo also has helpful videos in their library, found at the bottom of their Investment Courses page.

Bull Versus Bear Markets

- **Market:** The place where investments like stocks or bonds are bought and sold. This term is often used to refer specifically to the stock market. Market indicators like the Dow Jones Industrial Average, S&P 500, and Nasdaq track how groups of major companies are performing and give us a snapshot of how the stock market is doing.

- **Bull market:** When the market rises 20 percent or more (historically lasts about 4 years)
- **Bear market:** When the market falls 20 percent or more (historically lasts about 1.5 years)

WHY IT MATTERS: Understanding these market cycles helps us stay calm during downturns. Historically, bull markets (growth) dominate, with the S&P 500 up 78 percent of the time over the last ninety years. Bear markets feel scary, but they are usually temporary blips. Seeing these historical charts helps shift our perspective from a short-term fear to a long-term confidence.

RESOURCE: For a visual history of market cycles—and maybe some perspective to help you sleep at night—explore: Morningstar's "What Prior Market Crashes Taught Us in 2020," Investopedia's "Understanding Bear Markets: History, Causes, and Opportunities," and Vanguard's "Bull and Bear Markets Over Time" chart.

Diversification and Funds

- **Diversify:** In simple terms, don't put all your pasture-raised eggs in one basket. This means spreading your money across many different companies, investments, or sectors, like tech, healthcare, and retail. If one investment performs poorly, you're protected because others might do well.
- **Mutual fund:** A collection of money from many investors like yourself, managed by professionals who pick the investments
- **Index fund:** A fund that automatically tracks a specific market index, like buying an index that tracks the whole stock market or companies in the S&P 500
- **ETF (Exchange-Traded Fund):** Like a mutual fund, it pools money from many investors. But you can buy and sell an ETF throughout the day like a stock.

WHY IT MATTERS: Funds let investors like you and me own hundreds of companies with one purchase, which gives us instant diversification. Diversifying is a way to manage risk and helps protect our investments if any single company struggles.

RESOURCE: Next Gen Personal Finance (NGPF) has a movement activity called Let's Make the S&P 500 that helps students conceptualize the idea of multiple stocks inside one fund. TradingView has a Stock Heatmap that gives students a visual of the S&P 500.

Compound Interest

- **Compound interest:** The interest you earn on both the money you put in and the interest it's already earned

WHY IT MATTERS: It makes your investments grow faster over time. It makes your money work for you. It's a key tool for wealth building, and it's awesome.

RESOURCE: Visual Capitalist has an excellent infographic called "Visualizing the Extraordinary Power of Compound Interest" in their Wealth 101 series.

How Emotions Affect Markets

Market movements are the result of millions of human decisions happening every day. When someone buys Netflix (NFLX) stock, they're betting that people will keep binging shows like *Bridgerton*—making Netflix more valuable over time. When someone sells, they've decided it's time to take their money elsewhere. The stock market is essentially a massive conversation where people vote with their wallets about what products or services they think are valuable or not.

This human element is the stock market's greatest strength—and its biggest source of drama. Investors, other humans just like us, are often driven by emotions like fear, greed, and hope. These feelings influence people's decisions, causing stock prices to move up and down, and sometimes in ways that don't always reflect a company's true value. Psychology plays a huge role in market movement because it influences what they believe a company is worth. That belief drives their buying and selling decisions.

Think about it this way: When people feel fear or uncertainty, they may decide to step back, protect their money, and sell their investments. When they feel excited or confident, they're more likely to invest in companies they believe will grow. These feelings influence their behaviors and ultimately influence how the larger market moves.

Staying Calm in a Sea of Red

The first day I planned to teach investing was also the day the Dow Jones Industrial Average fell nearly 4 percent, the Nasdaq declined almost 6 percent, and the S&P 500 fell 4.8 percent. These are just fancy ways to say the stock market was on the struggle bus. It was the worst trading day since 2020. My students walked in with questions: "Miss, is everyone losing their money?" "Should people sell everything? What if all stocks go to zero?"

This wasn't how I'd planned to start the unit, but it became the perfect entry point. We pulled up the Finviz.com heatmap, a tool that gives you an instant visual snapshot of the larger stock market. Green squares mean stocks are rising; red means they're falling. That day, the screen was entirely red. But I asked them to pause for a second and zoom out. I showed them a chart displaying bull and bear markets over time since 1945, as well as the S&P 500 data since 1970. We looked at market movements for one month, one year, five years, ten years, and sixty years. Suddenly, we could envision our red day becoming a tiny blip in an upward journey.

I had already anticipated what my students would ask. Earlier that day, some teachers burst into my office in a sweat: "Should I sell? Should I cash out my investments? What if my retirement never recovers?" I did some deep breathing with them and proceeded to show them the same historical charts I later showed my students. Our emotions are bursts of chemicals that are valid and that feel very real. But we can ground our emotions in facts and history, especially when it comes to long-term investing. I'm not sure what they ended up doing, but I was there to provide the historical context for emotional moments that seem world-ending-ish.

The Emotional Investor Checklist

Experiencing market volatility feels like a white-knuckle ride on the Scream Machine in the 1990s. It's impossible to suppress our emotions during these financial roller-coaster moments. I still feel discomfort when I see red numbers, and I get FOMO when friends share their latest investment wins. Instead, we can recognize when emotions might be driving financial decisions and pause long enough to think clearly. Before making any investment decision, I teach others to take a breath and ask themselves:

- What emotions am I feeling right now—excitement, fear, or fear of missing out (FOMO)? Are those feelings driving this choice?
- Am I making this decision because of something I just read or heard, or does it actually fit my long-term goals?
- If this investment wasn't the hot topic everyone's talking about, would I still want to own it?
- Am I sticking to the plan I made when my head was clear, or am I reacting to what's happening right now?

Fear is real. Emotions are valid, but they don't always make the best financial advisors. These questions help you check in with yourself before your money follows your feelings somewhere you didn't plan to go. When students develop this kind of emotional awareness around money, they're building skills that will serve them throughout their investing journey.

Historical Comebacks

Even with all this self-awareness, markets will still test our resolve to stay the course. For most of us, the 2008 crash is a vivid memory of economic pain, but for students, the COVID pandemic crash is the most applicable. I use this crash to show long-term recovery. During this time of worldwide fear and uncertainty, the S&P 500 fell 34 percent from its February peak to its March low. The streets were bare and apocalyptic, while people struggled with losses of all kinds. It makes sense that strong emotions caused people to look for safety, leading to a sell-off of stocks.

But for those who stayed invested, over the next five years, the S&P 500 went up 112 percent cumulatively, resulting in an above average return of 16.3 percent annually. That's why it is key to zoom out and look at history over time. Every market crash in history has been followed by new highs. Not sometimes. Every time.

Investing Made Simpler

Now you might ask, what about the popular investing mantra "Buy low, sell high"? Buying low entails handpicking individual stocks to find that diamond in the rough, and hope for huge returns. Of course, it is possible; people have done it before. Warren Buffett's name is often mentioned in this stock picking conversation. Buffett stuck to a simple approach: He bought stock in solid companies he understood, he bought when prices dropped (getting a discount), and he didn't freak out or sell during market downturns. I think it is important for students to have information on individual stocks as background knowledge. They should know where to find stock quotes on sites like Yahoo Finance and understand metrics like earnings per share (EPS), price-to-earnings (P/E) ratio, dividend yields, and long-term average annual returns on companies.

But in reality, picking stocks to buy low and sell high is really hard to do. Over 85 percent of fund managers underperform the S&P 500 over a ten-year span.[3] People like Warren Buffett are statistical outliers. His investment success is unbelievable, ridiculously rare, and difficult to replicate. Even for most experts who live and breathe earnings reports, industry trends, and market movements, they still struggle to pick consistent winners over time.

Funds offer an easier path for most investors to participate in the stock market. (Even Warren Buffett recommends that most people invest in funds.) By purchasing a share of an index fund or an ETF, you own slices of hundreds of companies at once. You don't have to become a market wizard and wrestle with your emotions as much with this investing strategy. Yanely Espinal shares with students the long-game perspective. She makes sure future investors know, "There's no consecutive twenty-year period where the S&P 500 has decreased. It's impossible to find it. You just don't see it. It always increases over time when you reinvest dividends and don't take them out." When we understand that funds allow us to grow our money without needing to obsess over stocks, we can feel more confident getting started.

What Dating Can Teach Us About Long-Term Investing

Love, sweet love. Yanely shared another powerful way to make long-term investing accessible to starry-eyed teens. She uses dating analogies that students instantly grasp: "You're talking to two people, right? One of them is known for ghosting—but everyone seems into them because they're good-looking and really popular." She compares this to trendy, volatile stocks like Tesla or Nvidia. Then there's the alternate option: the consistent partner who always responds to texts, shows up, and never leaves you hanging. That's your trustworthy index fund—maybe not the most thrilling pick but the one you actually want to bring home.

As Yanely explains, "You have data points. That's the whole point, don't just focus on the popularity and the hype right now. What have they done every single time you texted them for the last twenty text messages? They only responded to two, right? That's your data. For the last twenty years, for the last fifty years—that's the equivalent in investing. Looking at long periods of data, not just looking at one instance."

This analogy works because it connects to something students already understand—evaluating reliability over flashiness. The boring index fund that consistently shows up over decades becomes more attractive than the exciting stock that might be full of returns but also might ghost your portfolio. Using analogies like dating also work because, as Yanely says, "the stock market is a foreign concept. You can't start with the stock market. You have to start with something else that I do understand and make that a bridge to understanding concepts in the stock market."

Trading Versus Investing

Okay, long-term investing makes sense. But then I hear about all these other flashy things like day trading, margin calls, penny stocks, forex, call and put options, and those WallStreetBets. What does it all mean?

Even though viral trading trends give me slight FOMO too, I'm more of a passive, low-cost fund gal. However, many of my students are interested in these forms of trading. They might have family members who day-trade or who like individual stock picking. I won't ever knock something my students are interested in. I never want to make them feel silly for being open and sharing what they have heard about in their lives. Yet I do want to give them the information they need to understand how trading really works.

I start by being honest: Active trading topics aren't my specialty. I let them know that our lessons focus more on taking a long-term investing approach emphasizing the power of compound interest over time. But I also believe students deserve all the educational tools to make an informed decision for themselves. There is a good thirteen-minute episode called "Trading vs. Investing" on the *Popcorn Finance* podcast that cleanly explains the differences. If they are still interested in short-term investing, I point them to a Fidelity Learn article on trading versus investing or Moomoo's beginner-friendly videos on day trading, options, and forex (the foreign exchange market), so they understand what those strategies involve and the real risks they carry.

I asked Yanely what single investing concept could transform education. Her answer was clear: understanding the difference between trading and investing. "Trading is over there. Investing is over here," she replies. Young people see forex coaches and day-trading gurus on social media promising quick riches. "That stuff makes me cringe so hard," she admits, "because it's really this next generation that is the start of seeing stuff like that."

Yanely offers a straightforward way to teach investing to our students: "So many educators picture in their mind trading stocks when we say investing in the stock market. In their mind, they immediately make that equivalent to trading stocks. It's so important for educators to differentiate between active trading in the market and passive long-term investments, because if they understood, all you have to do is teach your students (1) what's tried and true historically, and (2) that fees have to be really low. If you can get those two things, I mean, you're literally equipping every single teenager in your classroom to become a millionaire or multimillionaire if they start using that right away, pretty much right when they get their first job."

PILLARS OF LONG-TERM INVESTING

Every financial expert will tell you that past results don't indicate future gains. Which is true. However, history is all we've got. We can only make the best decisions possible with the information we have. And as of 2025, the information we have tells us that over the past eighty-two years, the S&P 500 has delivered positive returns in every single ten-year period. So whether we're guiding students or ourselves, here are three pillars of disciplined investing to return to when emotions run high or headlines have you panicking.

1. **Start early, stay consistent**

   The compound interest penny exercise never fails in my classroom. Would you rather have $1 million today or a penny that doubles every day for thirty days? They always choose the million—until we do the math. By day thirty, that penny becomes $5.3 million. This becomes our foundation for understanding that time, not timing, creates wealth. As they say, time in the market beats timing the market.

   When students start investing young, even with small amounts, they get to experience the power of compound interest. A student who invests $50 a month starting at age eighteen could end up with more money than someone who invests $150 a month starting at thirty. Why? Because early money grows longer, and compound interest snowballs over time.

   Starting young also builds habits. It's about discipline over time. Students who begin investing early learn to stay consistent, ride out market dips, and trust the process. Even if they pause contributions later in life, that early start gives their money more time to grow.

   And if you haven't jumped into the investing pool yet, have no fear. You know what they say: The best time to invest was yesterday; the next best time is today. Time to get in the saddle.

2. **Invest like an Android: Use dollar-cost averaging (DCA)**

   Students won't understand this reference, but dollar-cost averaging is like Data from *Star Trek: The Next Generation*. You might remember that Data Soong was an android who calmly, and annoyingly, countered Starfleet's emotional reactions with his steady, unwavering logic. Similarly, DCA is a strategy that keeps your emotions grounded with a steady, rational path through market ups and downs.

   Dollar-cost averaging means investing the same amount of money at regular intervals, regardless of whether the market is up or down.

Instead of trying to time the market perfectly, which even professional investors struggle with, you invest $50 every month, or $100 every paycheck, no matter what dip or rally happens.

The best is to use automated features, which keeps you from having to manually click buttons and risk being emotionally swayed away from your trusty DCA over time strategy. When I first started investing, I would obsess over daily market movements. Many beginner investors do this. Red days felt personal, and I wondered if I was a "bad investor." Then years later, I discovered dollar-cost averaging. I set up automatic transfers: $100 every month into my index fund, no matter what. Even during the 2020 market crash, my automatic investments kept buying shares at lower prices.

Don't get me wrong. I wasn't thrilled about DCA-ing when the 2020 downturn was happening. It felt very uncomfortable, and a bit dumb, to continue investing during the lowest points. But when the market recovered, those DCA crash purchases became some of the best-performing investments. I didn't time it perfectly. I just white-knuckled it through the fear, which statistically has been the best plan for long-term investors.

3. Volatility is normal: Learn how to ride the wave

After our stock unit, one of my eleventh-grade students asked for a book to read more about investing. I recommended the excellent *Friends That Invest* by Simran Kaur, which she read (for fun during her winter break). During the market drops we experienced, she came up to me and said, "You know how I invested in the S&P 500 right? Yeah, I'm keeping my money in. This is just a drop like any other drop." Let me tell you, I couldn't hold back the cheesiest smile. It was such a mature response that came with knowledge and confidence in a young investor. Can you imagine being this aware of staying the course during market volatility . . . at sixteen years old?

My student's Data Soong–like response reflects exactly what Andrew Kadjeski, head of brokerage and investments at Vanguard, observes, "Young people today are more engaged with investing than many would assume."

But he also understands why market volatility can feel overwhelming, especially for those who witnessed their parents' struggles. Andrew explained that every generation is impacted by the generation before them. Millennials and Gen Zers watched their parents or grandparents endure the financial crisis of 2008, seeing very real impacts—from home foreclosures to the loss of retirement savings. So it's natural to feel discomfort during volatile stock movements.

Investors can't control market volatility; it's the rule of engagement. That's why people of all ages need to study how markets have behaved over decades. Having this bird's-eye perspective and being able to compare long-term bull markets to short bear markets is critical. It turns scary black swan events like the 2020 crash into potential sales on future wealth. Zooming out sways us all from emotional investing decisions and keeps us focused on the long game. As Andrew says, "When you stay invested with a long-term view, the buy-and-hold approach almost always comes out ahead."

WHY TEACH INVESTING LITERACY

The results of my students' Money Mindset $urveys speak volumes: Twenty-seven of thirty took the class to learn about the stock market. Teaching investing democratizes access to one of the most powerful tools for building generational wealth. It's my favorite unit to teach, though I say that about every unit.

Because Wealth Should Reflect Their Values

Values reenter the conversation when we ask questions like: Why do we actually want to build wealth? What are our goals? This matters deeply. As author Bill Perkins asks in his fascinating 2020 book *Die with Zero: Getting All You Can from Your Money and Your Life*, are we optimizing for accumulation's sake, or for life fulfillment? I ask myself that often, and I want my students to reflect on it too.

Investing in the stock market is one of the most powerful levers for building wealth over time. We can teach students some impressive math: Saving $100 a month starting at age eighteen can grow into over $1.1 million by retirement, assuming a 10 percent annual return over forty-seven years. But life isn't just about accumulating money so you can swim in it like Scrooge McDuck.

I teach my students that investing and building wealth is a way to live a life that is meaningful to their values. I ask them to envision their future selves: What does financial freedom look like to you? Maybe it's the flexibility to choose meaningful work over just high-paying work. Maybe it's the security of knowing you will have retirement funds in your older age. Maybe it's the ability to support causes you care about or take care of aging parents. Many of them want to buy their mom a house one day, some want to travel the world, others want to support their community, and most want to ensure they never experience the financial stress their families faced. When we connect to these deeper values, we can set investment goals and brainstorm a strategy that is purposeful for their lives.

Because They Deserve Better Information

Students connect to investing because it's happening now and feels tangible to them. They see GameStop trending, hear about stock crazes, and watch influencers talk about their trades on Robinhood. But they're only getting pieces of the whole puzzle—and often dangerous ones.

Their interest in taking finance classes shows they want trusted guides. We can leverage their curiosity about day trading and market volatility to teach larger principles and provide the complete picture. We become the bridge between the good, bad, and ugly content they encounter, giving them tools to navigate investing for their benefit.

We teach the difference between speculation and investment, the psychology of market movements, why time in the market beats timing the market, why most day traders lose money, why TikTok investment advice can be misleading, and ultimately, how to get started investing.

What matters most is that students get access to the information they need to make their own informed choices. Some will still try day trading—and that's okay. They'll have the knowledge to pave their own way, or pivot to more long-term strategies. Others will skip the WallStreetBets and go straight to boring, beautiful index funds. Both groups will be informed in choosing their path.

Because They Need Transparency, Not Perfection

We're not financial advisors giving stock tips. Our job is education, not prescription. But I've found tremendous power in being transparent about my own investing journey, including my past fears and mistakes.

There's always a point when students are like, "Okay okay, I get it. I want to be an investor. So how do I do that? How do *you* invest, Miss?" When students ask this inevitable question, I tell the truth. We've all just wanted to ask a relatively normal person to be real with us and share what they actually do. First, I let them know I am not giving them advice. My purpose is to educate them so they can make their own decisions. Then I share that my investing is boring on purpose: I use low-cost index funds that track the whole stock market. For example, I personally use a total stock market index fund because it lets me own a tiny piece of thousands of companies at once.

"Some will fail, some will do well, but overall, American businesses tend to grow," I explain. I talk about my timeline, my comfort with market drops, and the fact that I won't need this money for decades. I also tell them what kind of investor I am: I don't have time nor the emotional bandwidth to research and buy individual companies, and I don't trust myself to outsmart professional traders. I'd rather spend my energy watching professional wrestling than monitoring stock tickers all day.

Your comfort level with transparency is personal. Some educators keep investments private, and that's valid. Others, like me, find that demystifying our choices helps students understand that investing doesn't require complex strategies or insider knowledge. We can all be investors.

The goal is to build decision-making skills students can take with them. When they ask, "Should I buy Apple?" instead of giving a yes-or-no answer, I guide them to think critically: "What do you like about the company? What's your timeline? What's your goal? How much risk feels right for you?" We're teaching them to think like investors, not telling them what to invest in.

Because Every Barrier Has a Bridge

Our students face the same barriers I once did. But you know how in *Wicked* when Elphaba realizes she had the power to fly all along and never needed the Wizard in the first place? That's exactly how it feels when knowledge suddenly makes investing barriers seem surmountable. Are educators the broom? Are we Glinda? Unclear. What I do know is that the financial barriers are the Wizard, an intimidating force that gatekeeps knowledge and keeps people feeling small and excluded.

Here are some barriers we can help students overcome:

"I DON'T UNDERSTAND ANY OF THIS." The jargon used in financial spaces is often an intentional barrier designed to keep people out. We translate the complicated language into concepts they already understand, making investing relevant to their everyday lives.

"I NEED THOUSANDS TO START." Although most students list investing as their top interest, they believe massive capital is required. We shatter this myth by showing how fractional shares let you own companies for one dollar, how many apps have no minimums, how twenty dollars weekly can build serious wealth over time, and how their employer's 401(k) match is free money.

"THE MARKET IS RIGGED." When students express this frustration, we acknowledge the real systemic problems while helping them understand that opting out guarantees exclusion. Opting in with knowledge creates possibilities. The system has flaws, but learning how it works gives you power within it.

"MY FAMILY SAYS IT'S GAMBLING." We shatter this myth immediately by distinguishing between speculation and long-term ownership. One tries to get rich quick with odds stacked against you. The other builds wealth slowly and surely with decades of odds in your favor.

Because One Student Can Change Communities

Teaching investing creates ripple effects beyond portfolios. When young people understand how markets work, they become better informed consumers, voters, and community members. They start to think critically about the companies they use, and the types of products they want to put their money into.

Additionally, just like Yanely Espinal and Trevor Rozier-Byrd, learners become agents of change in their families and communities. Students who learn compound interest teach siblings. Those who understand index funds guide parents. The most powerful moments can occur outside of class. A parent comes to conferences and says, "My son won't stop talking about index funds to me. I'm looking into it now." Or an uncle lets you know at graduation, "After your class, she really wanted to open a Roth IRA. I'm going to open one for myself also." Financial education is transformative for our communities. And it starts in our classrooms with knowledge that becomes power.

Because Time Is on Their Side

Oddly enough, students really like the retirement lessons. Out of all the topics, this is the last one I expected to hit, but it does. When we watch the Netflix *Money, Explained* episode about the three-legged retirement stool (Social Security, employer plans, and personal savings), they get really locked in. It is probably because they have heard the terms their whole lives from family, grandparents, or society, and now their knowledge makes them feel a part of the conversation. It's empowering to understand terms that went over your head for years.

Students start asking their parents about 401(k) matches and social security benefits. As one of our college advisors told me, "We knew you taught them about retirement today. Three different students asked us about pension jobs!"

Many students are also surprised to discover that retirement planning automatically makes them investors. Most have no idea their future 401(k) will be invested in the stock market. Most think retirement money gets sucked into an abyss for forty years and never comes out until they are elderly, if they're lucky. This misconception isn't just for teenagers; many adults never check their 401(k) or 403(b) because they assume the investments are out of their control. (Shout-out to Dan and Scott, creators of 403bwise.org, which helps educators figure out if their 403(b) plans are worth their hard-earned money!)

Learning about retirement turns abstract investing concepts into "Oh, wait, this is about *my* future?" Plus, young people have the greatest investing superpower of all: decades of time ahead of them.

SELF-REFLECTION: YOUR RELATIONSHIP WITH INVESTING

During my educator workshops, teachers share, "I haven't even been contributing to my 403(b)," or "I've never invested before. How can I teach this?" That self-doubt is real, but the great thing is that our transparency matters more than expertise.

Before we can teach investing authentically, we need to examine our own stories. I've shared mine—the nervousness, the small miracle of $120, the early withdrawal, the years of feeling locked out. Your story might be different, but the emotions are often similar. What messages did you inherit about investing? Take a moment to reflect.

Personal Reflection

- $ Do you hold stocks or funds as investments? Why or why not?
- $ Do you know any family members who buy stocks? What have you observed?
- $ Did you grow up learning or talking about investing? Why do you think that was?
- $ What emotions come up for you when thinking about or participating in the stock market? How do you manage them?
- $ What areas of investing do you want to learn more about?
- $ Have you ever experienced or witnessed financial stress or hardship? How did it influence your approach to finances and investing?

Educator Reflection

- $ What do you need to know about investing that will make you feel more confident teaching it?
- $ Do you focus more on the potential rewards or risks of investing in your teaching? Do you present a balanced view of both?

- $ How can you incorporate more hands-on, experiential learning activities related to investing?
- $ What do you think students know, or don't know, about investing? How will you find out if your assumptions are true?

TEACHING APPLICATIONS: INVESTING

Unit Overview

Investing education requires addressing both the technical and emotional sides of building wealth. Our job is to democratize access to wealth-building tools while helping students develop the emotional intelligence to stay disciplined during market volatility.

Just as we approached budgeting through values rather than categories, we teach investing by connecting to companies that students already know and love, then building toward understanding market psychology and long-term strategies. Throughout this unit, I apply the RICH framework to ensure all students see themselves as potential investors.

Representation means featuring diverse financial voices and investment stories beyond traditional Wall Street narratives. **Inquiry** encourages students to question assumptions about who can invest and why certain investment advice exists. **Connection** links investing concepts to companies and values students already understand. **Holistic thinking** recognizes that students bring different forms of wealth and different definitions of financial success to their investment journey.

This unit connects to the Investing standard from the National Standards for Personal Financial Education, helping students understand how people can invest money in financial assets to achieve long-term financial goals while learning about risk, return, and the benefits of compounding over time. I spend about three to four weeks on this unit, structured around these core topics:

- **The Human Side of Markets:** Understanding that stocks represent real companies, analyzing stock quotes, and recognizing how emotions drive market movements
- **Long-Term Wealth-Building Strategies:** Exploring values-based investing, time vs. timing, dollar-cost averaging, and the three pillars of disciplined investing, distinguishing between speculation and long-term ownership, and planning for retirement
- **Risk and Reward:** Understanding different types of risk, learning about funds, how diversification works, and why boring often beats exciting
- **Making It Accessible:** Breaking down barriers, starting small, and building investing habits

Empowering Educator Talk

Suggestions for language that welcomes every learner into investing conversations

Students bring diverse experiences. Some believe investing is risky, while others think it's only for the wealthy. Inclusive language creates safe spaces for learning and opens new possibilities. Here are some simple, welcoming phrases:

- "Your family may not have invested in stocks, but they've built wealth in other ways like through relationships, education, and community."
- "It doesn't matter if you start with $1 or $1,000. What matters is starting. Every investor started somewhere."
- "Markets rise and fall, but they've grown over time. We're in it for the long run."
- "Investing means claiming your seat at the table. You belong here."
- "It's normal to feel nervous. Most fear comes from not yet understanding how it works."
- "If investing seems like gambling, let's break down the difference between trading and long-term ownership."
- "Plenty of people started late or made mistakes and still built wealth. You're right on time."
- "There are no dumb questions. Your questions are the same ones that successful investors asked when starting out."
- "Investing isn't about being perfect with money. Just be consistent and willing to learn."

Student Discussion Questions

Quick prompts designed to ignite student conversation

- What do you think of when you hear "stock market"? Where did those ideas come from?
- If you could own part of any company, which one would it be? Why?
- Would you take $1,000 now or $10,000 in ten years? What influences your choice?
- How is saving different from investing? When would you choose each?
- Someone promises to double your money in a month. What would you ask them before agreeing to give them money?
- What money advice has your family shared? How do you decide if it's good advice?
- How would you feel if your investments lost 20 percent? What if they gained 20 percent?
- What worries you about investing? Where do those worries come from?

Quick Activities (5–15 minutes)

Perfect activities for warms-ups, transitions, or when you have extra time

- **Investing Myth Busters:** Present common investing myths on slips of paper ("You need $10,000 to start investing," "The stock market is just gambling," or "You should only buy individual stocks"). Students research reality and share findings.
- **Stock Ticker Detective:** Give students a list of cryptic stock symbols (PLAY, META, DIS, SBUX) and have them guess the companies. Reveal answers to see how many companies students can identify. You can also discuss how stock symbols often tell stories about company branding.
- **Investment Time Machine:** Ask students, "If you could go back twenty years and invest in one company, which would it be?" Use Stoculator to research past returns of a stock of their choosing. Amazon's $1,000 would be worth $150,000 today. Discuss: Can we predict the next Amazon? Is it worth it to try? Why or why not?
- **Investment vs. Speculation Speed Round:** Give rapid-fire scenarios that students quickly categorize as "investment" or "speculation" with a thumbs up or down. Examples: Day-trading meme stocks, investing in index funds, purchasing shares in a company with strong fundamentals, or betting on a start-up with no revenue but high potential
- **Risk Tolerance Emojis:** Give different investment scenarios and have students respond using emojis only. Share patterns and discuss how personality affects investing style. Examples:
  - Stock drops 15 percent in one month. You're still invested = 😣
  - You're offered stock options at your start-up job = 😎
  - You hear a hot stock tip from a friend = 😬

Standalone Activities (20–50 minutes)

Exercises that can fit into any lesson, with added discussion to extend learning

- **Stocks IRL:** Students list ten products they use daily, such as Nike, Gatorade, and Cheetos, then research which publicly traded companies own them. "You're already supporting these companies . . . what if you could own them?" Create quick visual maps showing how their daily purchases connect to potential investment opportunities.
- **News to Opportunity Pipeline:** Students read current Sherwood News or Market Briefs entries, identify mentioned companies, and research their investment

potential, creating real-time connection between news events and market opportunities.

- **Risk Levels and Life Goals:** Students build personal risk pyramids using different investment types (savings accounts, individual stocks, and index funds) and customize them based on their goals and timeline.
- **Company Deep Dive:** Use the "Jim's Birthday Present" activity from The Stock Market Game or the "Stocks IRL" activity as a starting point. Have students choose one company they already support and conduct thorough research on its stock (CEO, performance history, financial health, recent news, competitors, and growth potential) using Yahoo Finance.

EDUCATOR RESOURCES

Curriculum Resources

Free, ready-to-use lesson plans and activities to ground your investing unit

- **Jump$tart Clearinghouse:** Search "Investing"
- **Intuit for Education:** Investing Unit
- **Investopedia:** Investopedia Simulator (stock market simulator and beginner-friendly investing tutorials)
- **Junior Achievement:** Take Stock in Your Future (five-session curriculum and the optional JA Stock Market Challenge)
- **Khan Academy:** Personal Finance Unit 6 (Stocks and Bonds) and Unit 7 (Investment Vehicles, Insurance, and Retirement)
- **Next Gen Personal Finance (NGPF):** Unit 3 (Investing)
- **Vanguard:** My Classroom Economy (investment simulator)

Classroom Book Resources

A curated selection of books students can read to enrich their understanding of investing

- ***Friends That Invest: Your Guide to Financial Independence Through Shares and Stocks*** by Simran Kaur (the whole book, but at least part I)
- ***Get Good with Money: Ten Simple Steps to Becoming Financially Whole*** by Tiffany Aliche (chapters 7 and 9)
- ***I Want More Pizza: Real World Money Skills for High School, College, and Beyond*** by Steve Burkholder (chapter 3)
- ***I Will Teach You to Be Rich: No Guilt. No Excuses. Just a 6-Week Program That Works*** by Ramit Sethi (chapter 3)

- ***Mind Your Money: Insightful Stories and Strategies to Help You Reach Your #MoneyGoals*** by Yanely Espinal (chapter 7)
- ***Money Out Loud: All the Financial Stuff No One Taught Us*** by Berna Anat (chapter 6)
- ***Rich AF: The Winning Money Mindset That Will Change Your Life*** by Vivian Tu (chapter 5)

CHAPTER 10

BUILDING REAL ESTATE LITERACY

Now let me take you on an unofficial New York City real estate tour. Some days I risk it all and bike eight miles to work, from Queens to Brooklyn. On these rides, I hustle through multiple construction sites breaking ground for new apartment buildings. There is a stretch of the commute in an industrial area, with trucks loading timber and drywall for renovations. There will be at least ten buildings where scaffolding rises on yet another new development. I pass tons of real estate signs featuring agents who reflect the culture of each neighborhood. There are brownstones and multifamily homes going for millions at this point. For each shiny new floor-to-ceiling window I pass, there will be a renter paying at least $4K a month to live there. As I dodge potholes and pigeons, I'm aware of how real estate is omnipresent in our lives. Just like the bull on Wall Street, buying, selling, and renting is integral to my city.

When I travel to other cities to present on teaching financial empowerment, I notice the impact of real estate there as well. During a conference in Cleveland, a taxi driver shared how new construction was drawing more residents to the city. After a beautiful run in Redondo Beach, I was momentarily inspired to switch coasts, until a rideshare driver let me know homes were in the multimillion-dollar range. In New Orleans, a former educator discussed the suburban housing trend with me on the way to the airport. Yes, I am chatty during my travels. (Shout-out to hardworking drivers who indulge me with their real estate knowledge!)

For us and our students, real estate involves understanding two interconnected worlds. Residential real estate is where we live—the apartment we rent, the family home we grew up in, or the place we dream of owning someday. Investment real estate is the business side—properties bought specifically to generate income and build wealth.

When Students Don't Know They Know Real Estate

Our students notice when rent goes up, when families move away, when new construction changes their block. They understand property values through lived experience: watching friends leave because of rising costs, sharing rooms with extended family, and observing their neighborhoods shift.

Through countless one-on-one conversations, I realize that our students already have sophisticated knowledge of real estate. They just don't recognize it yet. Our role is to help them make those connections. When real estate is grounded in their lived experiences, it becomes more relevant and personal.

I remember talking with Ari, an eleventh-grade student, about her family's living situation. "My grandmother owns the house," she told me matter-of-factly. "We all live together. Different floors, and different rooms and we give her money. Actually, less money now because she owns it, and I think my mom owns it too."

I paused, wanting her to recognize what this meant. Then I said, "Ari, you know you're actually describing a strategy called house hacking. Your family is combining resources to pay off property and build generational wealth. Your grandmother and mom are real estate investors." *House hacking* is one of those new terms for something families have been doing for thousands of years.

"That's the same as real estate?" she asked. I grinned, "Yeah, girl. That's the definition of real estate." Ari looked at me, surprised. "Oh, I never knew they were considered real estate owners."

That same day, I spoke with Alejandro. When I asked what he knew about real estate, he shrugged. "Nothing really." I asked about his parents. "Well, my father owns land, but that's in Mexico. Nothing is built on it or anything, so I never thought about it as real estate." When it comes to investment real estate, our students often hold more knowledge than they realize.

These two conversations stood out to me. Ari and Alejandro believed they knew nothing about real estate, when in reality, the knowledge from their lived experience was a valuable entry point. Ari's multigenerational housing reflects a strategy many financial advisors promote. Alejandro's father owns raw land, a long-term investment requiring market understanding. Yet both students unintentionally dismissed this wisdom because it didn't match the textbook version they'd imagined.

Whether their family owns or rents, the two students understand housing stability in deeper ways. What they need from us is recognition that they're *already* part of real estate conversations. They need vocabulary to name what they've observed, tools to analyze what they've experienced, and confidence to see themselves as capable of building on generational knowledge.

DEFINING RESIDENTIAL REAL ESTATE

For many people, buying property is one of the biggest financial decisions they'll ever make. Understanding residential real estate means knowing how property functions both as the shelter we need, and as a vehicle for building long-term wealth. I always start with residential real estate because housing is personal and has immediate relevance to our lives.

I often think back to my own apartment hunt years ago: late nights envisioning finally holding my own front-door key and obsessing over mortgage calculations. I remember the fabulously priced three-bedroom, two-bathroom apartment in a perfect location that I loved and wanted to renovate with all my Pinterest ideas . . . even after discovering it was infested with bugs. After seeing those *cucarachas*, my mother shut that idea down fast; it was the end of my home-design dream. In hindsight, she saved me from a very expensive mistake—my thinking I could be like HGTV without any experience or the renovation budget. Real estate education isn't just about properties and numbers. It's about helping students navigate their values during one of life's most significant crossroads.

RESIDENTIAL REAL ESTATE introduces familiar topics such as:

- How homeownership builds generational wealth and fits into long-term financial goals
- Pros and cons of buying vs. renting with honest discussion of both paths
- Basic mortgage concepts and calculations
- True costs of homeownership including taxes, insurance, and maintenance

From Beignets to Borrowing: A Very Brief History of Real Estate and Wealth

Fun fact to impress your friends: The Louisiana Purchase was America's first major real estate deal. We bought 827,000 square miles from France in 1803 for about $15 million. Merci beaucoup for doubling our country's size—and for introducing us to beignets. (I eat a socially unacceptable amount of those things as soon as I land in NOLA.)

Property ownership has been a marker of success and stability across cultures and societies for millennia. In early America, the average person couldn't afford to purchase a home. Banks didn't lend out money for homes, so you had to have cash to buy. Everything changed after the National Bank Acts of the 1860s stabilized our banking system. Suddenly, banks could do something revolutionary: Lend money to buy homes. By the 1890s, early versions of the mortgage were beginning to open the door to what would eventually become the traditional American Dream. Over the course of the twentieth century, the white picket fence became cultural shorthand for success, even if that dream wasn't accessible to all.

Much of America's wealth lives in housing. In 2024, the US housing market was valued at $49.7 trillion—an increase of $2.5 trillion in just one year.[1] Real estate remains one of the most powerful ways to build generational wealth. In 2022, the median wealth gap between homeowners and renters reached almost $390,000. These new highs emphasize the profound impact property ownership has had on family finances for decades. Since 1989, homeowners saw their median wealth increase by almost $165,000 and average wealth grow by $900,000. For renters, the increases were more modest: $5,800 in median wealth and $56,000 in average wealth.[2]

That's why we talk about homeownership with such intensity. It is why grandparents sacrifice everything to buy that first house. And why parents stress about down payments and credit scores. Real estate doesn't just provide shelter. It is the foundation for many families to pass down ownership and build legacy.

The Foundation of Wealth

For many people, a home represents their largest asset and most significant wealth-building opportunity for several reasons:

- **Equity:** Every mortgage payment builds ownership stake. With every mortgage payment you make, you are paying down the mortgage. Your mortgage payments gradually transfer property ownership from the bank to you, the homeowner. As a renter, your payments provide housing, but your payments don't allow you to own the home as an asset.
- **Appreciation:** Historically, homeowners can expect property values to increase by 3 percent to 4 percent annually on average, though housing markets vary throughout the country. Particular circumstances can also affect appreciation. For example, during the pandemic period, existing home prices increased by 45 percent between December 2019 and June 2022.[3]
- **Tax advantages:** Homeowners benefit from multiple tax breaks. For example, homeowners can take deductions on mortgage interest and property taxes. Another powerful tax incentive is that for an individual homeowner, the first $250,000 of profit is exempt from capital gains taxes when selling a primary residence. This bumps up to $500,000

for a married couple filing jointly. Mortgage interest deduction allows homeowners to deduct the interest they pay on mortgage debt.

- **Intergenerational transfer:** Passing down real estate to the next generation compounds family wealth. Sixty-eight percent of real estate investors plan to leave their properties to heirs. This creates a foundation for the next generation's financial security and wealth building.[4]

Validating Diverse Housing Experiences

When teaching about real estate, I open with the big question: Should you rent or buy? While the wealth-building potential of homeownership is well-documented, I point out that renting can sometimes be the better choice. Buying or renting depends on location, life circumstances, and personal values. High property costs in certain areas, the need for job mobility, or a desire for more flexibility can make renting a smarter choice.

Validation is critical for this topic especially because where we live is very personal. We are talking about decisions their loved ones have made. I've noticed that when we discuss renting versus buying, students initially assume the "right" answer is homeownership. But when we examine the drawbacks of buying—maintenance costs, reduced mobility, market risk—I see heads perk up, particularly among students from renting families. This moment validates their families' housing choices and helps them understand that renting can be an intentional, strategic decision.

It's essential to create space for all family experiences. I make it a point to validate families who choose to rent because they don't want to deal with maintenance issues. I equally validate families who have worked hard to achieve homeownership and those who combine resources in multigenerational housing arrangements. Just like many aspects of personal finance, there isn't a one-size-fits-all approach to housing decisions.

The key educational goal is helping students evaluate these trade-offs based on their unique situations rather than blindly accepting their housing choices. Many students come from families that rent by choice, while others come from families that would prefer to buy but face financial barriers. Both experiences are valid. I want students to understand that their families are making decisions with the information and resources available to them, doing their best within their circumstances. Students can then decide whether they want to follow similar paths or pursue different housing strategies in their futures, but they should know their families' experiences are legitimate regardless.

This nuanced approach prepares students to make informed decisions that align with their values, circumstances, and goals. And these factors might lead them toward homeownership, or to strategic renting, or to an alternative arrangement that best serves their financial futures.

When discussing renting versus buying, it's also important to be mindful of students who may be experiencing housing instability or temporary living arrangements. These students might feel uncomfortable participating as they don't see their experience reflected in the traditional housing discussion. I'm sure I don't always get it right, but I try not to assume anyone's living situation. I also try to make space for all experiences by emphasizing with intentional language that housing decisions—whether by choice or necessity—are shaped by many factors, and all deserve respect.

My goal is to help students understand how the housing system works and equip them with the facts and vocabulary they'll need if they choose to engage with it in the future.

How Does Someone Actually Buy a Home?

Every year, I ask a local real estate agent to walk my students through the home buying process. Outgoing people by trade, they are happy to come talk to students to demystify the process. Some of my students are interested in being real estate agents, so this is like a mini career day for them also. I ask agents to share their own first-time buyer stories, their mistakes, and their victories. They talk about balancing wants with what's affordable. Students realize that most people start unsure, confused, and intimidated. But if you are disciplined, determined, and flexible, you can build something lasting through homeownership. One agent asked, "Raise your hand if you think buying a home is possible." Half of the hands went up. By the end of our session, those same students were asking about credit scores and down payment programs. I love to see the shift. Homeownership transforms from a distant, adult thing into something they can actually picture for themselves.

To build on that interest, I share resources like the "Your Home Loan Toolkit" guide from the Consumer Financial Protection Bureau (CFPB). Many students even take the resources home to share with their families. For anyone beginning the homeownership path, there is also a helpful online CFPB guide, *Buying a House: Tools and Resources for Homebuyers*, which simplifies the home buying journey and connects users to practical tools. They break it down into four steps:

1. **Prepare to shop:** This is where dreams start to meet reality. Future buyers have tools to check their credit, track their spending, and assess what they can afford honestly.

2. **Explore loan choices:** Once buyers know their budget, they can imagine making this purchase. They begin to explore rates and meet lenders. It's the first step in a major financial commitment.
3. **Choose a loan offer:** They've found their home. Now it's time to find their mortgage. Buyers can compare loan estimates. Comparing loan estimates becomes an exercise in values: What does this purchase mean, monthly and long-term? After a loan offer, buyers get an underwriter who tracks their life to the penny in order to approve them for the loan.
4. **Get ready to close:** The paperwork marathon finally ends at the closing. Many don't know about the closing process and costs associated. There are tools like the Closing Checklist to help.

Modern Homeownership Trends for Gen Z

Even with practical tools and knowledge, homeownership today looks different for Gen Z. There are rising home prices and interest rates, stagnant wages for many, and limited affordable housing. Many cannot save independently to purchase a home. In fact, nearly one in five young buyers live with family or friends just to accumulate enough funds for a down payment.[5]

The path is more complex, but not impossible. Just like all our juicy financial tidbits, knowledge creates empowerment. Families have long adapted to economic challenges in creative ways, and one of those timeless strategies now has a trendy name: house hacking.

HOUSE HACKING is an old-school approach: literally living with everybody and their mother to reduce expenses and increase savings. So, living with family now to save for a home later isn't a step backward? Absolutely not. It can be a smart, strategic move toward ownership. You may just want to invest in some noise-canceling headphones and a good stress ball while you're at it.

Additionally, I've seen students' eyes twinkle when they discover that there are also programs that could help them own homes one day. These programs can make homeownership more attainable for first-time buyers:

- **Federal Housing Administration (FHA) Loans:** Require as little as 3.5 percent down with flexible credit standards.
- **US Department of Veterans Affairs (VA) Loans:** Offer zero down payment for eligible military families, a benefit many students don't realize their families have earned.
- **US Department of Agriculture (USDA) Loans:** Provide zero down financing for homes in rural and suburban areas, expanding options outside expensive cities.

- **Neighborhood Assistance Corporation of America (NACA) Housing Program:** Offers housing counseling as well as no down payment, no closing costs, and lower interest rates to make homeownership more accessible for those who have been historically underserved.

Keeping It "Real" Estate

Twenty-four years ago, I learned how finicky owning a home could be. My sister Irene and her husband had just moved into their new home and asked me to fetch some baby toys from their attic for my sweet little nephew, Jacob. Being a young and nimble college kid, I volunteered to climb up there while Irene and our parents waited below, ready to assembly-line all those toys down to the living room.

That's when—Crash!—my big athletic foot went straight through the ceiling, sending drywall, batting, and dust raining down on their brand-new kitchen. While fighting for my life in that musty attic, I had forgotten to step on the beams, not the soft unsupported areas. My father spent weeks repairing that hole. It was never the same. Every visit afterward, I'd point to the clearly off-color paint job and sheepishly repeat, "Sorry about that." She'd give me a side-eye and a pointed "Mmhmm." She has since sold the house, so all is forgiven.

Homeownership is quirky. One day you are overjoyed at your new kitchen appliances, the next day your sister's foot is hanging down through your ceiling. And as the owner, it's your responsibility to fix it. When I bought my apartment, I budgeted for the down payment, but not for the closing costs, or the kitchen sink needing to be unclogged, or the surprise building sewer repairs. It's not a question of if but when these things will happen.

Students enjoy when I share my own real estate story with them. I include the pros and cons of my decision to buy ten years ago, the sewer surprises, and the sneaky fees at closing. They see possibilities, but they also see reality. Shiny marble countertops go hand in hand with cleaning dirty gutters on Saturday mornings. But what about equity, appreciation, tax benefits, and being able to pass down a home to the next generation? That's real too.

The Equity of Equity

The benefits of homeownership are clear, but the opportunity to own property hasn't been equally available to everyone. According to the US Census, in 2025, white homeownership rates were 74.2 percent, compared to 62 percent for Asian Americans, 47.8 percent for Hispanic Americans, and 44.7 percent for Black Americans.[6]

These gaps aren't random. They're the unfortunate legacy of policies like redlining, exclusionary zoning, and biased lending. As described by Federal Reserve History, redlining marked certain neighborhoods—often in red on maps—as "high risk," and lenders used those maps to deny credit in communities of color.[7] Biased lending practices meant families of color faced higher interest rates or were straight-up denied for loans, even with similar credit profiles. The effects persist today: Black households typically buy homes later in life, purchase less expensive properties with higher debt burdens, and face greater challenges maintaining homeownership over time.[8]

I share these realities not to discourage, but to acknowledge that owning a home has a complex history for many. Understanding these realities helps us teach real estate in ways that recognize barriers while empowering all students to build wealth through property ownership if they choose to buy.

DEFINING INVESTMENT REAL ESTATE

Beyond primary residences, investment real estate offers additional wealth-building opportunities. In conversations, students would casually mention aunts who "just own a store and an apartment" or uncles who "rent out the basement." They'd describe grandparents collecting rent or parents who bought a two-family home "so the other side could help with the mortgage." Many of our students' families are already aware of or participate in investment real estate, even if they don't use that terminology yet. Once students have the words for what they're seeing at home, the whole topic becomes far less intimidating.

The Essentials of Real Estate Investing

HOW RENTAL PROPERTIES MAKE MONEY: Properties can provide owners with monthly cash flow and equity over time. Future investors need to know the real numbers around property ownership, because trust me, it's more complicated than it looks on HGTV. Cash flow is the money left over after paying all expenses like mortgage, taxes, insurance, and repairs. Equity is the portion of the property you truly own as you pay down the loan and the home's value appreciates, or grows. Learning how to analyze these numbers is essential to understanding whether a property will actually make you money.

KEY REAL ESTATE INVESTMENT STRATEGIES

- **Buy and hold:** Owning a property and collecting rental income from residents to build equity over time

- **House hacking:** Living in one unit while renting others to reduce personal living expenses
- **Fix and flip:** Renovating and selling for a profit, which requires construction knowledge and capital
- **Short-term rentals (like Airbnb):** Higher income potential but more intensive management and different regulations
- **REITs (real estate investment trusts):** A way to invest in real estate without owning property directly

UNDERSTANDING HOW LEVERAGE WORKS: Leverage means using a smaller amount of your own money to gain control of a larger asset. For example, if you have $100,000 to invest, you can buy $100,000 worth of stocks. But with real estate, you can use leverage and use that same $100,000 to make a 25 percent down payment on a $400,000 property. This allows you to benefit from the growth of a much larger asset with that same $100K investment, which can increase your potential returns.

Investment Real Estate for Rookies

Here's what I want every educator to know: You don't need to be a real estate investor to facilitate these conversations. For example, I don't flip houses, and honestly, I'm not interested in doing it. But I recognize it's a successful strategy for many investors, so just like other topics, I want to facilitate that learning for my students. I present them with the pros and cons so they can decide if it fits their financial future. Then we give them pathways to learn more.

Just as we know with much of our content, we can't teach real estate investing comprehensively in our limited time. What we can do is spark curiosity, provide foundational knowledge, and connect students with quality resources for deeper learning. I point them toward podcasts for real investor stories, recommend Ashley Kehr's 2023 book *Real Estate Rookie: 90 Days to Your First Investment* for practical first steps, and show them how to use online calculators to analyze deals. My goal is to make them informed enough to continue learning on their own.

When you are getting started in understanding investment real estate, it can be intimidating. Especially if you didn't come from a family or community where it is common. It can be hard to find content that meets you where you are. When I started learning, a lot of content was way over my head. People talking about being accredited investors who had thousands of properties, syndication deals, and portfolios with commercial real estate. I was lost. It is easy to believe this world wasn't meant for people like you.

During a birthday weekend, my brother told me about BiggerPockets, which is an online community and education hub known for their forums and calculators. People join to connect with others who are about building wealth through real estate investing. Soon after, they started a podcast for beginners. I tuned in and learned a lot from people in different circumstances with different strategies, and their life stories.

The hosts—Ashley Kehr, who specializes in buy-and-hold rental properties, and Tony J. Robinson, who focuses on short-term rentals—offer a balanced view of two approaches to building wealth. They give listeners honest advice and real-life challenges, which helps make investing feel less intimidating and more achievable.

To deepen this learning for educators and students, I was excited to interview Ashley and Tony on their July 15, 2025, episode, "Teaching Real Estate Literacy."[9] They shared amazing insights from helping thousands of first-time investors start their journeys. When I asked them what educators should teach about real estate investing, their advice was categorized into two critical skill sets that we might not see fully on TV or social media:

Technical Skills Required

- Financial analysis and spreadsheet modeling ("I would have to teach them how to analyze a deal and to understand the numbers," Ashley Kehr told me.)
- Understanding local market conditions and trends
- Knowledge of financing options and lending requirements
- Basic understanding of construction and repair costs
- Legal knowledge of landlord-tenant laws
- Tax implications and depreciation strategies

Ashley emphasized that students need to understand "what buying a piece of property can do for you as far as appreciation, building that equity, that long-term wealth but also the cash flow." She stressed the importance of being able to map out deals on paper and show exactly where the money comes from and goes.

Soft Skills, Often Overlooked

- Communication with tenants, contractors, and lenders
- Problem-solving under pressure
- Patience and long-term thinking
- Emotional regulation when deals fall through

- Network building in your local market
- Time management and prioritization

Tony added a crucial perspective about mindset, explaining that he would focus on and what the alternative would be if not investing in real estate? He emphasized that without building something alongside W-2 income, you'll have to get up and go to work every day until you're many years old.

Students see real estate "success stories" on social media and are enticed by the glamour. Flipping looks exciting when it's done with a team of experts, and with the gift of video editing, problems disappear within thirty minutes on TV. But this strategy is not passive. You need construction knowledge, project management skills, and significant capital reserves when things go wrong—and something always goes wrong. Our job is to help them evaluate the good, bad, and ugly about real estate, analyzing if what they see is what is real.

There are countless real estate "moguls" that claim to own thousands of properties or flash big checks for their flip. Tony addressed this directly during our interview: "Don't believe everything you see on social media . . . there's so many young people on social media who are talking about how easy it is and how much money they're making . . . But there's so many of those people who aren't necessarily making money in real estate, but they're making money by teaching other people how to do this thing they did one or two times."

Ashley, who is also author of *Real Estate Rookie: 90 Days to Your First Investment*, reinforced this reality check, emphasizing that "in most cases, this isn't a get-rich-quick scheme." She noted that while you might make money on one flip, you could lose money on the next deal that "basically wipes out that profit you had made from a previous year." Instead, she encouraged focusing on "the long-term play of real estate and how that can impact your life of just building retirement, building generational wealth."

What is unsaid is if those checks are even real, how many hours went into that deal, the blood, sweat, and tears that went in, if they had partners, and a whole slew of other questions to validate their claims. But students, and adults, don't always know the questions to ask to determine if those posts are real. So it is again our job to make sure they discern the real from the fake and enter investment real estate with knowledge and tools to navigate if they so choose.

Tony shared a personal example: His son set a goal to complete his first wholesale deal in one semester. Tony encouraged him, but added a dose of realism: "I love that you're doing this, but I don't think you're going to do it in the five months you have for this semester . . . You'll be lucky if you get one deal before the year is over."

This example is a lesson for all new investors: The timeline for success in real estate is rarely quick and is far from the instant success promised on social media. (Shout-out to Tony and his son for embracing the long game and passing knowledge forward to the next generation!)

WHY TEACH REAL ESTATE LITERACY

Real Estate Has Ingrained Relevance

Our students are immersed in real estate daily, whether they realize it or not. And they want to know more. Out of everything we explored this year—including love and money, scams, advertising, money mindset, budgeting, saving, and investing in stocks and cryptocurrencies—every single student said they wanted more time for real estate. Each one of my twenty-nine students chose it as their favorite.

Before diving into mortgage calculations and cap rates, I take a moment to recognize that students already know a lot about real estate. Just like us, they walk through neighborhoods noticing new construction, rising rents, and changing communities. As one of my eleventh graders noted, young people today are "thinking about our future" and hoping "to raise enough money for a house, a car, and be able to raise our parents." Real estate isn't abstract to them. It's deeply connected to their dreams and family experiences.

It Meets Students Where They Live

Students often arrive with a deep, if informal, understanding of how property shapes their communities. Think of the ways the built environment influences what they know:

- Urban students might walk past construction sites, luxury high-rises, appreciating brownstones, and multigenerational homes
- Suburban students might witness single-family homes, condominium communities, and new business developments
- Rural students might observe agricultural properties or farmland, vacation homes, and small-town commercial business

Every student has a real estate story, whether it's their own family's homeownership journey or rental experiences, or simply watching their neighborhood change. This universal connection makes the learning immediate and personal.

The most fun aspect about teaching the topic of real estate is that it is flexible and adapts to meet students exactly where they are. As educators, we know our students' cultures and communities in ways that generic curriculum can't capture. We understand which families have multigenerational wealth tied to property, which students navigate rental instability, and which communities have been affected by new developments. This intimate knowledge allows us to make real estate education deeply relevant to each classroom's specific context.

It Addresses Real Concerns

When Lia from my course mentioned that "we hope to raise enough money for a house," she articulated what many young people are thinking. When students express hopes of buying homes and supporting their parents, real estate education provides practical frameworks for achieving homeownership goals.

During a "Do Now," a quick routine used to activate prior knowledge, I shared an article about a new policy where NYC allows ADUs (accessory dwelling units), and I asked students to think of someone who could benefit from this. We shared stories about basement apartments, converted garages, and grandparents moving into additions. Real estate policy became personal. Teaching real estate can address their actual living situations and offer real solutions.

It Builds on Community Wealth

Real estate conversations naturally invite family financial histories and cultural approaches to homeownership. Students begin seeing their backgrounds as financial assets rather than obstacles. The strategies their families already employ become launching points for deeper learning.

Ask around and tap into the knowledge of your community. Invite colleagues with real estate experience to speak to students and share stories that go beyond their content areas. One of my students' favorite lessons was when I invited a teacher in my school who flips houses to come in and share his experience. He shared the costs, the unseen costs, the rewards and benefits, and the high level of work involved in his flips.

We can encourage students to bring family stories of homeownership, renting, or investing into the classroom. Create space for parents to join via virtual calls and share their own real estate journeys.

It Prepares Future Investors

The research is clear: Homeownership remains a primary wealth-building path, the homeowner-renter wealth gap keeps widening, and real estate offers both appreciation and cash flow opportunities outside traditional investments.

Whether students rent a place, buy a home, or invest in property, understanding real estate markets, property values, and investment basics will serve them throughout their lives. Plus, as digital natives, they enjoy using apps and online tools to analyze properties as it feels natural to them.

Real Estate Education Works

And if those reasons aren't enough, look at what my students said at the end of the course:

- Kalisa: "I loved real estate. I didn't know anything about that before. I liked learning about different prices in different areas of the country."
- Jo: "I liked real estate most because my aunt flips houses. I didn't even know until I was talking to my mom about it."
- Sky: "I loved learning about flipping houses. I had no idea all the costs that went into flipping, but I'm interested in it."
- Alan: "I liked real estate the best because I want to do this in the future as an agent, and I didn't know what it would look like before."

Their reflections told me everything I needed to hear. Real estate education connects students to possibilities they can see, touch, and literally, build.

SELF-REFLECTION: YOUR REAL ESTATE EXPERIENCE

If you're new to real estate concepts, you have an advantage. Your learning journey alongside students can model the curiosity and research skills needed for sound property decisions whether that's residential or investment real estate. Teaching real estate effectively requires honest self-reflection about your own property experiences and potential biases. Consider these questions.

Personal Reflection

- $ Do you own or rent? How has this shaped your perspective on real estate as an investment?
- $ Do you view homeownership as essential to wealth building, or do you see valid alternatives?
- $ How do you feel about owning, or possibly owning, real estate? Do you feel secure, proud, or anxious?
- $ Does anyone in your family own real estate? What do they say or feel about it?

- $ Are there any emotional attachments or memories associated with real estate in your life?
- $ Do you have any financial goals related to real estate? Are you looking for wealth accumulation, rental income, or a place to live?
- $ How do you envision your relationship with real estate evolving in the future?
- $ What assumptions do you hold about who can be a real estate investor?

Educator Reflection

- $ What motivates you to teach real estate? What do you find personally rewarding about this subject?
- $ What is your level of comfort about sharing your knowledge and expertise in real estate with your students?
- $ What are the biggest challenges you face in teaching real estate? How can you overcome these challenges?
- $ How well do you understand the real estate market in your students' communities?
- $ How can you bring real estate learning from the outside into the classroom?

TEACHING APPLICATIONS: REAL ESTATE

Unit Overview

Teaching high schoolers about real estate is an overlooked, but critical piece of the financial puzzle. Financial education classrooms can give students a foundational understanding of real estate as both a personal or business decision—helping them decide if ownership aligns with their values and long-term goals. Whether they know it at the beginning or not, they'll be informed by the end. Just as we approached budgeting and investing through personal values, we begin real estate by anchoring it in their lived experiences. From there, we build toward understanding market forces and investment strategies.

I approach real estate education through the RICH framework to ensure every student sees themselves as capable of participating in property wealth building. **Representation** means featuring diverse real estate professionals and investors whose stories reflect various paths to success. **Inquiry** encourages students to question assumptions about who can own property or invest in real estate. **Connection** links concepts to the neighborhoods and housing experiences students already know. **Holistic thinking** recognizes that students bring valuable community knowledge and different definitions of real estate success to their learning.

This unit integrates multiple National Standards for Personal Financial Education, particularly Spending (housing decisions), Investing (real estate as an investment vehicle), and Managing Credit (mortgages and financing), while helping students understand how real estate impacts personal wealth building.

I spend about two to three weeks on this unit, structured around these core topics:

- **Real Estate as Community Wealth Building:** Exploring how property shapes communities and family legacies, recognizing diverse housing experiences, and connecting neighborhood observations to economic concepts
- **Housing Decisions That Align with Life Goals:** Understanding buying vs. renting analysis, examining true costs of homeownership, and evaluating housing choices based on personal circumstances and values
- **Real Estate Investment Fundamentals:** Analyzing real estate markets using online tools, understanding cash flow and returns, and exploring strategies from house hacking to rental properties
- **Making Real Estate Accessible:** Identifying barriers and solutions, exploring first-time buyer programs, and connecting family stories to wealth-building strategies

Empowering Educator Talk

Suggestions for confidence-building language in exploring real estate topics

- "If real estate feels overwhelming, that's normal—most people start out unsure."
- "Everyone is new at first. Let's focus on learning the fundamentals and building knowledge over time."
- "Whether you want to buy, rent, invest, or simply understand how housing shapes wealth, you belong in these conversations."
- "Your neighborhood knowledge is valuable. You understand your community in ways that outside investors never will."
- "Renting is a valid and strategic choice. It can offer stability and flexibility while you work toward other goals."
- "You don't need perfect credit or a huge down payment. There are programs designed to support first-time buyers from many backgrounds."

Student Discussion Questions

Quick prompts designed to ignite student conversation

- What are your personal experiences with real estate, such as renting, owning a home, or seeing family members invest in property?
- Are you interested in owning your own home? Are you interested in becoming a landlord? Why or why not?

- How does real estate align with your personal financial goals and values?
- How might real estate investing positively impact your life and the lives of others?
- What ethical considerations should you think about when investing in real estate?
- What's the difference between paying rent and paying a mortgage?
- How does gentrification affect your community?
- What questions would you ask before buying your first property?

Quick Activities (5–15 minutes)

Perfect activities for warm-ups, transitions, or when you have extra time

- **Home Search Challenge:** Give students a fixed budget (e.g., $150,000, $300,000, $750,000, or $2 million). Students find a home that fits their needs and values. They compare what different regions offer: size, location, walkability, climate, and community features. Discuss how the cost of living, geography, and local economies shape housing prices.
- **Real Estate Math Lightning Round:** Short, clear prompts that build numeracy and vocabulary without overwhelming students. You can even turn it into a friendly competition, if that energizes your class. Examples: If rent increases 3 percent each year, what will it be next year? If property taxes are 1.2 percent of the home price, how much is that on a $350,000 home? A home costs $400,000. What's a 10 percent down payment? A 20 percent down payment?
- **Property Pitch Speed Round:** Students get a real listing and two minutes to pitch it as an investment or a place to live. Rotate quickly to hear different perspectives. Vote on the most convincing pitch or the best deal.
- **Neighborhood Snapshot:** Students choose one address in their neighborhood (home, school, or a nearby building). They look it up on Zillow/Redfin/Realtor.com; note the estimated value, property type, and year built; and reflect on changes they've observed over time.

Standalone Activities (20–50 minutes)

Exercises that can fit into any lesson, with added discussion to extend learning

- **Real Estate Career Exploration:** Students explore careers in the real estate field.
    - Research different real estate careers (agent, investor, property manager, appraiser, and developer) using CareerOneStop.org.
    - Find required education, typical earnings, and day-to-day responsibilities, and present findings if time permits.

- **First-Time Homebuyer Simulation:** Students get hands-on experience and analyze real costs of residential real estate.
  - Use real local listings found on sites like Zillow or Redfin.
  - Calculate total costs of homeownership including down payment, closing costs, monthly payments, insurance, taxes, and maintenance using the mortgage calculator on calculator.net.
- **Investment Property Analysis Using Four Square Method:** Students analyze investment properties and evaluate whether they are good deals or not.
  - Students choose a market based on their "Where Should I Live?" inquiry.
  - Find a property to analyze within that market.
  - Use BiggerPockets Four Square Method PDF to evaluate the investment potential.
  - Allow students space to showcase their analysis and share if they found a cash flowing property.
- **Zip Code Detective:** Explore neighborhoods using maps and charts from the US Census Bureau or niche.com/places-to-live. This connects personal experience with real estate, demographics, and economic data.
  - Enter your home zip code into data.census.gov.
  - Examine maps, charts, and reports that describe your community's population trends, housing characteristics, income and employment, education levels, homeownership rates, and racial and ethnic diversity.
  - Reflect on the discoveries: What information feels familiar based on your lived experience? What surprises you or feels new? What patterns do you notice? How might these insights affect how people buy homes or build wealth here?

EDUCATOR RESOURCES

Curriculum Resources

Free, ready-to-use lesson plans and activities to ground your real estate unit

- **Intuit for Education:** Credit Unit (Mortgages)
- **Khan Academy:** Personal Finance Unit 6 (Housing)
- **Next Gen Personal Finance (NGPF):** Buying a House Mini-Unit

CHAPTER 11

NAVIGATING WEB3

The most exciting—and possibly most intimidating—chapter is here: teaching Web3. Web3 is a decentralized version of the internet. It's built on blockchain technology, where people can own digital assets, make transactions directly with each other, and participate in new digital economies. If that definition feels like a lot to you, you're not alone. Educators are charged with explaining what is undoubtedly the most uncomfortable topic in financial literacy. The newness, expansiveness, and digital nature of this topic make it overwhelming for many teachers. This is exactly why it needs to be featured in a financial education text. We break down the basics in this chapter because adult fears cannot outrun how quickly Web3 will impact our students' lives.

This year, I started my crypto unit by walking in wearing my son's LED light up mask. I clicked through the options to find the scrolling binary matrix numbers glowing in bright blue and green, turned off the lights, and frantically waved my arms while intoning in a deep voice, "It's time for emerging technologyyyyy."

I lean into the mysterious nature of cryptocurrency and Web3 because I like to get a cheap laugh. But I also know the blossoming Web3 world feels cryptic and overwhelming to many of us. Personally, I'm excited—I think it has the ability to change our world entirely, and there are so many fascinating uses for new technology—*and* it still scares me. I'm excited to explore in this chapter how we can teach it in a way that addresses our discomfort and benefits our students.

Blockchain and cryptocurrency put most of us out of our comfort zone completely. It's a whole new financial world that is changing our lives and teaching instincts. I have watched countless Coin Bureau YouTube videos and read books from various perspectives, including *The Truth About Crypto* by Ric Edelman, *Bubble or Revolution?* by Neel Mehta, *The Future of Money* by Eswar S. Prasad, *Three Steps to Quantum Wealth* by Linda P. Jones, and *Number*

Go Up by Zeke Faux, yet I still need to refresh my memory every single time I teach it. And that's okay. We don't need to be sages on stages, especially in this topic. We can model curiosity, flexibility, and humility while navigating a digital world in real time alongside our students.

DEFINING WEB3: BEYOND THE HYPE

As educators, we are in the perfect moment to immerse ourselves in learning about Web3 at its genesis. Interestingly enough, this topic is a lot more digestible for students, most of whom have been raised since birth in a largely digital world.

The urgency of understanding emerging tech is real. My students are already hearing about Bitcoin from social media, YouTube, and their older siblings. This isn't some tinfoil hat theory; it's already part of their financial world. As the world moves at whiplash speed, we can embrace a growth mindset and join the journey. Let's co-learn, co-question, and cocreate spaces where Web3 is a little intimidating but also empowering.

What Is Web3?

Web3 is described as the next evolution of the internet. It aims to be more decentralized, meaning no single company owns or controls it. And the goal is to be user-controlled, giving people more say over their own information and online experience. Supporters believe this new internet could give people more power over their online money and data and offer new ways of doing business. Web3 is still being built, so it requires educators to be more vulnerable in learning alongside their students for much of the ride.

To make sense of baby Web3, let's start with its internet ancestors.

Web 1.0 (1990s–2000s): The Static Web

This was the first iteration of the World Wide Web. Web 1.0 was like a digital bulletin board. It was static, read-only, and built for browsing rather than interaction. Websites like Netscape.com or early Yahoo pages offered basic info with no commenting or sharing features. You'd visit, read, and leave. No logins, no likes, just access.

Web 2.0 (2000s–2020s): The Interactive Web

This is the internet that most of us know and understand—interacting through social media, blogs, streaming, and comments. Websites became spaces for connection and creativity. You could post, share, and build communities instead of just browsing. Do you still remember your AIM screen name? Mine was Toofresh28—don't judge me. But behind the interaction, centralized platforms—run by big tech companies like Facebook, Google, and Amazon—make money off your data. In this version of the web, you and I are using the internet, and we are also part of what's being sold.

Web3 (2020s and Beyond): The Decentralized Web

This iteration has its building blocks in place, and the shift is happening. In this decentralized version of the internet, users own their data, digital assets, and online identity. Instead of companies controlling data and processes, the control is distributed across networks of users. It's sort of like going from renting your digital life to owning it.

Understanding the Shift from Centralized to Decentralized

In most shifts in society, every action is a reaction. Web3 is emerging in response to both the positive and negative aspects of Web 2.0. Centralized systems are like traditional banks—one institution controls your money, makes the rules, and can freeze your account. All your transactions flow through that single gatekeeper.

Web 2.0 mostly works the same way: Big companies control the platforms we use every day. There are pros and cons to this model, but understanding how centralized systems work helps us understand why the shift toward decentralization is happening. Here are the pros and cons of centralized systems:

- **Easy to use:** Familiar platforms offer smooth interfaces.
- **Customer support:** Help is usually available if something goes wrong.
- **Security measures:** Large organizations invest in protecting users.
- **Less control:** Companies can change policies or even block access.
- **Privacy concerns:** User data may be tracked and sold.
- **Fees and restrictions:** Middlemen often charge for services.

Decentralized systems are more like a group of peers keeping a shared record of transactions. Everyone has a copy, and the group has to agree on decisions. No single person or company is in charge. Web3 works this way by spreading control across a network instead of relying on one central authority. Here are the pros and cons of decentralized systems:

- **More control:** Users often own their identities and assets.
- **Greater transparency:** Rules and data are typically visible to everyone.

- **Censorship-resistant:** Harder for any single authority to block access or information.
- **Lack of support:** There's usually no built-in customer service to help.
- **Security risks:** Losing your private "key" or access can mean losing your assets.
- **Scams and bugs:** Open systems can attract bad actors and have technical issues.

Is Web3 Just a Fad?

My principal, Noah, has a running "joke" where he surprises me by popping into my room and yelling "Scam!" whenever I teach Web3. No matter how many blockchain or crypto articles he asks me to explain, he's deeply skeptical of these abstract, rapidly evolving changes. Plus he loves a dad joke, so round and round we go. It's similar to how people reacted to the internet when it first came out, like that 1995 *Newsweek* article "The Internet? Bah!" or when the *Daily Mail* in 2000 wrote that the internet "may be just a passing fad."[1]

I suppose it's the contrarian in me, but whenever there's a lot of fear, I get curious. Fear has been at the core of every revolution. Think about Web 1.0 and Web 2.0. We couldn't imagine sending text to someone's computer. Who would want to do that? In a 1995 interview, David Letterman questioned Bill Gates about the internet: "What the hell is that exactly?" Gates explains how people can have their own homepages and send emails. Letterman is doubtful, but then Gates mentions you can listen to a baseball game on your computer. Letterman fires back, "Does 'radio' ring a bell?" The crowd laughs. Then Gates tries to explain that you can also listen to the game "whenever you want," leading Letterman to quip, "Do 'tape recorders' ring a bell?"[2] More audience laughter. In case you forgot, there was plenty of initial confusion and skepticism surrounding the internet's value in its early days.

Their exchange is so funny because now, no one can imagine a world without the internet. In just about thirty years, our whole lives have completely changed because of this technology. I don't know if it will be the same in the next thirty years, but I do know that we need to prepare ourselves and our students to be knowledgeable about emerging technology and able to navigate the world as it evolves. What helps me see the value of Web3 is understanding how it can be used in the real world. Let's think about how we can continue to make the mental shift and open our minds to the possibilities of Web3.

Key Web3 Building Blocks

To be sure, the transition from a centralized to a decentralized internet requires a big mental shift. It can feel completely abstract. To truly understand its potential, we need to see how it affects the lives of people like us. In this section, we'll break down common Web3 terms and connect them to tangible, real-world applications. When these concepts feel relevant to our lived experiences, that mental leap becomes much easier, and the ideas start to click IRL.

BLOCKCHAIN: A digital ledger, or record book, shared across many computers, built as a chain of blocks containing transactions. Each block is locked to the previous block with cryptography. So if someone tries to change information in an old block, it would break the chain and everyone would notice. Imagine if every student has a copy of the classroom attendance and someone tries to change their attendance after the fact; everyone else's copy would show the fraud.

Real-world examples: A hip coffee shop records every step of its beans' journey on the blockchain, so customers can easily see if their oat milk latte was ethically sourced. A nonprofit uses blockchain to track donations, making sure all the charitable funds are spent as promised.

SMART CONTRACTS: Software programs stored on a blockchain that run automatically when specified conditions are met. Think of it like a vending machine: You put in money, select your item, and the machine delivers it without a human in the middle.

Real-world examples: A freelance graphic designer sets up a smart contract to automatically get paid as soon as their client approves their work. A college student creates a crowdfunding agreement where their tuition payments are released only after they achieve a specific GPA.

DIGITAL ASSETS: Items you can own digitally, from cryptocurrencies to digital art to virtual real estate. Unlike most digital files, which can be copied infinitely, these assets have proof of ownership built into the blockchain.

Real-world examples: A gamer buys a galactic sword in an online game that only they own and can trade or sell to other players. An artist creates a digital comic with limited editions, and each one comes with a verifiable certificate of ownership.

CRYPTOCURRENCY: Digital money protected by cryptography, designed to work independently of banks or governments. Bitcoin was the first cryptocurrency, but now there are thousands with different purposes, like sending money quickly, running apps without a company in charge, or helping people keep their finances private.

Real-world examples: Someone sends money to family overseas using cryptocurrency like bitcoin (BTC) or USDC, a stablecoin, to avoid money transfer services fees. A traveler books an international hotel using Ether (ETH).

NFTS (NON-FUNGIBLE TOKENS): Digital certificates of ownership for unique items—often digital art but could be anything from concert tickets to virtual trading cards.

Real-world examples: NBA Top Shot sells NFTs of official game highlights, letting fans own a specific iconic moment, like a LeBron dunk, forever. Bored Ape Yacht Club are digital art collectibles that double as membership passes to exclusive events —their dramatic rise and fall in value offers a real-world lesson in the volatility of digital assets.

DEFI (DECENTRALIZED FINANCE): Peer-to-peer financial services like lending, borrowing, and trading that work without banks or middlemen. Instead, everything runs on decentralized blockchain networks.

Real-world examples: A college student supplies some of their crypto (for example, ETH or USDC) on a platform such as Aave and earns interest, all without needing a bank. A small business owner borrows funds by using their digital assets as collateral, rather than going through a traditional bank.

DAOS (DECENTRALIZED AUTONOMOUS ORGANIZATIONS): Digital communities run by code, where members use tokens to vote on decisions. Rules are built into smart contracts, so operations happen automatically. No single person is in charge.

Real-world example: A charity DAO designed for philanthropy where members pool crypto funds for good causes. They vote on where donations go, and smart contracts ensure funds are sent automatically and transparently.

DAPPS (DECENTRALIZED APPLICATIONS): Apps that run on blockchain networks instead of centralized servers.

Real-world examples: A music app lets fans vote on which artist gets funding, and each token they own holds decision power. A ride-sharing service app operates without a central company, and drivers and riders share profits directly.

When I learned about these real-world applications, or use cases, it became clear to me that Web3 is bigger than just meme coins. The way we use and exchange money is changing completely. Students will find these Web3 building blocks in their games, social media, and even future careers. Learning about these tools means getting the digital money skills they'll need for their future jobs and finances. All of these exciting possibilities are powered by a foundational technology: blockchain.

UNDERSTANDING BLOCKCHAIN TECHNOLOGY

Emphasize not what blockchain is, but what it can do for you.

—RIC EDELMAN, financial advisor and author

While cryptocurrencies are the most widely known Web3 concept, we have to understand the underlying blockchain technology that powers them. Blockchain is a secure digital ledger shared across many computers. It records transactions in blocks that are linked together, making it nearly impossible to change past data. It's the infrastructure, or the railroad tracks, that cryptocurrencies ride on.

The Blockchain Trilemma

As Ric Edelman, renowned financial advisor and author of *The Truth About Crypto* (highly recommended for understanding this wonky world), explained to me, blockchain technology is really just software. Students need to understand "what this technology is, how it works, why it was developed, what it is being used for today, and what it is expected to be used for in the future."[3]

One of the most helpful concepts Edelman shared with me is what he calls "the trilemma." He explains that the goal in financial systems has always been "to move money as fast as possible, as safely as possible, and as inexpensively as possible, and to do all of that at scale." The challenge is that "it's easy to accomplish two of those three. It's very difficult and in fact, nobody has yet figured out how to do all three, so this is the big dilemma and distributed ledger technology is the most advanced solution to date."

Think about it. You might use Venmo because it is fast and cheap, but it requires trust in a centralized company—PayPal. Cash is private and doesn't require intermediaries, but it's not practical for large transactions across distances. Credit cards work globally but have high fees and security risks. Blockchain technology attempts to solve all three challenges simultaneously.

Making Blockchain Tangible: A Hands-on Experience in Decentralization

The biggest challenge I face teaching blockchain is that it's completely digital and abstract. Bitcoin is a purely digital asset behind a screen. There is nothing physical that you can connect it with. That's why we start this learning with a hands-on activity, so students can actually visualize the core ideas of blockchain and decentralization.

Here's how I present it in class: You'll work in small groups, acting as nodes, like individual computers in a vast network. Each group gets a ledger (a lined sheet of paper) to keep track of everyone's money, with lines for debits and credits. I'll assign each of you a random amount of money to start.

Now, when someone wants to make a transaction—say, Kalisa is buying a bacon, egg, and cheese—your group (node) has to decide: Can this transaction happen? Does Kalisa have enough money? To "verify" it on our "blockchain," we need consensus. Everyone in the class, acting as their own node, has to approve the transaction. If there's a disagreement, you'll have to show your math (that's our cryptography) to prove if it's right or wrong, until we all reach consensus. Once approved, you'll highlight that line on your ledger, showing it's added to our "blockchain" of shared transactions.

This is an intentionally simplified activity—not a perfect model but enough to make the abstract click. Here's what you just experienced:

- **Decentralization:** Instead of one person (like me, the teacher) holding all the official records, every node (small group) has an identical copy of the ledger. This means no single person or company controls the information. If one copy of the ledger got crumpled up in a book bag or lost, everyone else would still have the correct history.
- **Consensus:** For any transaction to be added, the majority of the nodes (groups) had to agree it was valid. This ensures honesty and prevents cheating.
- **Cryptographic security (the "math" part):** Just as you had to show your math to prove a transaction was valid, real blockchain uses complex math to link each new transaction to the previous ones. If someone tries to change an old entry, it breaks the mathematical chain, and everyone on the network knows something is wrong.

BEYOND CURRENCY: REAL-WORLD APPLICATIONS

Blockchain technologies aren't just for digital money. They also have real-world applications that directly impact our daily lives. Companies are already working to create and implement these very uses. In fact, blockchain might even open up new jobs for students, jobs that don't even exist today. Ric Edelman's advice to "emphasize not what blockchain is, but what it can do for you" resonates with me. To truly understand what it can do for us, let's explore some everyday scenarios where this technology is already making a difference.

Transparent Supply Chains

- What's the real story behind your fish dinner? Imagine scanning a QR code on your salmon's package to see its entire journey. You'd see the catch date, the boat's name, whether it was wild-caught or farmed, and every step of its handling from the ocean to your plate.
- Who made your clothes? You scan a QR code on your shirt to instantly see its path from raw material to factory to store. You could verify what its material sources are and if it was made ethically.

Medical Records

- Have to fill out another medical intake form and blanked on half your medical history? Think about your entire medical history securely stored on a blockchain — ensuring your care providers always have your latest, most accurate records no matter where you get treatment, and giving you complete control over who sees it.

Real Estate and Property Records

- Buying a home, simplified? Imagine if buying or selling a house becomes faster and safer. Property records on a blockchain could prevent fraud and speed up transfers between seller and buyer. Steps like verifying ownership and transferring title that took months could be reduced to weeks or even hours, giving you clear, undeniable ownership.

Automated Smart Contracts

- Pay rent and need repairs? Let's say a renter and landlord set up a smart contract where the rent is automatically released from the tenant's account to the landlord's only after the landlord confirms a repair has been completed.

- Is your flight delayed? What if an airline set up a smart contract that automatically sends you a refund or compensation if your flight is delayed by more than three hours, based on verifiable flight data.

Digital Identity and Voter Verification

- Is your vote truly counted? Imagine a voting system where your unique digital identity ensures your vote is securely recorded and instantly verifiable by anyone. This makes elections incredibly transparent and highly resistant to fraud.

Digital Ownership (NFTs)

- Is that event ticket real or fake? Picture buying a concert ticket that's an NFT. It's truly yours, can't be counterfeited. You could even resell it directly to another fan, with the artist getting a small cut automatically.
- Is that signed jersey authentic? A significant portion of signed memorabilia is fake. But what if you bought a signed sports jersey and an NFT acts as its digital certificate of authenticity? You could scan a code and instantly verify the athlete's signature and the item's entire ownership history.

CRYPTOCURRENCY BASICS: BITCOIN AND BEYOND

Now that we understand the blockchain foundation, it's time to introduce its lead singer: cryptocurrency. Students have already heard about people making—or losing—fortunes with bitcoin and meme coins. This is where students' eyes light up because they are eager to connect their prior knowledge with education.

What Makes Cryptocurrency Different

Traditional fiat money, like the US dollar, is issued and controlled by governments. Cryptocurrencies, however, are created and maintained by networks of computers running blockchain software. You can buy, sell, and trade these cryptocurrencies on exchanges like Coinbase and Binance. No single entity controls them, which is both their strength and their challenge.

This decentralized "no single entity controls them" situation means you become your own bank, and you hold the responsibility for taking care of your crypto. A seed phrase is a series of twelve to twenty-four random words that acts as the master key to your cryptocurrency wallet.

Try this experiment. Take one minute to memorize this seed phrase: trot, sword, where, noodle, joy, eagle, shimmer, tuna, backbone, museum, gossip, river. Now, cover the words up and see how many you can remember in order.

No matter how much ginkgo biloba you drink, it's not going to happen. This is why you must write your seed phrases down and never lose them. Unlike in traditional banking, there's no customer service to call if you lose access. Lose the seed phrase to recover your private key, and your cryptocurrency is gone forever. Just ask poor James Howells, a British man who accidentally threw away a hard drive with the private key for eight thousand bitcoins in 2013. He's been digging through landfills to find it ever since. To put that in perspective, eight thousand bitcoins multiplied by today's price adds up to hundreds of millions of dollars. To be fair, I'd still be digging too. The same thing happened to me, though it was a far less valuable coin; it irks me to this day I lost the seed phrase.

Bitcoin: The Original Cryptocurrency

Bitcoin was created in 2009. It's considered digital gold because it's a store of value that can't be controlled by any government or institution. You can read its famous white paper (only nine pages!) describing why it was created after the 2008 financial crisis. It was written by Satoshi Nakamoto, whose identity is still a mystery.

Here's why Bitcoin is unique:

- **Limited supply:** Only twenty-one million bitcoins will ever exist, making it scarce like gold.
- **Decentralized:** No central bank, government, or single company controls it.
- **Digital:** It exists only as data on the blockchain. There's nothing physical to hold.
- **Global:** It works the same way everywhere in the world, 24/7.

Altcoins: Beyond Bitcoin

After the success of Bitcoin, more than ten thousand alternative cryptocurrencies, or "altcoins" have been created. While some altcoins are designed for real-world applications and specific technologies, others are created primarily for speculation or entertainment, with little or no underlying purpose. It's important for students to understand that not all coins are created equal.

Here are some common types of altcoins you might hear about:

- **Ethereum (ETH):** This platform was developed for smart contracts and decentralized applications, and its native cryptocurrency, ether (ETH), is used to pay for transactions and computations on the network. It's the second-largest cryptocurrency after bitcoin.
- **XRP:** Designed for fast, low-cost international money transfers—often used by banks to move money across borders quickly.
- **Stablecoins:** These are designed to maintain a stable price, usually by being tied, or pegged, to a real-world asset like the US dollar. This makes them useful for everyday transactions or for avoiding the price swings of other cryptocurrencies. USD Coin (USDC) is an example of a stablecoin.
- **Utility tokens:** These altcoins give you access to specific services or features within a particular blockchain project. They are like tokens for an online arcade. Chainlink (LINK) is a utility token example that connects blockchains to real-world data.
- **Meme coins:** Created often as a joke or based on internet memes, like Dogecoin or Shiba Inu, these altcoins usually don't have a specific technological purpose but gain value from community popularity and social media trends.

Central Bank Digital Currencies (CBDCs)

Central bank digital currencies (CBDCs) are often in the same conversation as cryptocurrencies. While they are a form of digital money, CBDCs are fundamentally different from cryptocurrency like bitcoins and altcoins. They are issued and controlled by a country's central bank, like the Federal Reserve in the US, not a decentralized network. CBDCs are mostly just a digital version of your country's paper money, still government-issued, still government-controlled, just in digital form.

Several countries have already embraced CBDCs and many more are on the horizon. The Bahamas was one of the first countries to officially launch a national CBDC, called the Sand Dollar. Nigeria was the first African country to launch a CBDC, eNaira. Many other countries, including the US and in Europe, are researching or piloting their own versions, like Sweden's e-krona and India's digital rupee.

Common Crypto Questions

Since cryptocurrencies and blockchain technology are relatively new, we all have a lot of questions about them. Here are some common questions I hear often:

"IS BITCOIN A SCAM?" Bitcoin itself isn't a scam, but many scams involve cryptocurrencies. The technology is legitimate, but like any new technology, it attracts both legitimate and fraudulent uses. As educators, we need to teach students about common scams like phishing, which tries to trick them into revealing private keys or seed phrases. The golden rule: Never share your seed phrase with anyone, ever. If you ever use cryptocurrency, write your seed phrase on paper (not digitally), store it somewhere secure, and remember that being your own bank means you're responsible for your own security.

"WHY DOES THE PRICE CHANGE SO MUCH?" Cryptocurrency markets are young and smaller than traditional markets. This makes them more volatile. Prices can swing dramatically based on news, government regulations, and even social media posts. It's important for learners and interested investors to understand that cryptocurrency is a very volatile asset that creates the possibility of big gains and also carries the real risk of big losses. This is why cryptocurrency is considered a speculative asset rather than a stable investment.

"SHOULD I INVEST IN CRYPTO?" That's a personal decision that depends on your financial situation, risk tolerance, and goals. Take time to research the white papers, so you can understand the function of the coins in which you are investing. And of course, never invest more than you can afford to lose.

Ric Edelman's practical approach helped me think about this question differently. Rather than getting caught up in hype or fear, he suggests a measured approach: Consider allocating 1 percent of your portfolio to cryptocurrency. This allows you to participate in the potential growth while limiting risk to your overall financial health.

EDUCATING FOR THE DIGITAL AGE: OUR ROLE IN WEB3

We need to help children understand how money works in a digital age and increasingly that money is going to work through blockchain technology.

—RIC EDELMAN, award-winning financial advisor and author

So how do we move past our knee-jerk dismissals and help students understand these concepts objectively?

Making It Real for Students

One of the biggest challenges I face teaching this unit is helping students grasp something that's entirely digital. Edelman discussed how the financial services industry "always has this dilemma because it deals in intangibles." He explained that fifty years ago, investing felt more concrete because "you received as an investor, a stock certificate or a bond certificate. You actually got a piece of paper that you held in your hands, and it was something real, but now we don't have that." With cryptocurrency, the challenge is even greater because "bitcoin is a purely digital asset. There is nothing physical that you can associate it with."

Instead of getting lost in the technical details of how blockchain works, I focus on what it can enable students to do. We talk about goals they might have—going to college, buying a car, traveling, starting a business—and explore how understanding these technologies might open new pathways to achieve those goals.

Addressing Our Own Discomfort

I'll be the first to admit that teaching Web3 topics regularly pushes me out of my comfort zone. Many educators worry about teaching topics where they don't feel expert-level confidence. This concern is valid but manageable.

Edelman points out that teachers "tend to be safer and conservative as opposed to entrepreneurs." (That makes sense: We are the people who chose a stable, pensioned career!) He clarifies that "is not incorrect. It's not invalid. It's simply a bias." We just have to be aware that our conservative investor bias may come through in conversations with students, potentially overstating the level of risk without even knowing it.

His outlook is also how I approach financial education: We should expose students to the entire "universe of content." This includes the pros and cons, the good and bad, and the risk-versus-profit spectrum for every asset class. In doing so, we provide a more balanced and comprehensive understanding.

This perspective transforms our role from crypto cheerleader or skeptic to critical thinking facilitator. We can explore Web3 technologies alongside our students, modeling intellectual curiosity while maintaining healthy skepticism. (Shout-out to NGPF's Cryptocurrency Certification courses, led by Yanely Espinal, for delivering unbiased, research-based content that balances opportunities and risks!)

From "Sage on the Stage" to "Guide on the Side"

One of my favorite insights from Ric Edelman came when I asked about how educators can start building knowledge themselves outside their comfort zone. He referenced a movement in educational circles about going from sage on the stage to guide on the side and explained that "since this technology is new to everyone, it might be better to learn with students side by side. They go through that journey, and they'll be able to learn together. The teacher can provide guidance as to what seems to be legitimate versus what seems to be a scam, what seems to be biased or incomplete information."

This approach inspires me in how I teach this unit. No pressure. I'm not pretending to be a cryptocurrency expert. I'm positioning myself as a fellow learner who happens to have some skills in evaluating sources, asking critical questions, and making connections to other financial concepts we've learned.

Take prediction markets, for example: Platforms like Kalshi and Polymarket allow people to bet on the outcomes of future events like elections, economic situations, weather, or even wars. These are emerging so rapidly that I'm often learning about new platforms, regulations, and use cases from my students. Rather than pretending to have all the answers on topics that change by the second, I embrace being comfortably uncomfortable in this messy middle. When a student asks, "Miss, do you bet on prediction markets?" I use my favorite move and answer their question with a question: "Should I?" The next day, we look at top prediction market headlines together, evaluate the technology's potential and risks, and have conversations about the ethics of each situation to build critical thinking. This is "guide on the side" in practice.

WHY TEACH WEB3 LITERACY

Although intimidating, avoiding these next-level topics leaves students vulnerable to misinformation, scams, and missed opportunities for understanding the evolving financial world.

Already Engaged with Web3

Our students will encounter Web3 technologies whether we teach them or not. They might receive cryptocurrency as gifts, encounter NFT projects in gaming, or be targeted by crypto scams on social media. The question is whether they'll navigate these experiences with knowledge or confusion.

Ric Edelman makes this point when he talks about how "we need to help children understand how money works in a digital age and increasingly that money is going to work through blockchain technology." Just as we teach students about traditional banking even though many have never written a check and barely use cash, we need to teach them about digital finance systems they're already encountering.

I also lean into the fact that students are, in some ways, better equipped to engage with Web3 than I am. Living and growing up in the digital age, they are comfortable with digital transactions, online gaming economies, and virtual relationships in ways that feel natural to them.

The Digital Economy Is Here

Understanding Web3 technologies is increasingly relevant for students' economic futures. Blockchain technology applications affect so many aspects of our economic world, like supply chain management and smart contracts for business transactions. These innovations are reshaping how people work, create, and earn.

A new wave of economic participation is also emerging, especially within the rapidly expanding creator economy. Many of our students are already part of this world. Web3 technologies are creating unprecedented ways for creators to monetize their work, offering career and entrepreneurial paths that didn't exist a decade ago:

- Artists can sell digital art as NFTs and earn royalties on future sales.
- Content creators can be paid directly by fans with cryptocurrency.
- Musicians can tokenize their work and share ownership with fans.
- Writers can publish on decentralized platforms and keep more of their earnings.

None of us imagined "influencer" or "content creator" would be jobs when we were kids. Your feelings about them as professions is beside the point. Just like the rest of our social constructs, if enough people believe it is a thing, it is a thing. Students who understand Web3's economic and career impacts will be better positioned to evaluate opportunities and participate meaningfully in this evolving digital economy.

Digital World, Real Money

We know that financial education works best when it connects to students' immediate reality and future goals, and Web3 technologies increasingly intersect with both. According to a 2024 Pew Research Center study, 17 percent of US adults have invested in, traded, or used cryptocurrency. Adoption rates are increasing faster among younger demographics, including 42 percent of men aged eighteen to twenty-nine.[4] More urgently, cryptocurrency and blockchain technology discussions dominate social media platforms where our students spend significant time, often in the absence of reliable educational context.

The goal isn't to convince students to invest in cryptocurrency. Our role is to ensure they can make informed investment decisions based on knowledge rather than hype or fear.

Spotting the Scams

From a pedagogical perspective, teaching Web3 is an opportunity to teach students how to critically analyze digital content. What they learn equips them to evaluate malicious tactics such as pump-and-dump schemes, where promoters hype up a coin or NFT to drive prices higher before selling their own holdings for profit, or shilling, where individuals promote a project without disclosing that they are being paid, artificially inflating interest.

Consider the warning from Lee Myung-gi (Player 333) in *Squid Game*, who, after hyping a failed crypto investment, reminded his angry followers, "Whenever you're investing, in the end, it's up to you to make the final call based on your own judgment." Those players were not eager to hear that, but it highlights the importance of teaching personal responsibility and informed decision-making.

Final Thoughts: Teaching Through Uncertainty

Teaching Web3 technologies requires embracing uncertainty while maintaining educational rigor. We can prepare students for a financial future shaped by technologies we can't fully predict. Thankfully, our role isn't to have all the answers—it's to engage honestly and equip students with frameworks to ask good questions, evaluate new information, and make thoughtful decisions as the landscape evolves.

Ric Edelman's perspective on technological adoption really resonates with me here. He talks about how when the internet first emerged, "the notion of purchasing a product on the internet and entering your credit card into a search engine—it was like that was the scariest thing in the world—who on earth would do that?" And today, "every investor in the country owns Amazon simply because it's inside every stock ETF and mutual fund, so the same experience is being observed in bitcoin."

According to Edelman, we have "fifteen years of experience, fifteen years of performance, fifteen years of data, and it's a very different scenario today." The question isn't whether digital financial technologies will continue to evolve—they will. The question is whether our students will be prepared to navigate that evolution with confidence, knowledge, and appropriate caution.

Our students will inherit a world where digital and traditional finance increasingly come together. By teaching Web3 literacy now, we're giving them the tools.

The future of money is being written in code, but it will be shaped by human decisions. Let's make sure our students are prepared to participate in creating that future rather than simply reacting to it.

SELF-REFLECTION: YOUR WEB3 DREAMS AND FEARS

Your uncertainty is a teaching strength. When educators model critical thinking, students learn valuable skills for navigating complex topics throughout their lives. Before diving into the Web3 curriculum, take a moment to examine your own relationship with these technologies.

Personal Reflection

- $ What's your earliest memory of encountering Web3, crypto, or blockchain?
- $ Do you own crypto or NFTs? How has that shaped your view?
- $ What assumptions do you have about Web3? Do you think it's revolutionary, risky, or overhyped?
- $ How do you typically engage with new digital financial trends?
- $ What do others in your life say about these emerging technologies?

Educator Reflection

- $ How comfortable are you teaching topics where you're not an expert, like Web3?
- $ What concerns do you have about teaching speculative financial topics?
- $ How do you balance presenting pros and cons of Web3 technologies?
- $ How do you address student questions when you're still learning about a topic yourself?
- $ How do you balance presenting multiple perspectives while helping students develop critical thinking skills?

TEACHING APPLICATIONS: WEB3

Unit Overview

This unit requires balancing multiple truths simultaneously: Web3 technologies offer fascinating possibilities and significant risks. Our job is to equip students with knowledge, critical thinking skills, and practical frameworks for making informed decisions about their digital financial future. We explore Web3 by first examining how financial innovation and technological change will impact students' lives, then building toward technical understanding.

I approach Web3 education through the RICH framework to ensure every student feels empowered to make informed decisions about emerging financial technologies. **Representation** means featuring diverse voices in the Web3 space, from your educator perspective to tech innovators to skeptical economists, from young crypto enthusiasts to traditional finance experts. **Inquiry** encourages students to question both the hype and the criticism surrounding Web3, developing their own analytical frameworks. **Connection** links these modern technologies to financial concepts students already understand, like using digital banking, saving, investing, and evaluating risk. **Holistic thinking** recognizes that students bring to their learning varied relationships with technology, experiences with risk, and comfort levels with financial innovation.

This unit extends the Investing standard from the National Standards for Personal Financial Education into emerging digital assets, teaching students to evaluate cryptocurrency and blockchain technologies as speculative investments while understanding their unique risks and potential returns.

I spend about two weeks on this unit, structured around these core topics:

- **Understanding Blockchain Technology:** Demystifying distributed ledgers and exploring blockchain applications beyond cryptocurrency
- **Cryptocurrency Basics: Bitcoin and Beyond:** Examining digital currencies as both technology and investment, understanding what drives crypto values, and comparing different types of cryptocurrencies and their purposes
- **Web3 Applications and Digital Assets:** Exploring NFTs, DeFi, and DAOs through real-world examples, evaluating applications that solve genuine problems vs. speculative opportunities, and connecting Web3 to creative and entrepreneurial possibilities
- **Evaluating Opportunities and Risks:** Developing critical thinking frameworks for new financial technologies, identifying red flags and legitimate innovations, and creating personal guidelines for engaging with Web3 based on individual values and risk tolerance

Empowering Educator Talk

Suggestions for reframing language to build confidence in exploring Web3 topics

- **Instead of:** "This is really complicated technology that's hard to understand."
  Try: "We'll break down this new world together, one step at a time."
- **Instead of:** "You probably won't need to know about crypto; it's very specialized."
  Try: "Knowing Web3 helps you make stronger financial decisions, whether you decide to participate or not."
- **Instead of:** "This is just speculation and gambling."
  Try: "Like any investment, there are both opportunities and risks that we need to understand."

- **When students share skepticism:** "Your questions mean you're thinking critically. That's exactly what smart investors do. Let's examine both the potential and the pitfalls together."
- **When students show excitement:** "Love that energy! Now let's make sure we don't miss the fine print."

Student Discussion Questions

Quick prompts designed to ignite student conversation

- Have you ever heard family or friends talk about cryptocurrency? What did they say?
- What does ownership mean to you? How might digital ownership be different?
- If you could create a digital currency for your school, what would you want it to do?
- What questions would you ask before investing in any new technology?
- Is any money real? Why or why not?
- What are your biggest concerns about new financial technologies?
- Who do you trust for financial advice? How would you research Web3 investments?
- What role should the government play in regulating new technologies like cryptocurrency?
- How might Web3 technologies affect different communities differently?

Quick Activities (5–15 minutes)

Perfect activities for warm-ups, transitions, or when you have extra time

- **Blockchain Building:** Students create a physical blockchain with paper and tape. Give them a series of simple, funny, or hard problems to solve. Each student's answer adds a "transaction" to the chain, showing how information connects and becomes permanent.
- **Crypto or Not:** Show students various digital assets (bitcoins, loyalty points, gift cards, NFTs, ETH, Fortnite V-Bucks, Starbucks rewards, music streaming tokens, or Robux). Students decide what counts as cryptocurrency and then defend their reasoning.
- **Future Predictions:** Students write one prediction about how they think Web3 technology will affect their daily lives in ten years. Have students share predictions and discuss what assumptions they're making. Show the Bill Gates and David Letterman TV interview from 1995 to make comparisons.

- **Trust or Verify:** Present scenarios where students must decide whether they need a trusted middleman (bank, government, or company) or could use a decentralized system. Examples: Sending money to a friend, buying concert tickets from a stranger online, proving you graduated high school, getting a loan from a lender, or voting in an election
- **Seed Phrase Memory Game:** Ask a volunteer student to pick twelve random words—or use this example: ***pumpkin, table, lilac, happy, forest, surfboard, quick, bright, dream, quiet, friend, journey***. Give students one minute to memorize them. Then, cover the list and ask them to write all twelve in order on a whiteboard or paper—illustrating that with decentralization, you must securely record your seed phrase because trying to memorize it is nearly impossible.

Standalone Activities (20–50 minutes)

Exercises that can fit into any lesson, with added discussion to extend learning

- **Blockchain Applications Beyond Money:** Pairs of students research one real-world blockchain application—such as tracking where food comes from (supply chains), proving identity online without a middleman (digital identity), securing elections (voting systems), or verifying carbon-reduction projects (carbon credits). They create a one-slide presentation explaining how it works and whether they think it's actually useful. Students compare applications and discuss which ones actually solve real problems
  - Discussion prompt: Which Web3 application do you think has the most potential to improve people's lives, and why?

- **Scam or Legit?** Present students with various Web3 investment opportunities (some legitimate, some obvious scams, and some in the gray area). Have students work in groups to identify red flags and create criteria for evaluating Web3 investments. Include examples like established cryptocurrencies, obvious pump and dump schemes, celebrity-endorsed NFT projects, and DeFi protocols with unrealistic returns. Groups share their evaluation frameworks and discuss how these principles apply to traditional investments too.
  - Discussion prompt: Would you invest in any of these projects? Why? What were the most common red flags your group identified as indicators of risk?

- **White Paper Challenge:** Students, working individually or in small groups, receive two or three contrasting crypto white papers (a strong example, a questionable one, and a meme example) along with a white paper checklist to identify key sections: problem statement, proposed solution, team information, token utility (tokenomics), and road map. They use the checklist to note what's included and, more importantly, to spot red flags like vague language, anonymous teams, unrealistic promises, or unclear purpose. If there's time, students could share their findings.

- Discussion prompt: What's the core idea of this cryptocurrency? What problem is this project trying to solve? What's one positive sign you found in the white paper? What's one major red flag or concerning element you spotted?

EDUCATOR RESOURCES

Curriculum Resources

Free, ready-to-use lesson plans and activities to ground your Web3 unit

- **Banzai:** Tech- and AI-focused professional development (*Bringing Financial Literacy to Life: Practical Tech and AI Tools for Educators* by Wally Luckeydoo and *The Bionic Educator* by Eric Curts)
- **Intuit for Education:** Investing Unit (Navigating Alternative Investment Opportunities)
- **Khan Academy:** Financial Literacy Unit 16 (How Blockchain Works and Finance and Capital Markets) and "Bitcoin" in Unit 8 (Money, Banking and Central Banks)
- **Next Gen Personal Finance (NGPF):** Cryptocurrency Mini-Unit

APPENDIX

YOUR FINANCIAL LEARNING TOOL KIT

This appendix is your starting line for continued learning, whether you're deepening your own financial knowledge or looking for resources to share with students, colleagues, or family members. I've organized these resources based on how they've shown up in my own journey and in conversations with other educators. There is a lot of great content out there now. For additional resources, updated materials, and supplementary activities, visit the online appendix at www.beacon.org/MoneyTalksAppendix.

BOOKS

These are the books that shifted my perspective, helped me heal my money wounds, and gave me language for concepts I felt but couldn't articulate. Some are deeply personal, others are practical guides, but all of them made me a better financial educator.

For Getting Started (Your Financial Foundations)

- *Cultura and Cash: Lessons from the First Gen Mentor for Managing Finances and Cultural Expectations* by Giovanna González
- *Finance for the People: Getting a Grip on Your Finances* by Paco de Leon
- *Get Good with Money: Ten Simple Steps to Becoming Financially Whole* by Tiffany Aliche
- *I Will Teach You to Be Rich: No Guilt. No Excuses. Just a 6-Week Program That Works* by Ramit Sethi
- *Mind Your Money: Insightful Stories and Strategies to Help You Reach Your #MoneyGoals* by Yanely Espinal
- *Stacked: Your Super-Serious Guide to Modern Money Management* by Emily Guy Birken and Joe Saul-Sehy

For Understanding Your Money Mindset

These books help you work through money beliefs, heal financial wounds, and develop abundance thinking.

- *Deeper Than Money: Ditch Money Shame, Build Wealth, and Feel Confident AF* by Chloe Elise
- *The Emotional Life of Money: How Money Changes the Way We Think and Feel* by Mary Cross
- *The Financial Activist Playbook: 8 Strategies for Everyday People to Reclaim Wealth and Collective Well-Being* by Jasmine Rashid
- *Happy Money: The Japanese Art of Making Peace with Your Money* by Ken Honda
- *A Healthy State of Panic: Follow Your Fears to Build Wealth, Crush Your Career, and Win at Life* by Farnoosh Torabi
- *MoneyZen: The Secret to Finding Your "Enough"* by Manisha Thakor
- *The Soul of Money: Transforming Your Relationship with Money and Life* by Lynne Twist and Teresa Barker

For Spending Less and Saving More

- *The No-Spend Challenge Guide: How to Stop Spending Money Impulsively, Pay Off Debt Fast, and Make Your Finances Fit Your Dreams* by Jen Smith
- *The One-Page Financial Plan: A Simple Way to Be Smart About Your Money* by Carl Richards
- *You Need a Budget: The Proven System for Breaking the Paycheck-to-Paycheck Cycle, Getting Out of Debt, and Living the Life You Want* by Jesse Mecham

For Stock Market Investing

- *The Elements of Investing: Easy Lessons for Every Investor* by Burton G. Malkiel and Charles D. Ellis
- *Friends That Invest: Your Guide to Financial Independence Through Shares and Stocks* by Simran Kaur
- *A Random Walk Down Wall Street: The Time-Tested Strategy for Successful Investing* by Burton G. Malkiel
- *The Simple Path to Wealth: Your Road Map to Financial Independence and a Rich, Free Life* by J. L. Collins
- *Wealth Warrior: 8 Steps for Communities of Color to Conquer the Stock Market* by Linda Garcia

- *We Should All Be Millionaires: A Woman's Guide to Earning More, Building Wealth, and Gaining Economic Power* by Rachel Rodgers
- *You're Already a Wealth Heiress! Now Think and Act Like One* by Linda P. Jones

For Real Estate Investing

- *First-Time Home Buyer: The Complete Playbook to Avoiding Rookie Mistakes* by Scott Trench and Mindy Jensen
- *Real Estate 101: From Finding Properties and Securing Mortgage Terms to REITs and Flipping Houses* by Michele Cagan
- *Real Estate Rookie: 90 Days to Your First Investment* by Ashley Kehr
- *Retire on Real Estate: Building Rental Income for a Safe and Secure Retirement* by K. Kai Anderson

For Understanding Cryptocurrency and Web3

- *The Bitcoin Standard: The Decentralized Alternative to Central Banking* by Saifedean Ammous
- *Bubble or Revolution? The Future of Bitcoin, Blockchains, and Cryptocurrencies* by Neel Mehta, Aditya Agashe, and Parth Detroja
- *Three Steps to Quantum Wealth: The Wealth Heiress' Guide to Financial Freedom by Investing in Cryptocurrencies* by Linda P. Jones
- *The Truth About Crypto: A Practical, Easy-to-Understand Guide to Bitcoin, Blockchain, NFTs, and Other Digital Assets* by Ric Edelman

For Unique Perspectives on Wealth

- *Die with Zero: Getting All You Can from Your Money and Your Life* by Bill Perkins
- *The Psychology of Money: Timeless Lessons on Wealth, Greed, and Happiness* by Morgan Housel
- *Rich Dad Poor Dad: What the Rich Teach Their Kids About Money That the Poor and Middle Class Do Not!* by Robert Kiyosaki
- *The Richest Man in Babylon: Timeless Strategies for Building Wealth* by George S. Clason
- *The Wealthy Gardener: Life Lessons on Prosperity Between Father and Son* by John Soforic

For Classroom Reads

These books work well in the classroom—as assigned reading, in literature circles at the end of a unit, as book club selections, or simply as resources to keep on hand for students who want to explore further. They align with the Classroom Book Resources recommended at the end of most application chapters. As always, read these books in advance and use your discretion based on the age and needs of your students.

- *Cultura and Cash: Lessons from the First Gen Mentor for Managing Finances and Cultural Expectations* by Giovanna González
- *Friends That Invest: Your Guide to Financial Independence Through Shares and Stocks* by Simran Kaur
- *Get Good with Money: Ten Simple Steps to Becoming Financially Whole* by Tiffany Aliche
- *How to Money: Your Ultimate Guide to the Basics of Finance* by Jean Chatzky and Kathryn Tuggle
- *I Want More Pizza: Real World Money Skills for High School, College, and Beyond* by Steve Burkholder
- *I Will Teach You to Be Rich: No Guilt. No Excuses. Just a 6-Week Program That Works* by Ramit Sethi
- *Mind Your Money: Insightful Stories and Strategies to Help You Reach Your #MoneyGoals* by Yanely Espinal
- *Money Out Loud: All the Financial Stuff No One Taught Us* by Berna Anat
- *Napkin Finance: Build Your Wealth in 30 Seconds or Less* by Tina Hay
- *Rich AF: The Winning Money Mindset That Will Change Your Life* by Vivian Tu

PODCASTS

These are the voices that have kept me company on my morning subway rides. They make complex financial concepts accessible, though most of them are geared toward adult listeners. As you listen, you'll notice the difference between your educator lens and your learner lens; use your judgment. Sometimes there are short segments you can bring into the classroom. When I do that, I usually stick to five to ten minute clips, often found on YouTube, so I can project the interview. An asterisk (*) indicates podcasts I've successfully used with young people.

For Personal Finance Foundations

- *Afford Anything* with Paula Pant
- *Brown Ambition** with Mandi Woodruff and Tiffany Aliche
- *The Clever Girls Know* with Bola Sokunbi

- *Everyone's Talking Money* with Shannah Game
- *Financial Feminist* with Tori Dunlap
- *Journey to Launch* with Jamila Souffrant
- *Money with Katie* with Katie Gatti Tassin
- *Planet Money: The Economy Explained* from NPR
- *Planet Money: Summer School** from NPR
- *Popcorn Finance** with Chris Browning
- *So Money* with Farnoosh Torabi
- *Unicorn Millionaire* with Charly Stoever

For Learning About Investing and Business

- *Be Wealthy and Smart** with Linda P. Jones
- *BiggerPockets Money** with Mindy Jensen and Scott Trench
- *Earn Your Leisure** with Troy Millings and Rashad Bilal
- *Friends That Invest: Your Guide to Financial Independence Through Shares and Stocks* with Simran Kaur
- *Real Estate InvestHER Show* with Liz Faircloth and Andresa Guidelli
- *Real Estate Rookie** with Ashley Kehr and Tony J. Robinson
- *Yo Quiero Dinero* with Jannese Torres

ONLINE COMMUNITIES AND LEARNING PLATFORMS

These are all free, high-quality resources designed to support both educators and learners.

Banzai: Interactive financial literacy curriculum with real-world simulations for K–12 students (teachbanzai.com)

ChooseFI Foundation: Curriculum and resources focused on financial independence education for pre-K–12 students (choosefifoundation.org/prek12)

Council for Economic Education: Research, curriculum resources, and professional development for economic and financial education (councilforeconed.org)

EVERFI: Digital lessons covering financial literacy, entrepreneurship, and other life skills (everfi.com)

Federal Reserve Education Resources: Educational materials (federalreserveeducation.org) and the Dallas Fed's Building Wealth curriculum (dallasfed.org/educate)

Federal Trade Commission Resources: Bulk-order materials on credit, debt, budgeting, and mortgages for students, families, and communities (bulkorder.ftc.gov)

Intuit for Education: Interactive financial literacy lessons with real-world simulations, including budgeting games and investing units (intuitforeducation.com)

Jump$tart Coalition: National financial education resources and state-by-state standards (jumpstart.org)

Khan Academy: Articles and video-based lessons on personal finance topics, including blockchain, banking systems, and foundational concepts (khanacademy.org/college-careers-more/financial-literacy)

Next Gen Personal Finance (NGPF): Curriculum resources, professional development, and the go-to for tracking financial education mandates across the US (ngpf.org)

Vanguard Classroom Tools: Classroom-ready tools that engage students in budgeting, saving, and investing through hands-on activities and a market simulator (myclassroomeconomy.org/home)

Visual Capitalist: Online graphs and data visualizations about markets and money (visualcapitalist.com)

Working in Support of Education (W!se): Certification programs and professional development for financial educators (wise-ny.org/programs-services/certifications)

FURTHER LEARNING: TOOLS AND RESEARCH

Self-Assessment and Reflection

- **Brené Brown's List of Values:** Comprehensive values list for classroom activities and personal reflection (brenebrown.com/resources/dare-to-lead-list-of-values)
- **FINRA Financial Knowledge Quiz:** Test your own financial literacy (finra.org/financial_knowledge_quiz)
- **Klontz Money Script Inventory:** Identify your unconscious money beliefs (bradklontz.com/moneyscriptstest)

Money News and Newsletters

Curated (and free) sources for staying current on financial topics

- ***Sherwood News***: Daily financial news newsletter written for modern investors (sherwood.news)
- ***Market Briefs Newsletter***: Concise daily market updates and financial news (marketbriefs.com)
- ***Morning Brew***: Accessible daily business news (morningbrew.com)
- ***The Hustle***: Daily tech and business news with personality (thehustle.co)
- ***Finimize***: Global financial news made simple and accessible (finimize .com)

Research and Articles Worth Reading

- Board of Governors of the Federal Reserve System, *Survey of Consumer Finances (SCF)*, 2023, https://www.federalreserve.gov/econres/scfindex.htm
- John Hope Bryant, "Financial Literacy Is the Civil Rights Issue of This Generation," *Time*, Feb. 13, 2024, https://time.com/6694236/financial-literacy-john-hope-bryant/
- Consumer Financial Protection Bureau, "Financial Well-Being: The Goal of Financial Education," May 30, 2019, https://www.consumerfinance.gov/data-research/research-reports/financial-well-being/
- Equifax, "How Long Does Information Stay on a Credit Report?" 2026, https://www.equifax.com/personal/education/credit/report/articles/-/learn/how-long-does-information-stay-on-credit-report/
- FINRA Foundation, *National Financial Capability Study*, 2024, https://www.finrafoundation.org/national-financial-capability-study
- McKinsey & Company, "What Is Gen Z?" Aug. 28, 2024, https://www.mckinsey.com/featured-insights/mckinsey-explainers/what-is-gen-z
- MoneyLion and Mastercard, *Health Is Wealth: The Hidden Link Between Finances and Physical Well-Being*, 2025, https://moneylion.nyc3.digitaloceanspaces.com/pdf/HIW_WhitePaper_Combined_PDF.pdf
- National Endowment for Financial Education (NEFE), *Personal Finance Ecosystem Framework*, 2026, nefe.org/initiatives/ecosystem/

A FINAL NOTE

This isn't an exhaustive list—it's a curated collection based on what has worked for me and the educators I've collaborated with. Some of these resources will resonate with you immediately; others might not fit your style or context, and that's okay. The goal is to keep learning, keep questioning, and keep building your own financial knowledge in ways that feel authentic to you. Remember: You don't need to consume everything on this list to be an effective financial educator. Pick what sparks your curiosity, aligns with your values, and meets you where you are. And please, share what you discover with others. That's how we share the wealth.

ACKNOWLEDGMENTS

This book exists because of everyone who said, "I wish I learned that when I was in high school." It exists because of super-passionate educators who live and breathe this work, bring creativity and vulnerability to every lesson, and know down to the core that financial education changes lives. It exists because of a growing community who believes we can do better for our young people. And it exists because of thousands of students who trust us to show them how money can work for them and the people they love.

It exists, too, because of many conversations with people who have an uncomfortable relationship with money. I hope you read this and be gentle with yourself. You're growing. And you're the best.

To KJ and Tuki. I'm really happy you're my children. You turned out to be nice, hardworking, fun people, and I love and like you *a lot*, which is frankly a huge relief. Thank you for tolerating my writing obsessions, and for teaching me about money, values, and living life. I'm proud to be your host. You make life more beautiful.

To Wallace. Thank you for understanding when I disappeared into my obsessive, Mamba-mentality writing zone for hours, days, entire weekends. Thank you for pretending to be interested when I explained the RICH framework for the millionth time, and for using all your delivery promos to order us food. Thank you for never making me feel weird or guilty for chasing my passions, even when it landed on your plate. You're the man.

To Mami, Papi, Turt, and Dave. Thank you for raising me by example to work hard, to be curious and keep learning, and to care deeply about others. Thank you for keeping me in check and humble when I get gassed up, while being completely supportive as I expand and grow. And of course, thank you for being funny and loco, which gives me great stories to share. Les amo tanto.

To Angie, Arivee, Carlita, and Steph. For always supporting me to write a whole book since day one! You knew I could do it before I did. And you kept that annoying imposter thing away from me. Spicy Mamis & Mujeres 5eva.

To my students at Brooklyn Preparatory High School. You are the real reason this book exists. For years you burst into my office asking to take the Money Move$ class, stopped me in the hallway to get my thoughts on stocks, and cornered me while my hands were full of papers to ask about credit cards. Every time you showed up excited to learn about money, you proved that young people want—and deserve—real financial empowerment.

To my colleagues at Brooklyn Preparatory High School who have walked most of this twenty-year journey with me. My admin team (S.A.N.D.) thank you for supporting me as I went to conferences, wrote, taught, and fully lived my joy of helping people understand how money moves. My legendary staff, you're the real MVPs. Thank you for the hallway conversations, for sharing your life stories, for bringing me treats and checking in when I stayed late to write. Thank you for always going above and beyond, and for inspiring me with your creative teaching. Special thanks to "my kids" who I hired as newbies and watched grow into the fantastic educators they are today. I'm grateful for your friendship throughout the years. Public education is hard, hilarious, and beautiful, and I'm honored to have done this work alongside all of you at BPHS.

To the educators and practitioners who generously shared their wisdom for this book: Tiffany Aliche, Halle Amore Bauer, Ian Brock, Joel Chrisler, Curt Cruz, Shanisha Dixon-Tyrell, Ric Edelman, Yanely Espinal, Karen Holland, Andrew Kadjeski, Ashley Kehr, Beth Kobliner, Alex Lamon, Vilda Vera Mayuga, Dan Otter, Courtney Pouquette, Tony J. Robinson, Trevor Rozier-Byrd, Nicole Russell, Christian Sherrill, Carly Urban, and Elvira Valdez. Thank you for honestly sharing your expertise and letting me learn from your gifts. You made this book more interesting and infinitely more useful. The field of financial education is better because you're in it.

To my former students Anais, Jennalissa, Lexi, Lia, Naiymah, Rachel, and Ryan—thank you for your eagerness, your humor, teaching me new slang words, and your willingness to share your stories. You make this work fun.

To the Council for Economic Education, Intuit for Education, and Next Gen Personal Finance. Thank you for welcoming and including my ideas through our collaborations, and for believing that financial literacy education can change lives. Your resources, platforms, and support make it possible for educators to empower more students.

To my editor, Rachael, who was energetic and excited about this project back when I was simply trying to ask if she had any financial literacy books for educators. Instead, she Jedi-mind-tricked me into writing the book I was looking for. Turns out she was right. Thank you for believing in this project from the very beginning.

To my Beacon Press team. Thank you for taking a chance on an unconventional, people-centered book about financial education. I appreciate every person on the team who understood my voice and was so gracious with feedback. Your kind words kept me motivated when it got hard.

And, finally, to every educator, parent, and caretaker who has ever felt underprepared, under-resourced, or overwhelmed at the thought of teaching other people about money: This book is for you. Every honest money talk makes a difference and matters more than you know.

Do your best. Your best is enough.

NOTES

INTRODUCTION

1. Paco de Leon, *Finance for the People: Getting a Grip on Your Finances* (Penguin Books, 2022).

CHAPTER 1: THE IMPACT: HOW FINANCIAL EDUCATION CHANGES LIVES

1. Emily Swaim, "Money Anxiety Is Common, but You Don't Have to Handle It Alone," *Healthline*, 2022, https://www.healthline.com/health/anxiety/money-anxiety#signs.

2. Nicole Russell-Wharton, *Breaking Generational Silence: A Guide to Disrupt Unhealthy Family Patterns and Heal Inherited Trauma* (Sounds True, 2025).

3. Swaim, "Money Anxiety Is Common."

4. Lauren M. Papp, Brian K. Brittain, and Sarah K. Goetz, "For Richer, for Poorer: Money as a Topic of Marital Conflict in the Home," *Family Relations* 58, no. 1 (2009): 91–103, https://doi.org/10.1111/j.1741-3729.2008.00537.x.

5. Morgan Housel, "Other People's Mistakes," Collaborative Fund, 2021, https://collabfund.com/blog/mistakes/, accessed May 10, 2025.

6. Paul Yakoboski, Anthony Webb, and John D. R. S. Abernethy, *College-Educated Millennials: An Overview of Their Personal Finances*, 2014, https://doi.org/10.13140/RG.2.1.2157.9689.

7. FINRA Investor Education Foundation, *Financial Capability in the United States: Highlights from the FINRA Foundation National Financial Capability Study, Fifth Edition*, FINRA Investor Education Foundation, 2022, https://finrafoundation.org/sites/finrafoundation/files/NFCS-Report-Fifth-Edition-July-2022.pdf.

8. Tim Kaiser et al., *Insights: Financial Capability*, National Endowment for Financial Education, 2022.

9. Jere Behrman et al., "How Financial Literacy Affects Household Wealth Accumulation," NIH.gov, 2013, https://pmc.ncbi.nlm.nih.gov/articles/PMC3554245/pdf/nihms-400812.pdf.

10. MoneyLion and Mastercard, *Health Is Wealth: The Hidden Link Between Finances and Physical Well-Being*, 2025, https://www.moneylion.com/learn/health-is-wealth/.

11. Board of Governors of the Federal Reserve System, *Economic Well-Being of U.S. Households in 2022*, 2023, https://www.federalreserve.gov/publications/files/2022-report-economic-well-being-us-households-202305.pdf.

12. Consumer Financial Protection Bureau, *Financial Well-Being: The Goal of Financial Education*, 2015, https://files.consumerfinance.gov/f/201501_cfpb_report_financial-well-being.pdf.

13. Consumer Financial Protection Bureau, *Financial Well-Being: The Goal of Financial Education.*

14. Idil Woodall, "Financial Literacy Statistics: Financial Knowledge by Key Demographics," *Moneyzine*, 2024, https://moneyzine.com/personal-finance/financial-literacy-statistics/.

15. Carly Urban, "Guest Post: What Happens When States Guarantee Personal Finance for All High Schoolers," *Next Gen Personal Finance (NGPF) Blog*, 2023, https://www.ngpf.org/blog/advocacy/dr-carly-urban-guest-post-what-happens-when-states-guarantee-personal-finance-for-all-high-schoolers/.

16. Carly Urban et al., "The Effects of High School Personal Financial Education Policies on Financial Behavior," *Economics of Education Review* 78 (Mar. 2020): 101786, https://doi.org/10.1016/j.econedurev.2018.03.006.

17. Naiymah Dickson, interview with author, Apr. 15, 2025.

18. Urban et al., "The Effects of High School Personal Financial Education Policies on Financial Behavior."

19. Consumer Financial Protection Bureau, "Consumer Credit Card Market Report of the Consumer Financial Protection Bureau, 2025," *Federal Register* 91, no. 4, Jan. 7, 2026, https://www.consumerfinance.gov/data-research/research-reports/the-consumer-credit-card-market-2025/.

20. Hannah Gdalman, M. K. Falgout, and David Silberman, "Overdraft, NSF Fees Bigger Burden Than Previously Estimated," Financial Health Network, Mar. 24, 2025, https://finhealthnetwork.org/research/overdraft-nsf-fees-bigger-burden-than-previously-estimated/?utm_source=copilot.com.

21. Consumer Financial Protection Bureau, "CFPB Closes Overdraft Loophole to Save Americans Billions in Fees," https://www.consumerfinance.gov/about-us/newsroom/cfpb-closes-overdraft-loophole-to-save-americans-billions-in-fees/.

22. Ryan Curry, interview with author, Apr. 14, 2025.

23. Urban et al., "The Effects of High School Personal Financial Education Policies on Financial Behavior."

24. Anais Vargas Pena, interview with author, Apr. 15, 2025.

25. Veronica Frisancho, "Spillover Effects of Financial Education: The Impact of School-Based Programs on Parents," *Journal of Financial Literacy and Wellbeing* 1, no. 1 (Apr. 28, 2023): 1–16, https://doi.org/10.1017/flw.2023.2.

26. Chris Melore, "Are You Financially Literate? Most Parents Wish They Knew More About Money Growing Up," Study Finds, Jan. 13, 2021, https://studyfinds.org/financially-literate-most-parents-wish-they-knew-more-about-money-childhood/.

27. Chase Media Center, "As More Schools Focus on Financial Education, Majority of U.S. Parents Are Teaching Kids About Money at Home," Chase.com, 2021, https://media.chase.com/news/as-more-schools-focus-on-financial-education.

28. Philip Gibson et al., "The Value of Financial Education During Multiple Life Stages," *Journal of Financial Counseling and Planning* 33, no. 1 (Mar. 22, 2021): JFCP-20-00017, https://doi.org/10.1891/jfcp-20-00017.

29. Ashley B. LeBaron-Black et al., "Parent Financial Socialization Scale: Development and Preliminary Validation," *Journal of Family Psychology* 36, no. 6 (Nov. 4, 2021), https://doi.org/10.1037/fam0000927.

30. LeBaron-Black et al., "Parent Financial Socialization Scale."

31. Gibson et al., "The Value of Financial Education During Multiple Life Stages."

32. Tiffany Aliche, interview with author, Apr. 29, 2025.

33. John Hope Bryant, "Financial Literacy Is the Civil Rights Issue of This Generation," *Time*, Feb. 13, 2024, https://time.com/6694236/financial-literacy-john-hope-bryant/.

34. Caroline Banton, "Network Effect," *Investopedia*, Dec. 9, 2022, https://www.investopedia.com/terms/n/network-effect.asp.

CHAPTER 2: THE MOMENTUM: POLICIES AND PRACTICES IN FINANCIAL EDUCATION

1. National Endowment for Financial Education, "Defining the Personal Finance Ecosystem," https://www.nefe.org/initiatives/ecosystem/default.aspx, accessed Nov. 5, 2025.

2. Hans Rosling, *Factfulness: Ten Reasons We're Wrong About the World—and Why Things Are Better Than You Think* (Flatiron Books, 2018).

3. Board of Governors of the Federal Reserve System, "Distribution of Household Wealth in the U.S. Since 1989," Distributional Financial Accounts, https://www.federalreserve.gov/releases/z1/dataviz/dfa/distribute/chart/, accessed Nov. 16, 2025.

4. Board of Governors of the Federal Reserve System, "Changes in U.S. Family Finances from 2016 to 2019," *Federal Reserve Bulletin* 106, no. 5 (2020), www.federalreserve.gov/publications/files/scf20.pdf.

5. Erik Hembre, "Homeownership Among Lowest-Income Households Climbs Near All-Time High," Federal Reserve Bank of Minneapolis, 2024, https://www.minneapolisfed.org/article/2024/homeownership-among-lowest-income-households-climbs-near-all-time-high.

6. Jung Hyun Choi and Amalie Zinn, "The Wealth Gap Between Homeowners and Renters Has Reached a Historic High," Urban Institute, Apr. 19, 2024, https://www.urban.org/urban-wire/wealth-gap-between-homeowners-and-renters-has-reached-historic-high.

7. Aditya Aladangady et al., "Greater Wealth, Greater Uncertainty: Changes in Racial Inequality in the Survey of Consumer Finances," Board of Governors of the Federal Reserve System, 2023.

8. Steve Maas, "Exploring 160 Years of the Black-White Wealth Gap," National Bureau of Economic Research, 2022, https://www.nber.org/digest/202208/exploring-160-years-black-white-wealth-gap.

9. Kim Parker, "A Booming U.S. Stock Market Doesn't Benefit All Racial and Ethnic Groups Equally," Pew Research Center, Mar. 6, 2024, https://www.pewresearch.org/short-reads/2024/03/06/a-booming-us-stock-market-doesnt-benefit-all-racial-and-ethnic-groups-equally/.

10. Mariko Chang et al., *Understanding the Gender Wealth Gap, and Why It Matters*, Federal Reserve Bank of St. Louis and Aspen Institute, 2023.

11. Consumer Reports, "What Is the Pink Tax?" last modified Oct. 18, 2021, https://www.consumerreports.org/money/what-is-the-pink-tax-a1270997218/.

12. Ana Hernandez Kent, "Gender Wealth Gaps in the U.S.," Federal Reserve Bank of St. Louis, Sept. 29, 2021, https://www.stlouisfed.org/open-vault/2021/september/gender-wealth-gaps-us-benefits-of-closing-them.

13. McKinsey & Company, *The Economic Impact of Closing the Racial Wealth Gap*, 2019.

14. Ani Turner, *The Business Case for Racial Equity: A Strategy for Growth*, W. K. Kellogg Foundation, 2018.

15. Carlos E. Cortés, "Renewing Multicultural Education: An Ancient Mariner's Manifesto: Adaptation of the Keynote Address Delivered at the 2024 National Conference of the National Association for Multicultural Education, Anaheim, California," *Multicultural Perspectives* 27, no. 2 (2025): 66–75, https://doi.org/10.1080/15210960.2025.2558492.

16. Idil Woodall, "Financial Literacy Statistics: Financial Knowledge by Key Demographics," *Moneyzine*, 2024, https://moneyzine.com/personal-finance/financial-literacy-statistics/.

17. Elvira Valdez, interview with author, Apr. 8, 2025.

18. Department of Consumer and Worker Protection, "DCWP Releases Updated Research Brief: 238,900 Households in NYC Are Unbanked," City of New York, 2025, https://www.nyc.gov/site/dca/news/027-25/dcwp-releases-updated-research-brief-238-900-households-nyc-unbanked.

19. Department of Consumer and Worker Protection, "DCWP Releases Updated Research Brief."

20. Vilda Vera Mayuga, interview with author, Apr. 28, 2025.

21. Andrew Kadjeski, interview with author, Oct. 7, 2025.

22. Dan Otter, "Teaching Financial Literacy in K–12 Schools: A Survey of Teacher Beliefs and Knowledge," UNM Digital Repository, 2010, https://digitalrepository.unm.edu/educ_llss_etds/30.

23. Financial Industry Regulatory Authority, "FINRA Foundation Releases State-by-State Financial Knowledge Findings," Apr. 9, 2025, https://www.finra.org/media-center/newsreleases/2025/finra-foundation-releases-state-state-financial-knowledge-findings.

24. Woodall, "Financial Literacy Statistics."
25. Financial Industry Regulatory Authority, "Financial Knowledge Quiz," 2025, https://www.finra.org/financial_knowledge_quiz.
26. Financial Industry Regulatory Authority, "FINRA Foundation Releases State-by-State Financial Knowledge Findings."
27. Annamaria Lusardi, Noemi Oggero, and Paul J. Yakoboski, *The TIAA Institute-GFLEC Personal Finance Index: A New Measure of Financial Literacy*, TIAA Institute and Global Financial Literacy Excellence Center, Mar. 2017, https://gflec.org/wp-content/uploads/2017/03/TIAA-Institute-GFLEC-P-Fin-Index-Report.pdf.
28. Lusardi, Oggero, and Yakoboski, *The TIAA Institute-GFLEC Personal Finance Index*.
29. Michelle Samuels-Jones, "The Importance of Equity in Financial Education," National Endowment for Financial Education, Aug. 7, 2024, https://www.nefe.org/news/2024/08/the-importance-of-equity-in-financial-education.aspx.
30. MoneyLion and Mastercard, *Health Is Wealth: The Hidden Link Between Finances and Physical Well-Being*, 2025, https://www.moneylion.com/learn/health-is-wealth/.
31. Next Gen Personal Finance, "LIVE U.S. Dashboard," 2025, https://www.ngpf.org/live-us-dashboard/.
32. Christian Sherrill, interview with author, Apr. 9, 2025.
33. Council for Economic Education, "FinEd50: Financial Education in All 50 States," https://www.councilforeconed.org/policy-advocacy/fined50/, accessed Nov. 5, 2025.
34. Council for Economic Education, *Survey of the States: Economic and Personal Finance Education in Our Nation's Schools*, 2024, https://www.councilforeconed.org/policy-advocacy/survey-of-the-states/.
35. Joel Chrisler, interview with author, May 6, 2025.
36. Carly Urban, *Best Practices Implementing Financial Education in High Schools*, Next Gen Personal Finance, 2022.
37. Carly Urban, interview with author, May 6, 2025.
38. Next Gen Personal Finance, "New Survey Finds 80% of Personal Finance Teachers Say Course Should Be Taught in 11th or 12th Grade," press release, Oct. 9, 2025, https://www.ngpf.org/blog/press-releases/new-survey-finds-80-of-personal-finance-teachers-say-course-should-be-taught-in-11th-or-12th-grade/.

CHAPTER 3: THE BELONGING: CREATING INCLUSIVE FINANCIAL SPACES

1. Aisha Nyandoro, "What Does 'Wealth' Mean to You?" TED, Oct. 16, 2023, https://www.ted.com/talks/aisha_nyandoro_what_does_wealth_mean_to_you?language=en.
2. Rudine Sims Bishop, "Mirrors, Windows, and Sliding Glass Doors," *Perspectives: Choosing and Using Books for the Classroom* 6, no. 3 (1990): ix–xi.
3. Tara J. Yosso, "Whose Culture Has Capital? A Critical Race Theory Discussion of Community Cultural Wealth," *Race Ethnicity and Education* 8, no. 1 (Aug. 23, 2005): 69–91, https://doi.org/10.1080/1361332052000341006.
4. Halle Amore Bauer, interview with author, Apr. 9, 2025.
5. Shanisha Dixon-Tyrell, interview with author, Apr. 14, 2025.
6. Curt Cruz, interview with author, Apr. 18, 2025.
7. Paulo Freire, *Pedagogy of the Oppressed* (Penguin Books, 1970).
8. Geneva Gay, *Culturally Responsive Teaching: Theory, Research, and Practice* (Teachers College Press, 2018).
9. Christopher Emdin, "Seven Cs for Effective Teaching," Association for Supervision and Curriculum Development, Sept. 1, 2016, https://www.ascd.org/el/articles/seven-cs-for-effective-teaching.
10. Consumer Financial Protection Bureau, "Effective Financial Education: Five Principles and How to Use Them," 2019, https://www.consumerfinance.gov/data-research/research-reports/effective-financial-education-five-principles-and-how-use-them/.

11. Jasmine Rashid, *The Financial Activist Playbook: 8 Strategies for Everyday People to Reclaim Wealth and Collective Well-Being* (Berrett-Koehler Publishers, 2024).

12. Michelle Samuels-Jones, "The Importance of Equity in Financial Education," National Endowment for Financial Education, Aug. 7, 2024, https://www.nefe.org/news/2024/08/the-importance-of-equity-in-financial-education.aspx.

CHAPTER 4: THE EDUCATORS: EXAMINING OUR OWN MONEY STORIES

1. Alex Lamon, interview with author, Apr. 14, 2025.

2. Wesley Wei et al., "In Debt: Student Loan Burdens Among Teachers," Learning Policy Institute, Feb. 4, 2025, https://learningpolicyinstitute.org/product/student-loans-among-teachers-brief.

3. Wei et al., "In Debt."

4. Elizabeth Heubeck, "Personal Finance for Students? Teachers Could Use It, Too," *Education Week*, Apr. 29, 2025, https://www.edweek.org/teaching-learning/personal-finance-for-students-teachers-could-use-it-too/2025/04.

5. Heubeck, "Personal Finance for Students?"

6. Heubeck, "Personal Finance for Students?"

7. Brad Klontz, "Klontz Money Scripts Test," https://www.bradklontz.com/moneyscriptstest.

8. Wendy L. Way and Karen C. Holden, "Teachers' Background and Capacity to Teach Personal Finance," *Journal of Financial Counseling & Planning* 20, no. 2 (2009).

9. Carly Urban and Melody Harvey, "How Confident Are Potential Personal Finance Teachers?" paper, Mar. 1, 2021.

10. John Pelletier, "Not Enough Teachers Know the Basics of Financial Education," *MarketWatch*, Apr. 18, 2019, https://www.marketwatch.com/story/not-enough-teachers-know-the-basics-of-financial-education-2019-04-18.

11. Beth Kobliner, interview with author, Apr. 22, 2025.

CHAPTER 5: THE FUTURE: HOW YOUTH NAVIGATE MONEY

1. Tom Wolfe, "The 'Me' Decade and the Third Great Awakening," *New York*, Aug. 23, 1976, https://nymag.com/article/tom-wolfe-me-decade-third-great-awakening.html.

2. "Living: Proceeding with Caution," *Time*, July 16, 1990, https://time.com/archive/6715389/living-proceeding-with-caution/.

3. Joel Stein, "Millennials: The Me Me Me Generation," *Time*, May 20, 2013, https://time.com/247/millennials-the-me-me-me-generation/.

4. WP Engine, "Generation Influence: Gen Z Study Reveals a New Digital Paradigm," *WP Engine Blog*, 2024, https://wpengine.com/press-releases/generation-influence-gen-z-study-reveals-a-new-digital-paradigm/

5. Ian Brock, interview with author, Apr. 14, 2025.

6. WP Engine, "Generation Influence."

7. Roberta Katz et al., *Gen Z, Explained: The Art of Living in a Digital Age* (University of Chicago Press, 2021).

8. McKinsey & Company, "What Is Gen Z?" 2022, https://www.mckinsey.com/featured-insights/mckinsey-explainers/what-is-gen-z.

9. Stanford News, "How Well Do You Know Gen Z?" Jan. 11, 2022, https://news.stanford.edu/stories/2022/01/know-gen-z.

10. Katz et al., *Gen Z, Explained.*

11. Deloitte, *2025 Gen Z and Millennial Survey: Growth and the Pursuit of Money, Meaning, and Well-Being*, Deloitte Global, 2025, https://www.deloitte.com/content/dam/assets-shared/docs/campaigns/2025/2025-genz-millennial-survey.pdf.

12. Deloitte, *2025 Gen Z and Millennial Survey*.

13. Mark C. Perna, "Gen Z Thriving: Entrepreneurship," *Forbes*, June 18, 2024.

14. Perna, "Gen Z Thriving."
15. Katz et al., *Gen Z, Explained.*
16. Perna, "Gen Z Thriving."
17. McKinsey & Company, "What Is Gen Z?"
18. Deloitte, *2025 Gen Z and Millennial Survey.*

CHAPTER 6: EXPLORING MONEY MINDSET

1. Shannah Game, "This Is Where the Receipts Start Talking," *Money Out Loud* (blog), May 12, 2025, https://receiptsplease.substack.com/p/this-is-where-the-receipts-start.
2. Linda García, *Wealth Warrior: 8 Steps for Communities of Color to Conquer the Stock Market* (Legacy Lit, 2023).
3. Jasmine Rashid, *The Financial Activist Playbook: 8 Strategies for Everyday People to Reclaim Wealth and Collective Well-Being* (Berrett-Koehler Publishers, 2024).
4. Lane Gillespie, "Survey: 47% of Americans Say Money Is Negatively Impacting Their Mental Health," Bankrate, May 9, 2024, https://www.bankrate.com/loans/personal-loans/money-and-mental-health-survey/.
5. Consumer Financial Protection Bureau, "Financial Well-Being: The Goal of Financial Education," May 30, 2019, https://www.consumerfinance.gov/data-research/research-reports/financial-well-being/.

CHAPTER 7: CREATING VALUES-BASED BUDGETS

1. Tiffany Aliche, interview with author, Apr. 29, 2025.
2. Tiffany Aliche, *Get Good with Money: Ten Simple Steps to Becoming Financially Whole* (Rodale, 2021).
3. Brené Brown, "Shame vs. Guilt," *Brené Brown* (blog), Jan. 15, 2013, https://brenebrown.com/articles/2013/01/15/shame-v-guilt/.
4. Chloe Elise, *Deeper Than Money: Ditch Money Shame, Build Wealth, and Feel Confident AF* (Penguin, 2023).
5. Elise, *Deeper Than Money.*
6. Bank of America Institute, "Paycheck to Paycheck: Slowing but Growing," Nov. 10, 2025, https://institute.bankofamerica.com/content/dam/economic-insights/paycheck-to-paycheck.pdf.

CHAPTER 8: DEVELOPING CREDIT CONFIDENCE

1. Beth Kobliner, interview with author, Apr. 22, 2025.
2. Megan DeMatteo, "My First Unsecured Credit Card Came with a $20,000 Limit—Here's Why That Is Rare Today," CNBC, July 22, 2020, https://www.cnbc.com/select/card-act-protections-for-young-people/.
3. Elizabeth Gravier, "Can Employers See Your Credit Score? How to Prepare for What They Actually See When They Run a Credit Check," CNBC, Mar. 25, 2025, https://www.cnbc.com/select/can-employers-see-your-credit-score/.

CHAPTER 9: ACCESSING THE STOCK MARKET

1. Yanely Espinal, interview with author, July 18, 2025.
2. Trevor Rozier-Byrd, interview with author, Apr. 1, 2025.
3. Bob Pisani, "Stock Picking Has a Terrible Track Record, and It's Getting Worse," CNBC, Sept. 18, 2020, https://www.cnbc.com/2020/09/18/stock-picking-has-a-terrible-track-record-and-its-getting-worse.html.

CHAPTER 10: BUILDING REAL ESTATE LITERACY

1. Erik J. Martin, "Beating the Generational Money Curse: How Homeownership Builds Your Family's Wealth," Bankrate, June 7, 2024, https://www.bankrate.com/home-equity/home-equity-and-building-generational-wealth/.

2. Board of Governors of the Federal Reserve System, *Survey of Consumer Finances (SCF)*, 2023, https://www.federalreserve.gov/econres/scfindex.htm.

3. Mike Hardwick, "Council Post: 3 Ways Homeownership Can Build Wealth," *Forbes*, Aug. 12, 2024, https://www.forbes.com/councils/forbesfinancecouncil/2022/08/03/three-ways-homeownership-can-build-wealth/.

4. Erik J. Martin, "Beating the Generational Money Curse."

5. Dana Anderson, "Nepo-Homebuyers: Aside from Paychecks, Family Money Is the Most Common Source of Young People's Down Payments," Redfin Real Estate News, July 14, 2025, https://www.redfin.com/news/young-homebuyers-family-money-down-payment/.

6. US Census Bureau, *Quarterly Residential Vacancies and Homeownership, First Quarter 2025*, Apr. 28, 2025.

7. Federal Reserve History, "Redlining," https://www.federalreservehistory.org/essays/redlining, accessed Jan. 15, 2026.

8. Jung Hyun Choi et al., "Three Differences Between Black and White Homeownership That Add to the Housing Wealth Gap," Urban Institute, Feb. 28, 2019, https://www.urban.org/urban-wire/three-differences-between-black-and-white-homeownership-add-housing-wealth-gap.

9. "Teaching Real Estate Literacy," *Real Estate Rookie*, BiggerPockets, podcast audio, July 15, 2025, https://podcasts.apple.com/us/podcast/real-estate-rookie/id1499646507?i=1000717358058.

CHAPTER 11: NAVIGATING WEB3

1. Clifford Stoll, "The Internet? Bah!" *Newsweek*, Feb. 27, 1995, https://www.nysaflt.org/workshops/colt/2010/The%20Internet.pdf; Regia Marinho, "Internet May Be Just a Passing Fad, The Newspaper Said 21 Years Ago," *Medium*, Dec. 20, 2021, https://regia-marinho.medium.com/internet-may-be-just-a-passing-fad-the-newspaper-said-21-years-ago-153aae2e0c2f.

2. "Bill Gates Explains the Internet to Dave (1995) | Letterman," YouTube video, Nov. 27, 1995, https://www.youtube.com/watch?v=fs-YpQj88ew.

3. Ric Edelman, interview with author, May 8, 2025.

4. Michelle Faverio et al., "Majority of Americans Aren't Confident in the Safety and Reliability of Cryptocurrency," Pew Research Center, Oct. 24, 2024, https://www.pewresearch.org/short-reads/2024/10/24/majority-of-americans-arent-confident-in-the-safety-and-reliability-of-cryptocurrency/.

INDEX